Whitetail Secrets:

Bachelor Life

ISBN-13: 978-17377620-8-9

ISBN-10: 1737762080

First Printing August 2023

Published by:

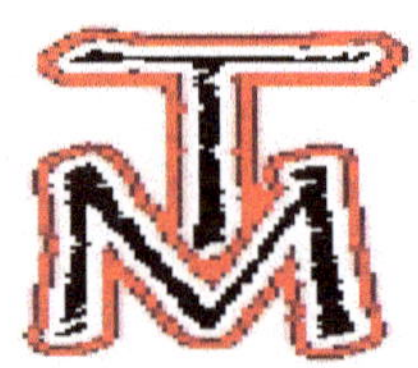

ThomasMax Publishing
P.O. Box 250054
Atlanta, GA 30325

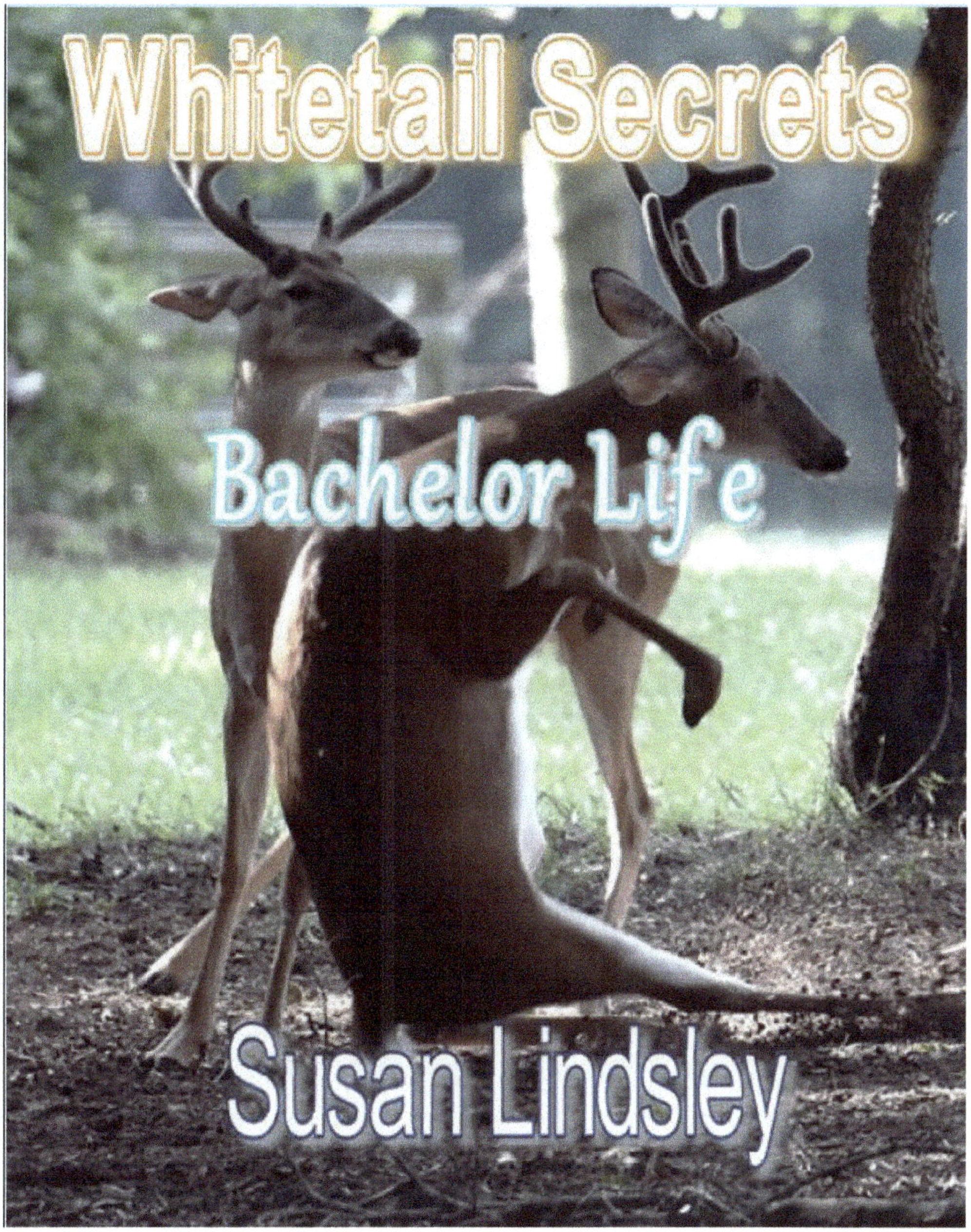

Whitetail Secrets

Bachelor Life

Susan Lindsley

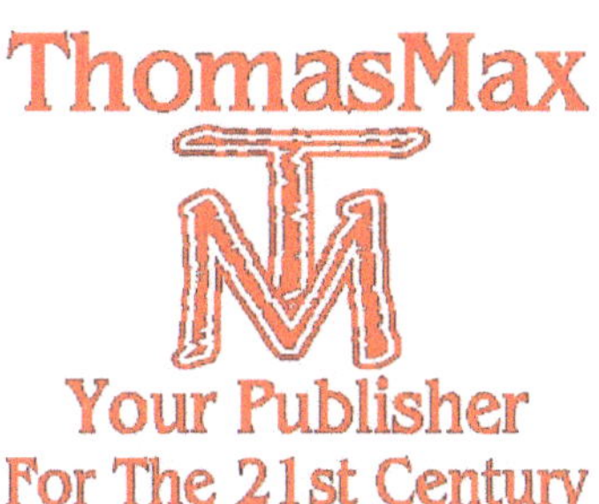

INTRODUCTION

This book is the result of several years of photographing deer and other wildlife, and a first draft of more than 600 pages. That length for a full-color 8.5 X 11-inch book would have put the cost beyond reasonable. So I cut some pictures, shrunk many, and consolidated material into two books: One deals with family life and one with bachelor life.

Unless otherwise noted, I took all of the pictures, most at my farm outside Milledgeville, in middle Georgia. I hope the pictures of the "nice" bucks do not tempt otherwise honest hunters to sneak onto my land to collect one of these critters. Maybe I need not worry, since a hunter told me he had been warned that poachers on my land went to jail, *IF* they survived. I have in fact guided a number of poachers to the local jail (see ***Possum Cops, Poachers and the Counterfeit Game Warden***).

Numerous deer come to the feeders, as many as eight or ten bucks at a time with racks any hunter would be happy to collect. And they come in daylight hours, which benefits my photography; I have 1,000 watts of floodlights, however, which enable me to photograph at all hours of the night.

Many years ago, when I just scattered feed, the deer learned the floodlights were their signal that food was available. Now the sound of the feeder throwing corn is their signal, but they anticipate the schedule and bucks, does and fawns often gather a half-hour earlier to be first to establish an eating site.

Unfortunately, many of these deer hang around day and night, and feed on browse and whatever else nearby, so they have created a shortage of natural food in the area. Therefore I now must run the feeders only in food-sparce winter months so the deer will circulate over a larger area and not hang around my yard and eat everything in sight while they wait for the feeder. Browse lines can indicate hungry and unhealthy deer.

The past few years have provided many hours of enjoyment as I watched and photographed animals, from small wrens to ten-point bucks. Flycatchers have hovered over deer to devour the pesky flies that so annoy deer in the summer months.

A photographer often remembers the picture missed: For me the one most remembered is the small-racked buck jabbing antlers into the rump of a large eight-pointer and running the larger buck into the woods.

I hope you enjoy these pictures and the knowledge I have gained through these observations and share here. I gain a lot of learning from putting these books together and from the deer experts who reviewed the drafts for me. Selecting photographs from more than some fifty thousand has not been an easy self-assignment.

This is only one of the two-book set: ***WHITETAIL SECRETS: Family Life*** and ***WHITETAIL SECRETS***: ***Bachelor Life***. May you find as much joy in the books as I had in my time with the critters, but also I hope you too will shed a tear over the difficulties the deer endured but also laugh a bit at their antics.

ACKNOWLEDGMENTS

Old friends and new have helped me with this book, from on-the-ground help to checking everything from my typing to my information. The "boys" (still boys in my 86-year-old mind) Wayne Barnes and Chuck Beaty have kept the feeders filled and done many mundane chores on site to help with my picture taking. Chuck has provided pictures of a buck carrying a crown of vines on his antlers, and Wayne has shown off his piebald buck.

New friend Professor Emeritus Dr. Karl V. Miller, now retired from the University of Georgia (and affectionally called the "Deer God of Georgia" by his students) read the manuscript and corrected my many misunderstandings and errors. I can never thank him enough for saving me from shame and disgrace should those errors have made it to the printed material. Patricia Blanks, classmate and retired librarian with an eagle eye, reviewed draft after draft. She has eagle eyes that can pick up the tiniest punctuation or spelling mistake.

Any typographical errors or errors of fact that did get through were added during revisions into the "final final" draft and did not pass through the hands of either reviewer.

Others who have helped me include David Waller, retired from the Department of Natural Resources here in Georgia; Vicki Yates of the Georgia Wildlife Federation, and Charlie Killmaster of Game Management, Georgia Department of Natural Resources, who provided statistical information and review. Technical assistance with formatting, as always, came from my patient publisher, Lee Clevenger.

As ever, my life partner Gail Cabisius has endured my many hours on the computer and days away on site with deer and camera, and on my return listening to me relate every move and action of every deer. Thank you, Gail, for your patient understanding and the many times you shared with your camera and pointed out another shot I should take.

When I managed to muddle the entire manuscript into a jumble of unsortable pages, I found computer help from Jim Cheuh of Sprint Print (Decatur) and also in Decatur from Sukru Aydin at Trend Tech Solutions. Thank you one and all.

For Richard and Shelia Key,

a pair of *deer* friends for a half-century

...and counting.

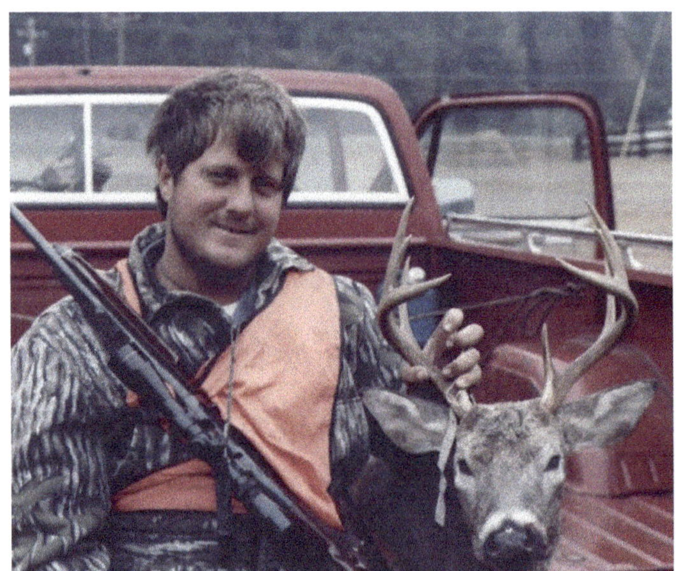
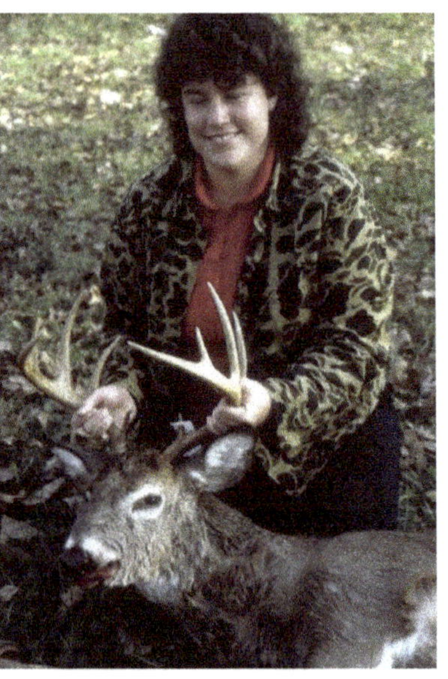

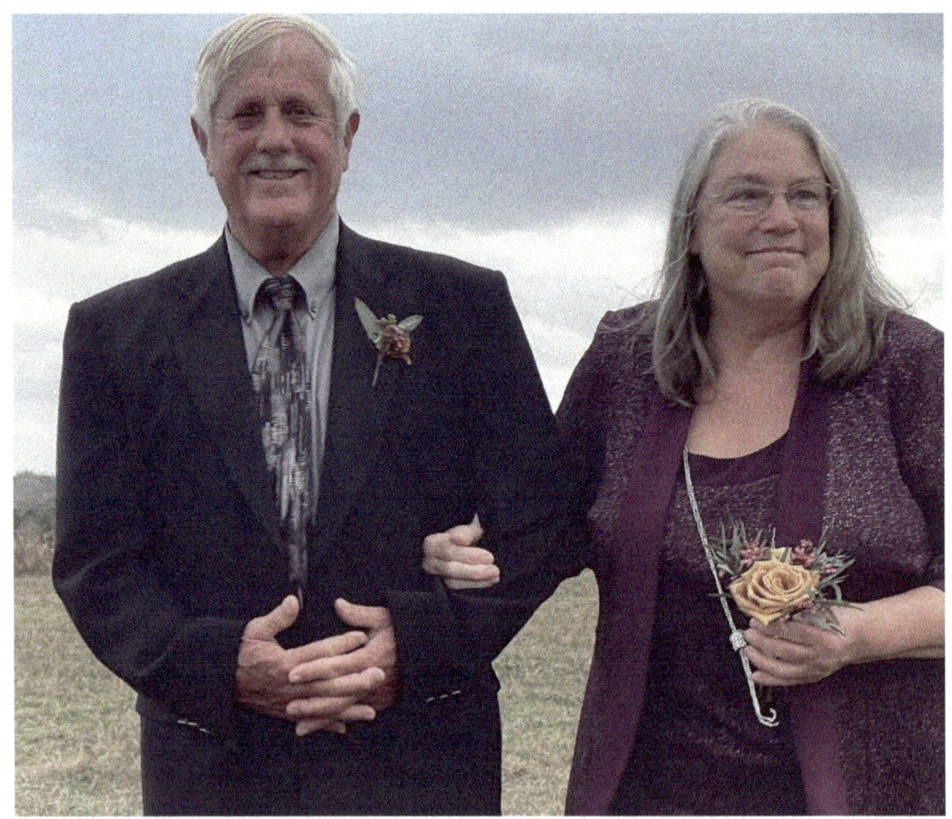

BOOKS BY SUSAN LINDSLEY

Novels, Southern historical
    The Bottom Rail
    When Darkness Fell

Memoirs
    Blue Jeans and Pantaloons in YESTERPLACE
    Possum Cops, Poachers and the Counterfeit Game Warden

Biography
    Susan Myrick of Gone With the Wind
    The Lindsleys of Westover
    Milledgeville's Sesquicentennial Murders

Collections of others' works edited
    Myrick Memories: From Plantation to Town (1900-1950s)
    Margaret Michell: A Scarlett or a Melanie? (Susan Myrick essays)
    Luther Lindsley: His Literary Works

Poetry
    O Yesterplace and other poems (out of print)
    Christmas Gift
    When Yestertime Was Now
    Whisper of Love

Short Story collections
    Emperor of the United American States
    Whitetails and Tall Tales
    Finding Bigfoot
    Tales Over Time

Specialty books
    Wildlife in Persimmon Paradise (photography)
    Whitetail Secrets: Family Life (photography)
    Whitetail Secrets: Bachelor Life (photography)

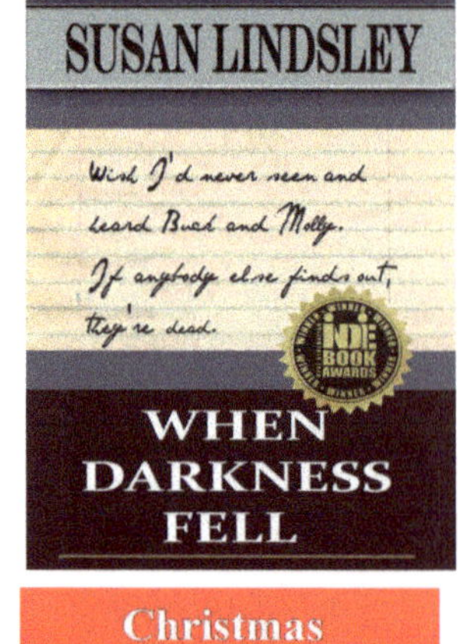

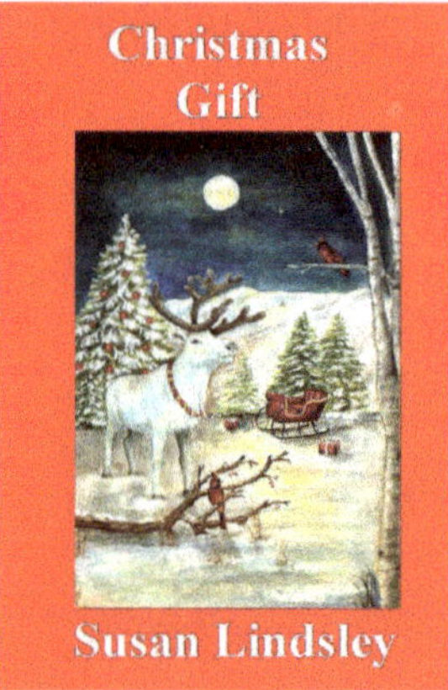

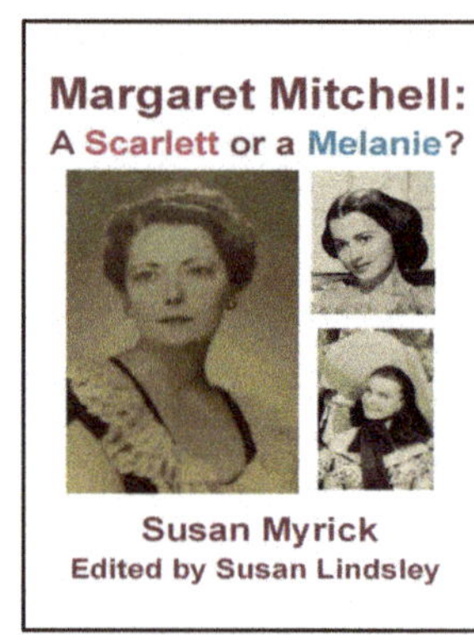

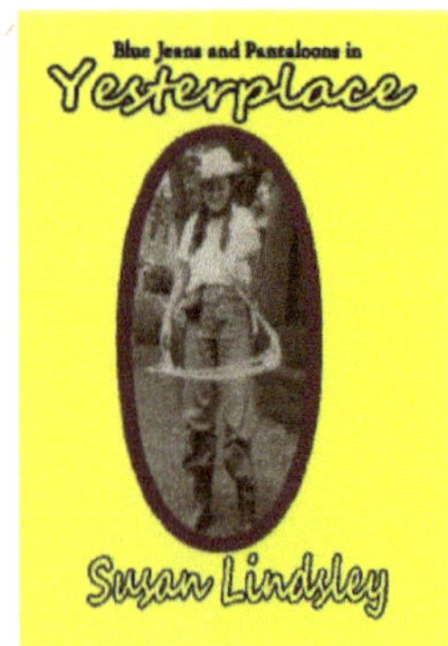

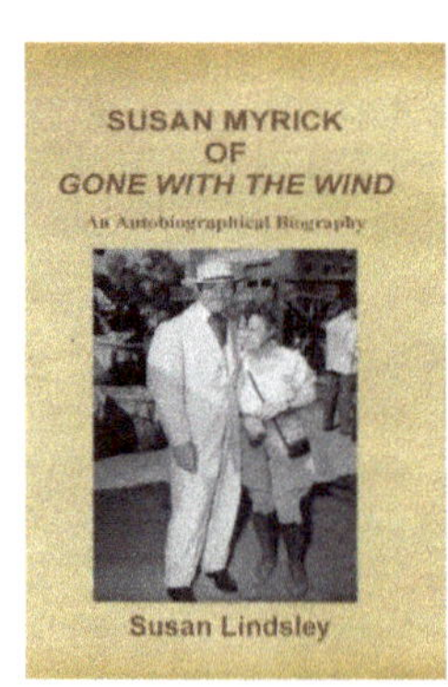

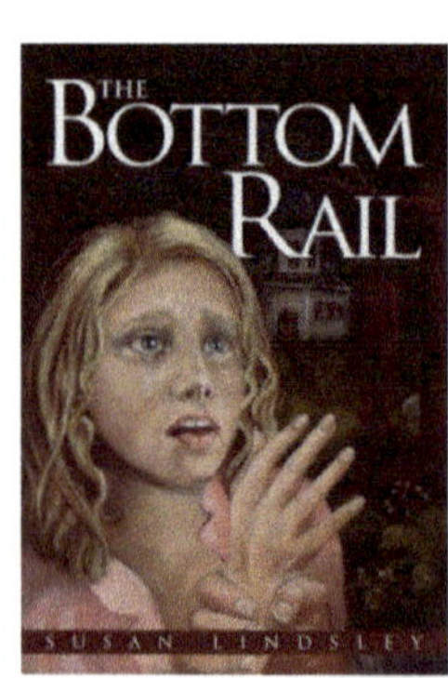

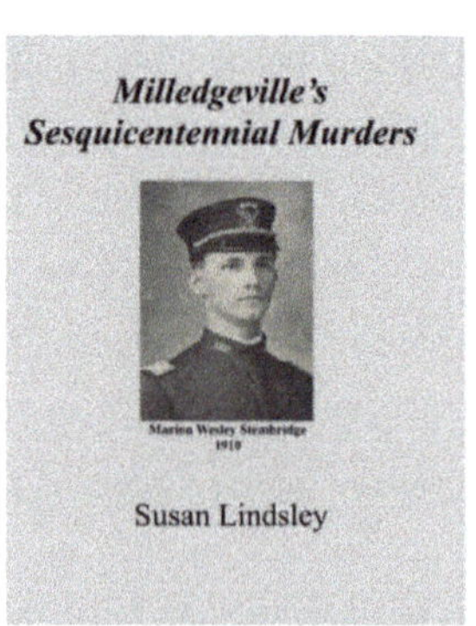

ANTLERS: BUCK'S GLORY, HUNTER'S DREAM

Antlers are the pride of the male whitetail, and are not the same as horns. Horns are permanent and grow for the lifetime of the animal. Antlers grow for a season like flesh, then harden into bone and soon fall off, to regenerate again the next spring. For a hunter, the antler size is important, for the larger the rack the greater the trophy. For the animal, the antlers are his attack and defense armament.

Although Georgia produces magnificent bucks, the antlers of our Georgia bucks do not score/rank quite as high as those of the rich soil and highly agricultural areas of the upper midwestern and central states, such as Wisconsin or Illinois, where some Georgia trophy hunters travel in search of a monster buck. After the whitetail was almost extinct in Georgia, it was reintroduced by both the state government and by some individuals, with many of the new animals coming from those midwestern states, as well as various other states. The genes came, but the acres of cornfields, alfalfa, soybeans and other highly nutritious crops were not that prevalent in Georgia, where soil was poorer and farmland was beginning a slow transition from annual crops to pulp and saw timber.

Still, hunters dream, and for some the dreams come true as the Georgia herd provides some trophies every year.

Some hunters provide acres of food plots to supplement year-round food sources, whereas some Georgia hunters provide an autumn-winter supply of corn to lure deer into range, and hope the bucks will show up during daylight hours in hunting season.

In recent years, politics in Georgia have resulted in allowing hunting over bait in the northern half of Georgia, as has been legal in South Georgia for a number of years, so many hunters provide corn from a few days or weeks before deer season and throughout the hunting season. I don't like that idea. Deer can be conditioned, like Pavlov's dogs. My yard deer congregate about a half-hour before the feeders go off; in 2022, as many as eleven bucks with six to ten points showed up for each feed.

Statistics from Georgia Game and Fish show an increase in "youth" (under 16 years of age) hunters who were successful, their numbers increasing annually from 3,911 in 2016-17 season to 6,206 in the 2021-22 season in the northern half of the state. On-line posts show some youths to be barely old enough to be in school; reports to Game and Fish include one youth's age to be *two* years. These children will not become "hunters," but "shooters" in adulthood if all they ever do is sit over bait.

Ironically, the number of successful adult *hunters* in the same northern half who harvested bucks with *fewer* than four points on one side rose the first year, from 29,477 to 33,808, then began to fall, down to 19,037 in the 2021-2022 season. During the same period, the number of bucks with four points or better on one side increased from 24,172 to 28,146 the first year, then dropped to 27,139 the second year. And increased annually thereafter. The number of does killed varied up and down in a similar pattern until the 2021-2022 season, when the number dropped by 5,000 over the previous year.

With hunters' desires for a trophy, some people wait for the big one to come by. Other hunters settle for the first legal deer; some for the eight pointer he has seen on a trail camera. And some hunters waiting for a trophy go home at season's end without a buck because the corn supply fed that monster in the night rather than in daylight hours.

A friend has not harvested a deer for the past three years because he waited for the big buck he viewed on his game camera to walk out near the feeder during shooting hours. Instead, the buck has been busy elsewhere during shooting hours.

Timber companies and some landowners plant thousands of acres in rows of pines, and thereby some portions of the state provide mixed blessings: Lush forage for the first few years, then shaded ground so less forage until the pines are thinned. The mixed pine and hardwoods of my land provide abundant soft and hard mast, in the form of acorns, mushrooms, dogwood seeds, persimmons and other natural foods. Undergrowth is heavy in some areas, where sunlight reaches through, and less so under thick timber. Many of my hunters plant summer and winter food plots; my home site is surrounded by about forty acres of Marshall ryegrass, planted to harvest for silage for cattle, which have kept neighborhood deer well fed for more than fifty winters.

Whatever his dreams, the hunter visualizes antlers. As does the housewife in the country who spots a buck in the yard, the tourists in game parks, and the child who has seen or read *Bambi*.

The white-tailed deer are found in all of the lower forty-eight states, although only sparsely in Utah and almost nonexistent in California and Nevada. The subspecies Key deer inhabit only Pine Key in Florida, with the few exceptions for those who have migrated to adjacent areas or keys.

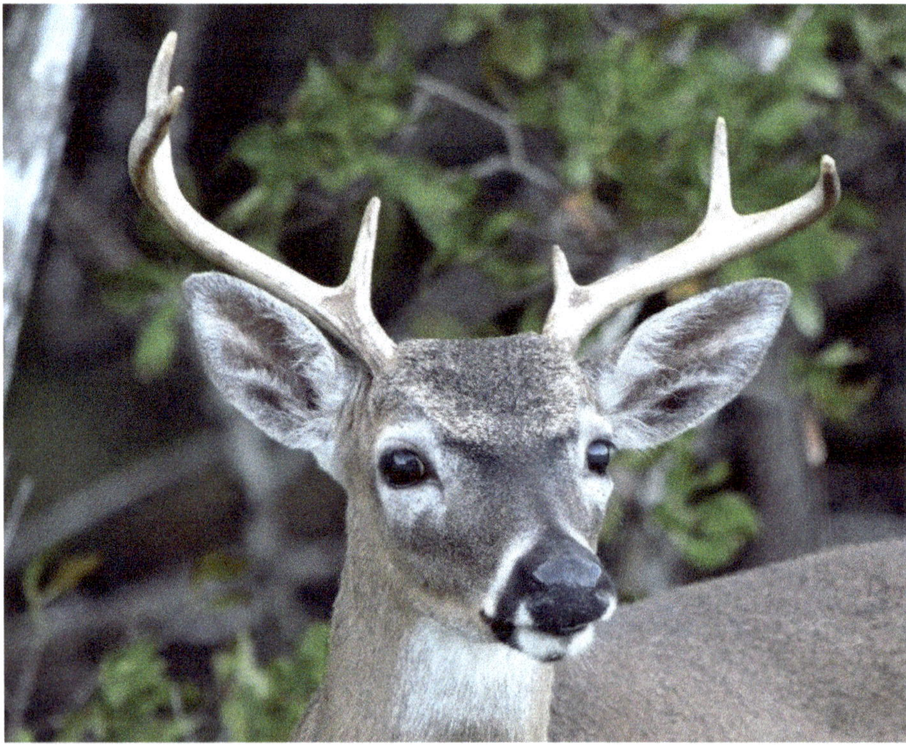

Key deer on Pine Key, Florida

ANTLERED RELATIVES IN THE U. S.

Mule deer and blacktail deer are western cousins. The big relatives in the lower forty-eight are moose and elk. Moose inhabit the Northeast and the West. Elk roam the west and have been reintroduced into the Southeast and thrive in the Cataloochee Valley; they also inhabit some areas in Virginia, West Virginia, Pennsylvania, and Kentucky.

Alaska is home to the wild caribou and the domesticated reindeer. A number of deer species have been imported, including the fallow deer and Sika deer.

ANTLER GROWTH

Male members of the deer family, and female caribou, grow antlers, the size and shape varying with deer species and individuals within species. Whereas the rack of a whitetail buck may weigh only three to nine pounds and have a spread of fourteen to twenty inches, moose antlers can grow to a spread of six feet and weigh up to forty pounds.

Antlers are the fastest growing of any animal material, flesh or bone. Needless to say, they grow faster in the moose since they grow so much larger. They also grow at different speeds in individual whitetails.

For the whitetail, antler growth depends on when he cast his previous antlers. If they cast early (from nutrition, genetics or otherwise) there will be a delay before the new ones begin to grow. Otherwise, they begin about two weeks after the buck sheds his previous antlers. The shape, size and speed of growth depend first on age and then on genetics, nutrition, minerals, overall health and injuries.

The growing antlers are highly innervated and vascularized and covered with a sheath called *velvet,* which is living flesh. When the antlers mature in the fall, they harden into bone and the velvet essentially dies, dries, cracks and dangles from the antlers until it falls off or the buck thrashes it off against brush.

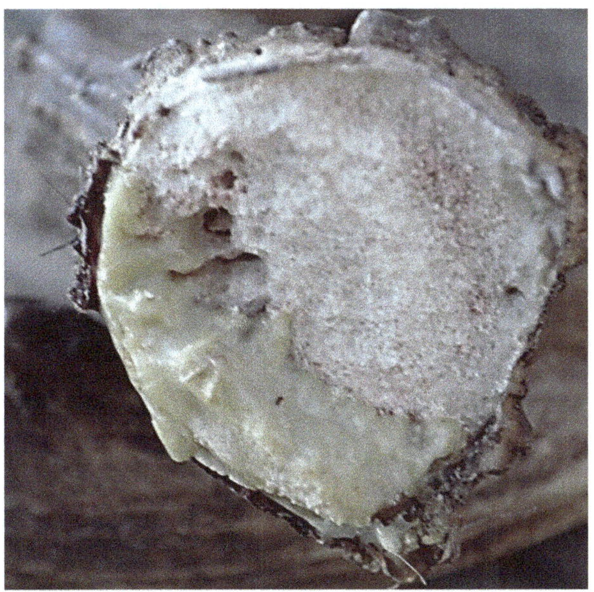

The holes in the base of this antler shed show where the blood vessels ran into the growing antlers to supply the nutrients needed for growth. The yellow here is pus and shows the buck had an abscess at the base of his antler.

Velvet gives the impression of large diameter and heavy mass, but the growing antler beneath is much smaller.

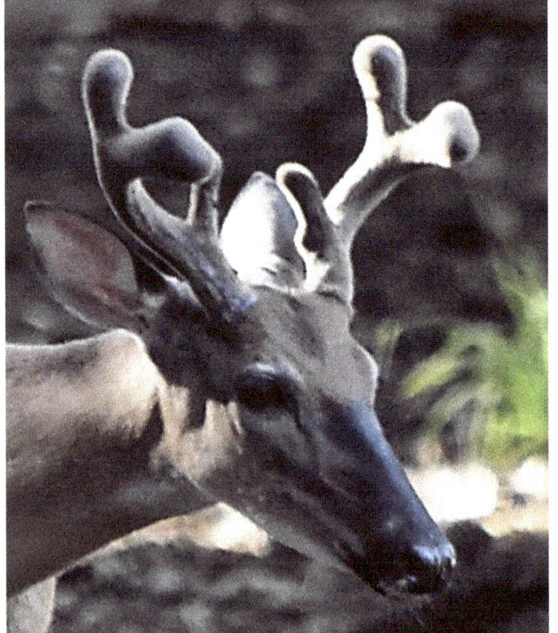
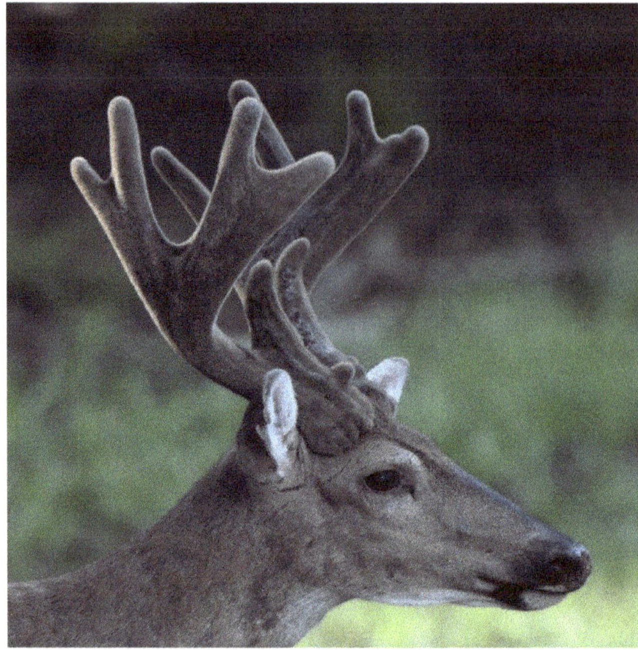

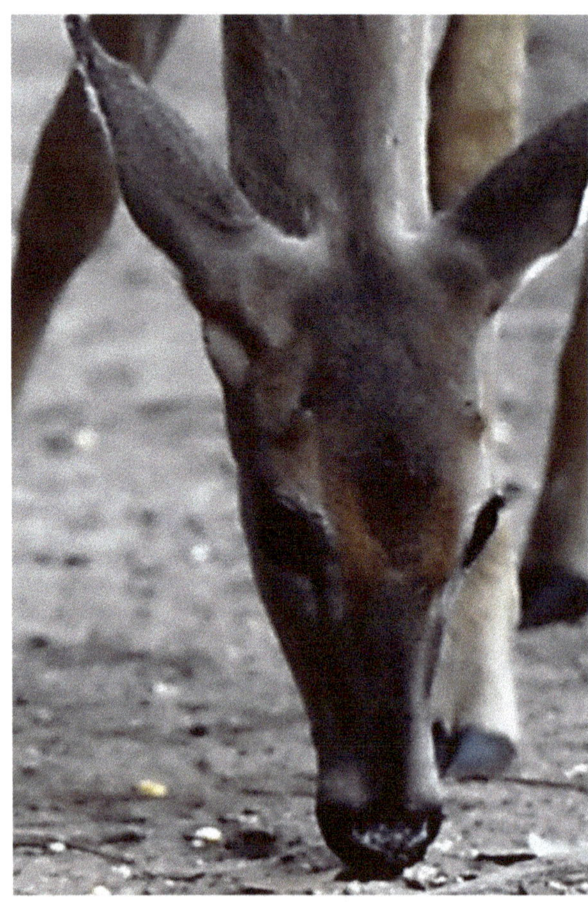

A spring fawn might have slightly visible antlers late in his first summer, but most have only budding pedicles (*buttons* or knobs) their first year, sometimes so small they are hard to see, like this youngster had in early September.

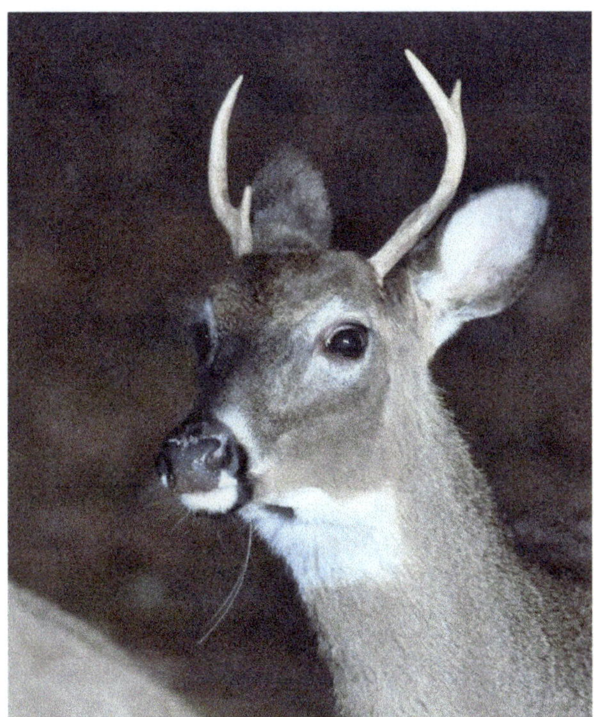

A whitetail buck begins growing his first antlers when he enters his first spring (after his birth spring), and by that fall, when he is eighteen months old, his rack may be only spikes or may be multiple points. The diameter of the main beam and the number of points do not depend on his age. He does not grow an additional point annually.

This boy is typical of most of the 18-month-old bucks in my neighborhood.

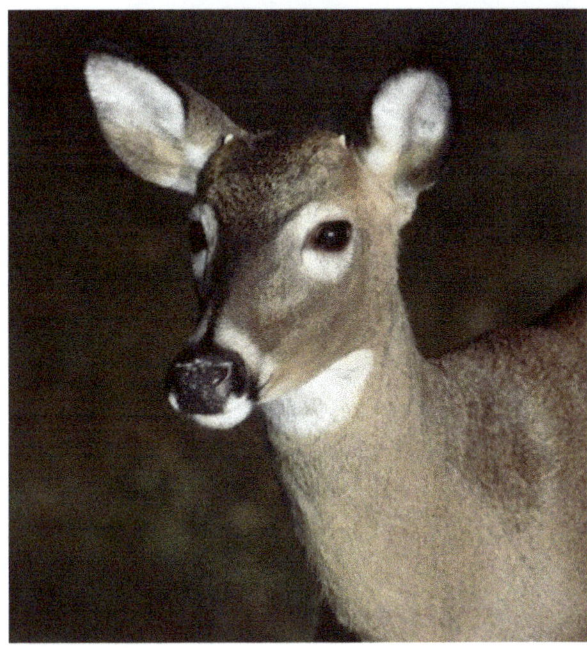

His buttons broke through his first September to show bone. He might be considered antlered and legal game in some states. He may have been born earlier in the spring than usual or may have better nutrition and/or super genetics for antler growth.

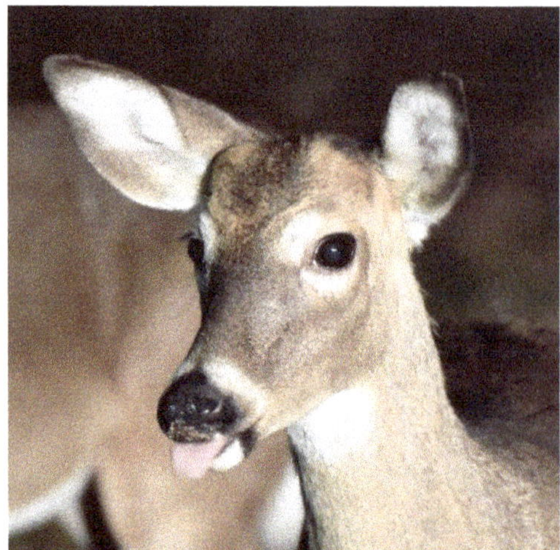

March 1. New antlers bulge.

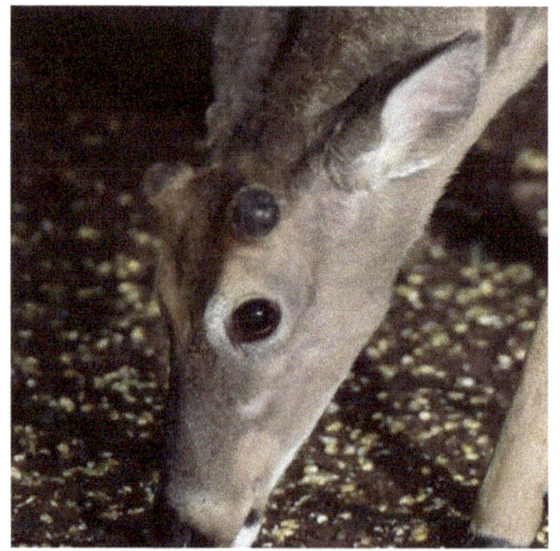

**March 25. Different buck. He had a
big rack that fall.**

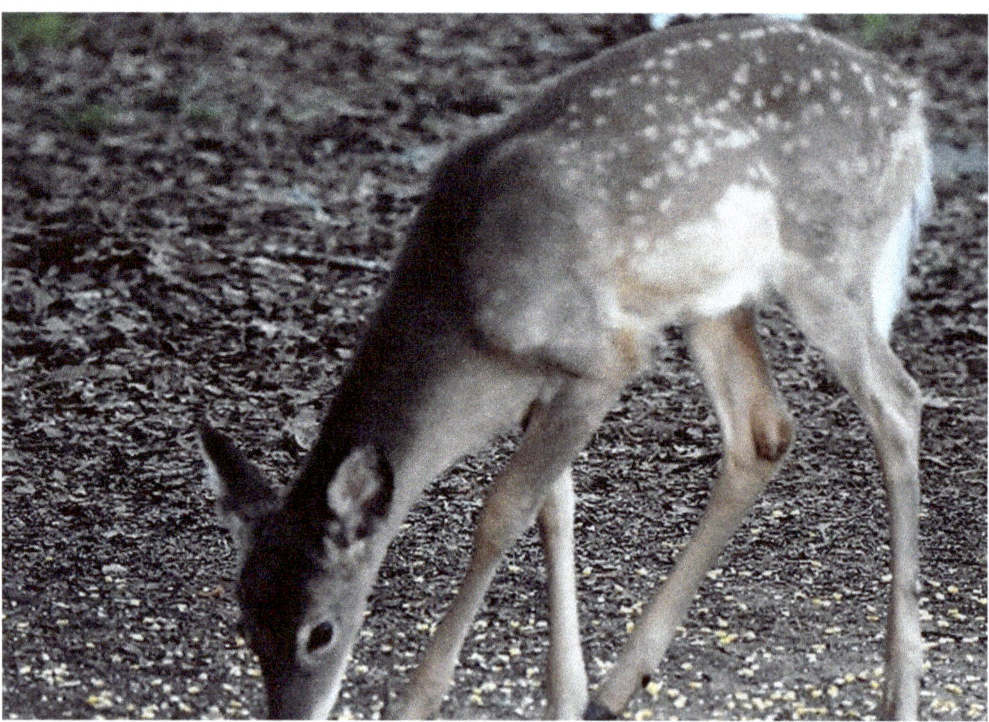

On March 14 and 30, 2022, this fawn in what looked like winter coat, showed up in the yard several times. I was able to identify it as a buck only when it walked away with its tail elevated. He was obviously too young to be a 2021 spring fawn; I figured his mother had been bred quite late, maybe even as the rut ended, and this fawn was born perhaps as late as November 2021.

On June 13, a youngster showed up with what appears to be a budding antler on the right side. It ran with an adult doe, probably its mother. On July 1, the budding antler showed on his left. By comparing the earlier photographs of the March spotted fawn, I was able to confirm this was the same buck and not a doe beginning to sprout antlers. His life pattern was out of kilter with the calendar. I am sure it was the same one from March 14 and 30. I did not see him after July 19.

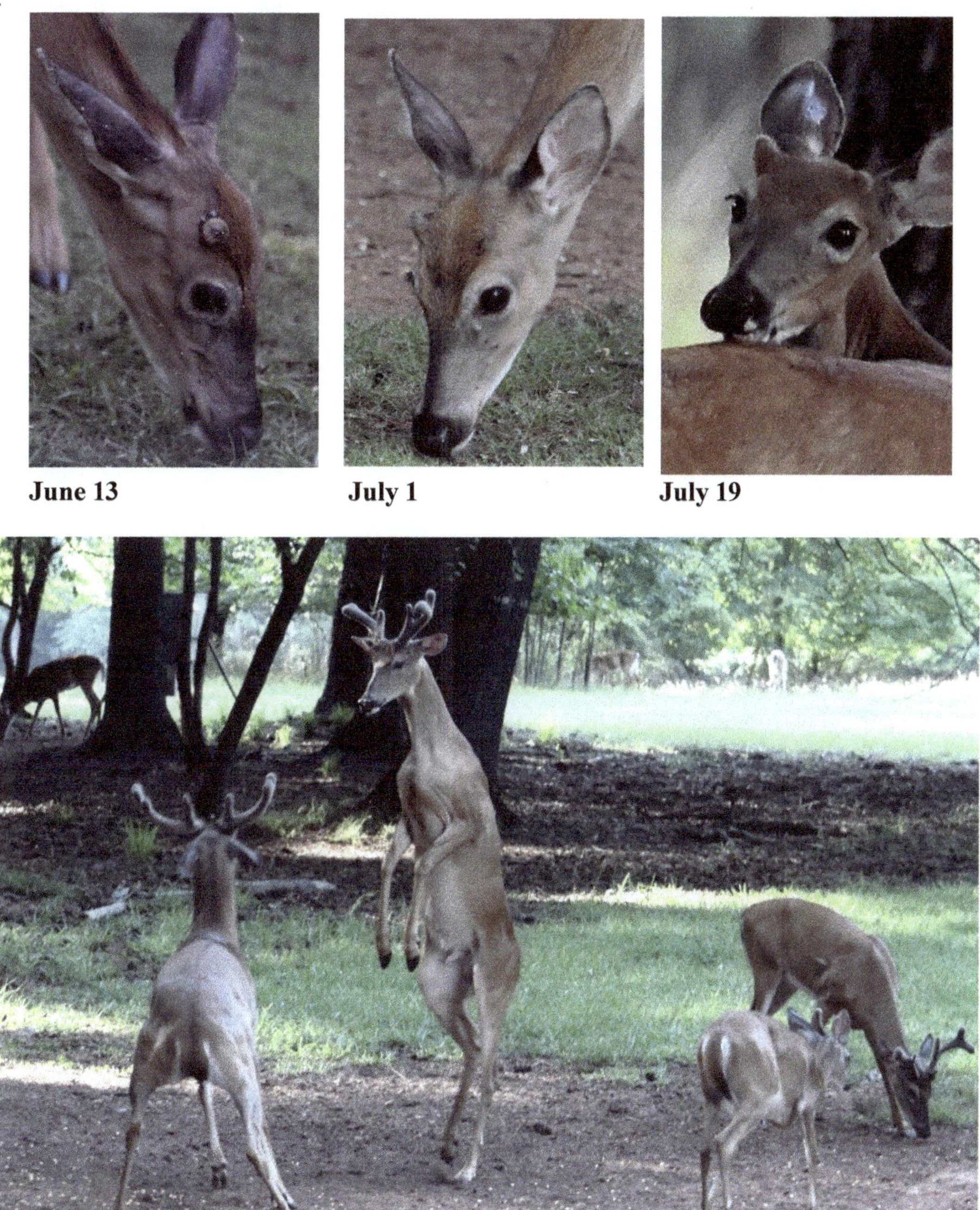

June 13   **July 1**   **July 19**

   While antlers are growing and still "flesh," bucks seem to know they must show dominance rather than prove it in battle; at times, however, the guy with the larger rack may yield to one with smaller antlers. The eight pointer fled the smaller six, and the nine pointer ran from a doe.

   Does seemed to have no fear of bucks when they are in velvet. Often in my yard, a doe would rear up at a buck and send him hiking. Somehow bucks seem to sense their antlers can be injured.

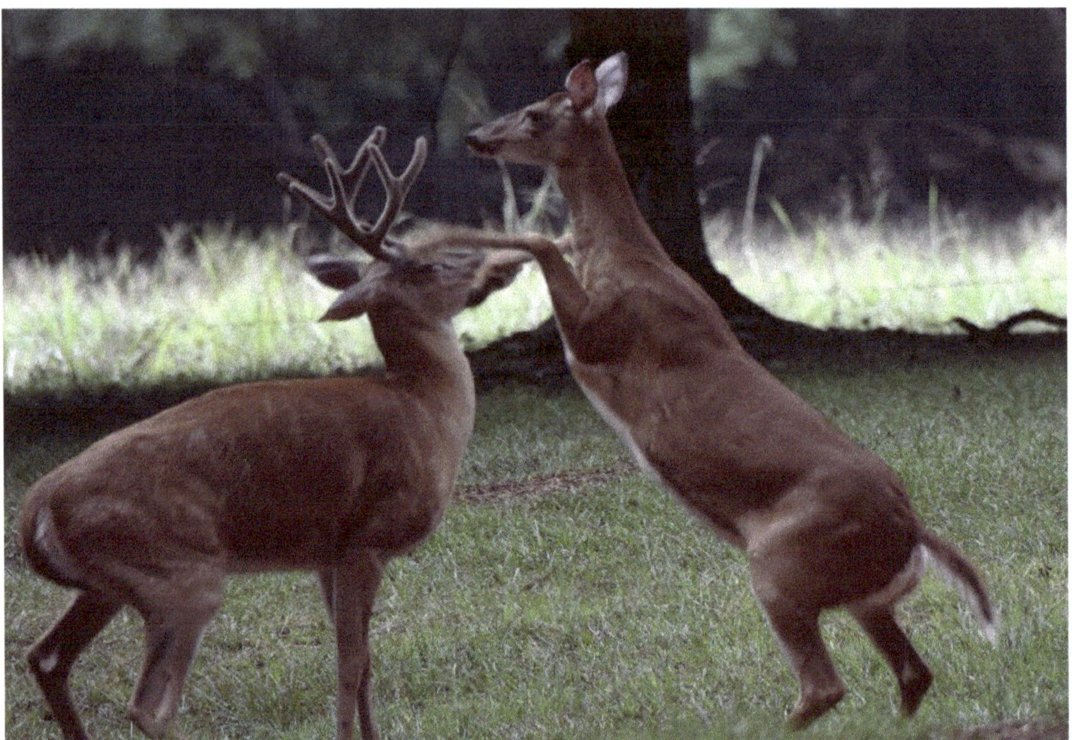

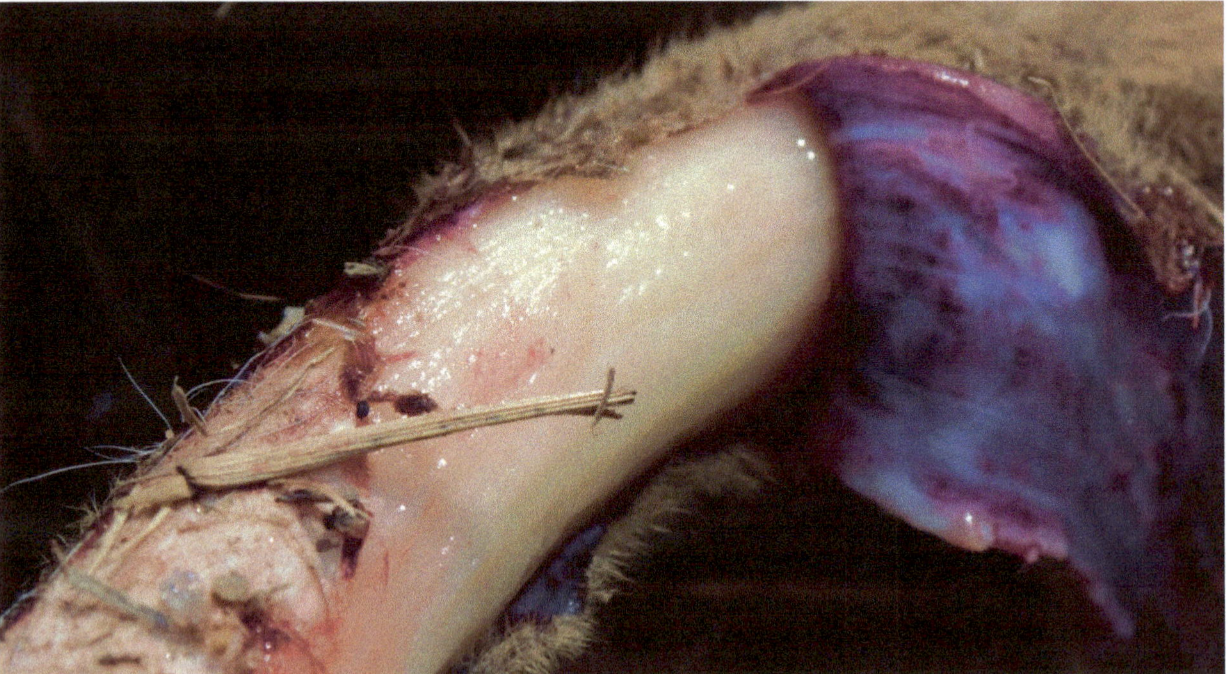

This spike buck was killed on the road on September 10. The antler had hardened but the velvet was not quite ready to be shed naturally.

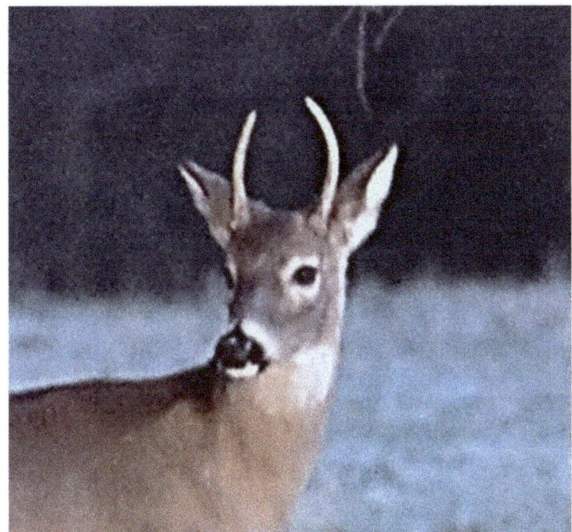
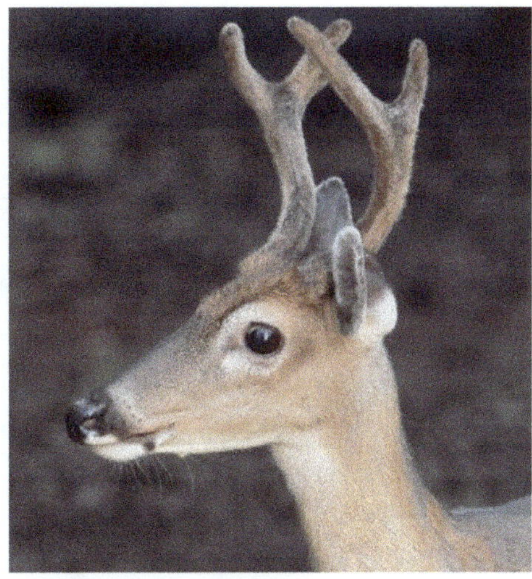

These boys are eighteen months and typical of that age in my area.

Antlered does are harvested every year, some in velvet and some with polished antlers. Even the Wall Street Journal and other newspapers carry stories about antlered doe whitetails. According to Joe Hamilton, founder of the Quality Deer Management Association, as quoted in *Grand View Outdoors.com*, October 15, 2015:

"Some velvet-antlered does reveal only external female organs and carry the male organs within the body cavity or just under the skin. Those with external male and female organs are referred to as hermaphrodites and could have enough testosterone to produce a normal antler growth cycle. Such deer are not expected to be successful at reproduction."

If a buck is castrated, perhaps when leaping a fence, and he is growing antlers at the time, the antlers probably will not harden in the fall and he won't drop them.

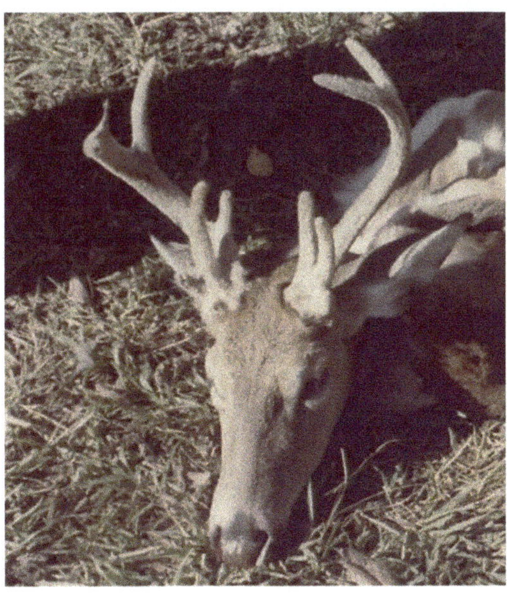

This buck was killed on my land in mid-November, but velvet is normally shed by mid-September; the hunter said he could not find visible testicles.

Bucks can injure each other in their battles for dominance while in velvet or during the rut when the antlers have hardened or in the late winter after they shed the antlers and still battle with slashing hooves. If they do more than simply play-shove, they can injure the pedicel, the base of the soon-to-grow antler.

                    Susan Lindsley

Injuries can affect antler development and shape. An injury to a growing antler will deform it for that year; injuries to the pedicle (the base left on the skull after the antler is shed) can also cause the antler on that side to deform, and that deformation may be permanent.

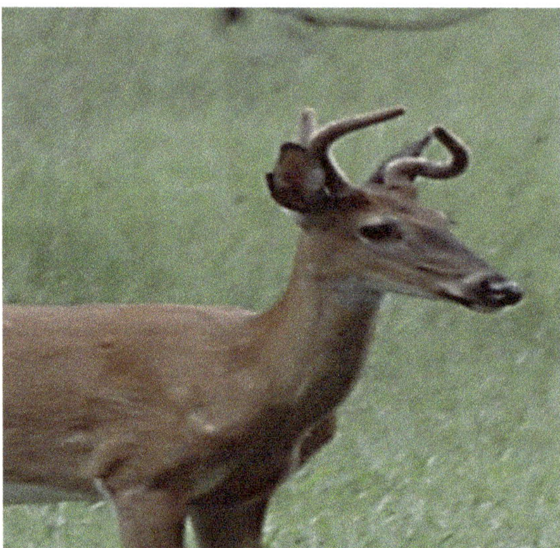

Snapshot in my yard, 1990s

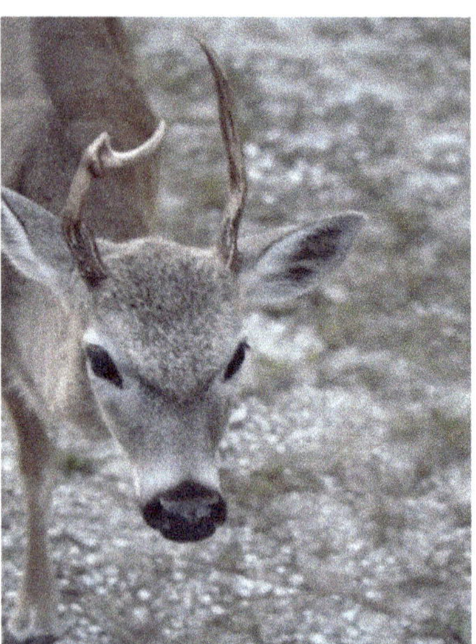

Key deer, early 2000

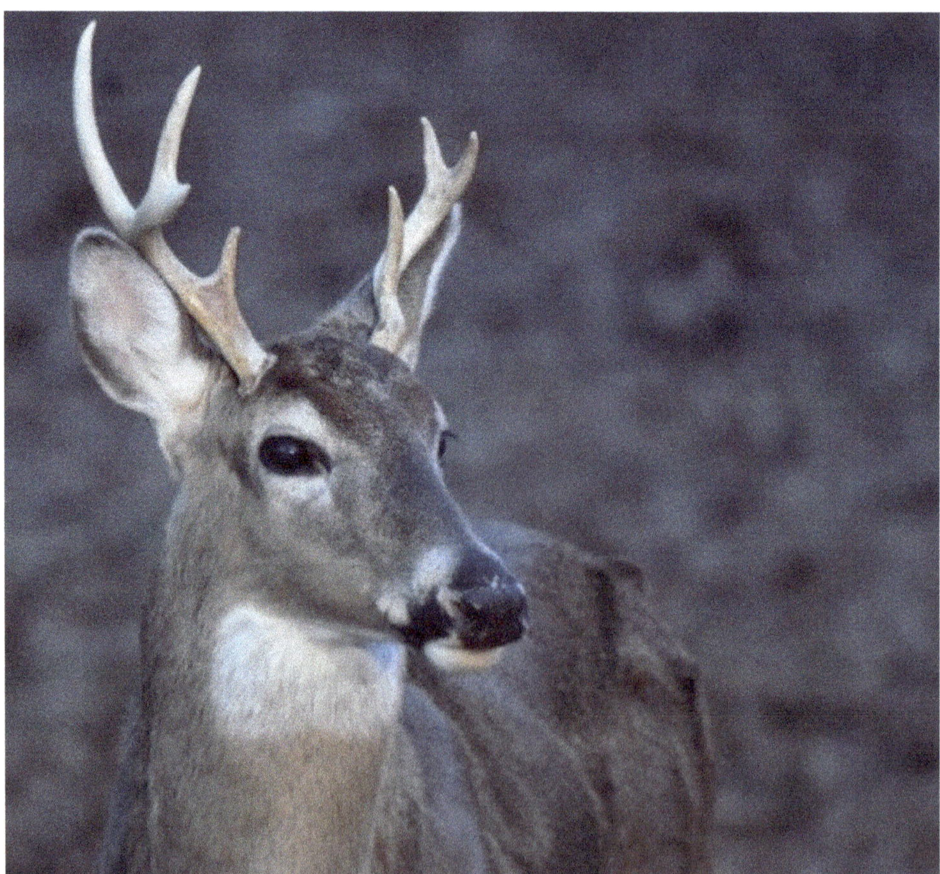

Yard deer

Leg injuries are another matter, and the relationship to the injury and antler is strange to say the least. A front-leg injury results in deformation to the antler on that side, but an injury to the back leg causes deformation on the opposite side. Again, how many years the deformation lasts are determined by the severity of the injury.

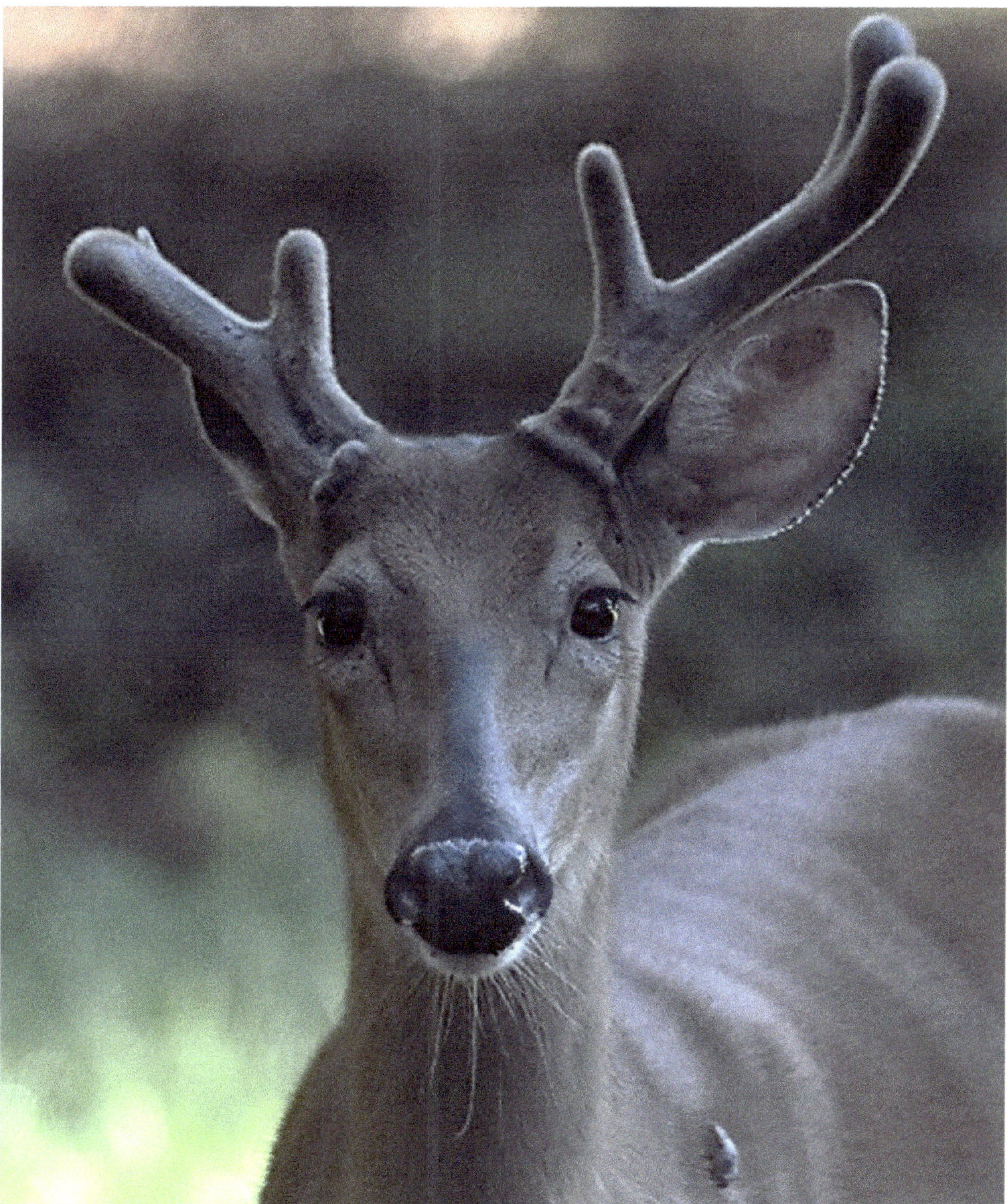

His unbalanced antlers didn't keep him from being a bully, even when in velvet.

These squabbling bucks were in the University of Georgia Research pens, which I was invited to visit by Joe Kurz, Game Management, Department of Natural Resources, in the mid-1980s. The buck at rest was in a penned preserve in Texas. For all, food was plentiful and balanced by biologists.

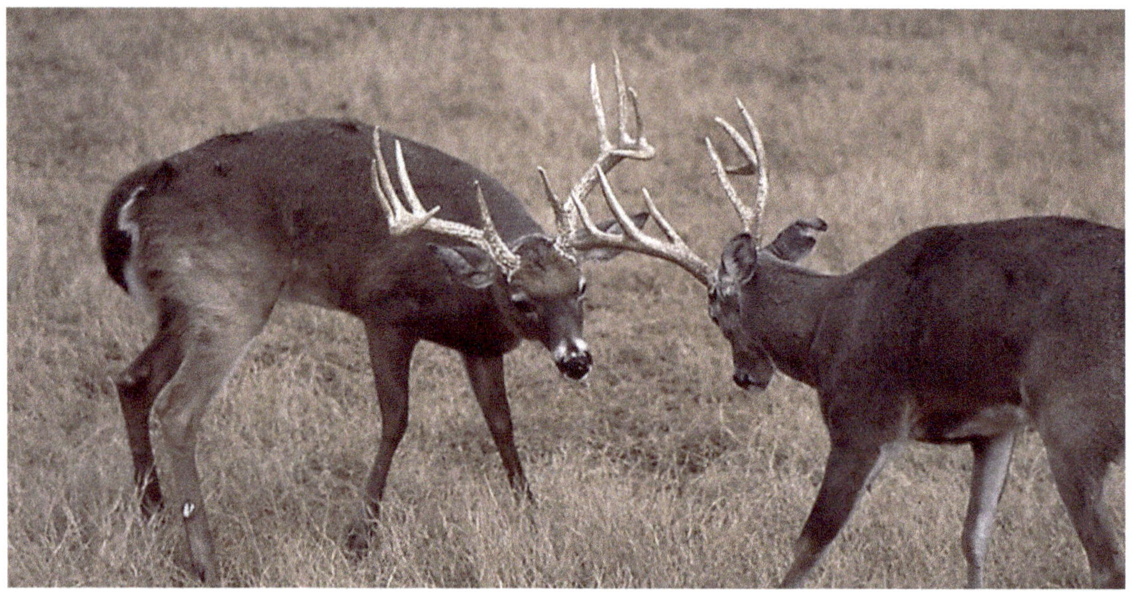

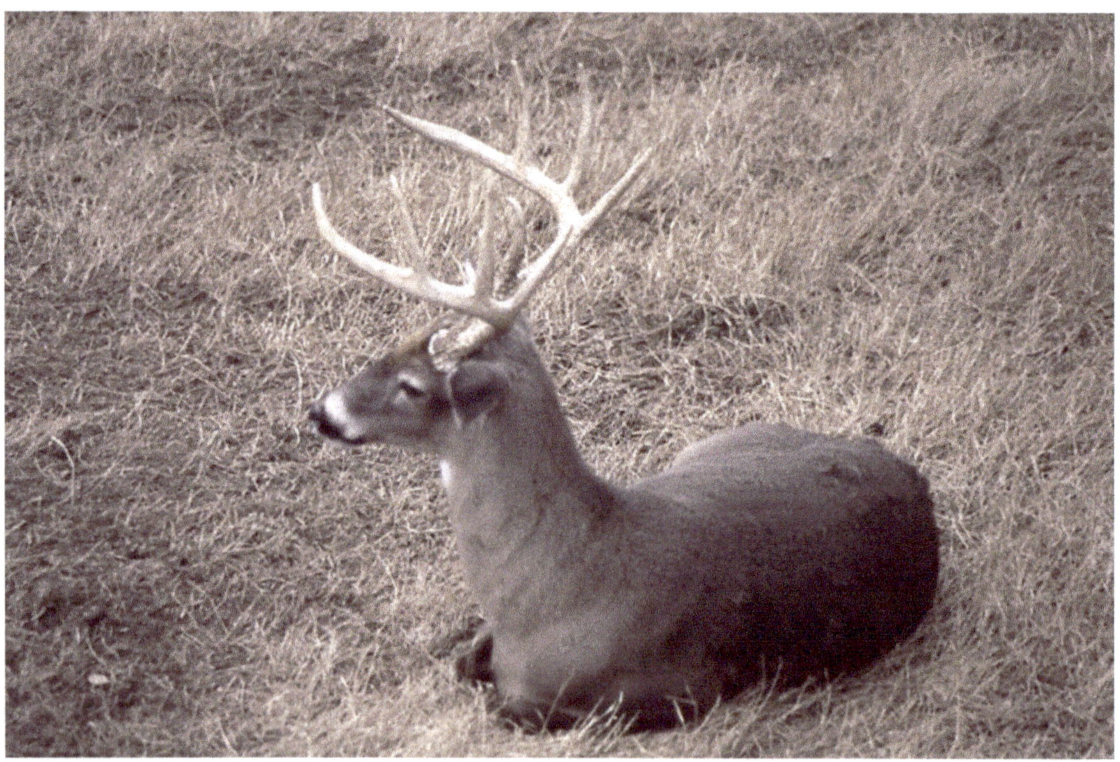

ANTLER TRAITS RUNNING IN THE HERD

Just as we humans have family traits passed from generation to generation, such as red hair or blue eyes, so do deer pass along antler patterns to future generations.

In my area, I have noticed a variety of antler patterns repeated over the years in the wild free-ranging bucks—absence of one or both brow tines or brow tines pointing off kilter as well as variations in the pattern of the main beams and other tines. Father-son and brother-brother patterns are obvious. A few of these pictures were taken with a three-megapixel point-and-shoot digital camera before 2010 and these early ones show how long an antler pattern can pass from generation to generation.

Biologists have named each prong (tine) on the antler with a series based on its location on the main beam, such as G-1, G-2, etc., but I do not use those terms here; I do however use the official term *brow tine* for the first tine on the main beam, close to the skull, and don't go into detail much about other tines.

It is easy to think a pattern is genetic when several deer show up with similar patterns, as I thought this flat-looking antler was genetic. But this is Two-Spot, and his next set of antlers showed a typical rack.

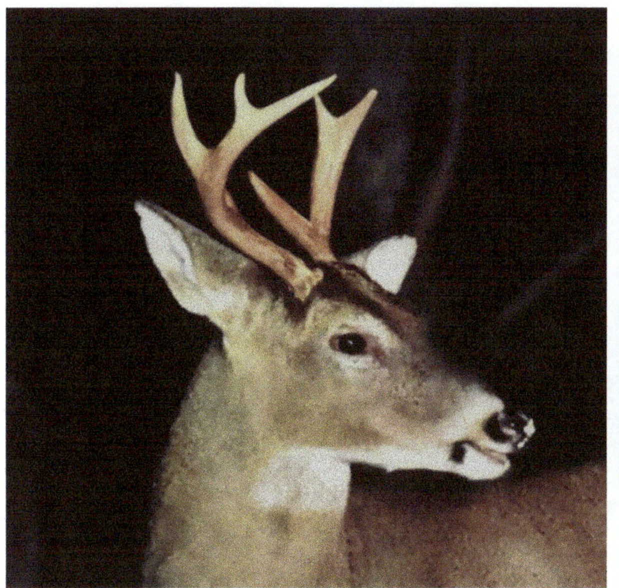

2021

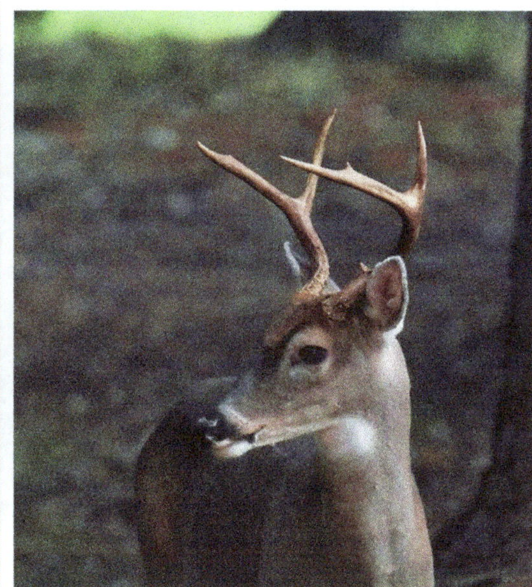

2022

Brow tines varied, from none to nubs to singles. Several six pointers had none. These guys showed up the same year.

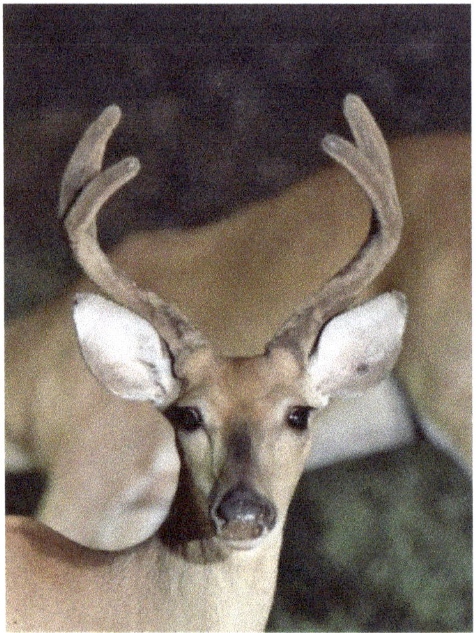
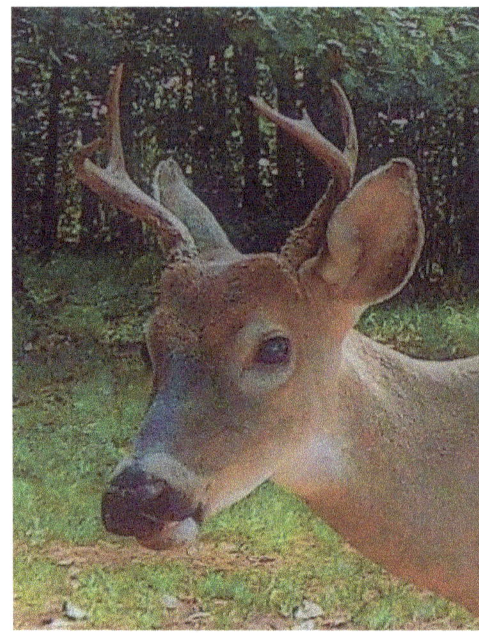

Little Six, on the right, showed up on the trail camera once and was killed by a car a few days later. Someone driving by stopped and cut off his antlers. It might be his angle to the camera, but his nose looks enlarged.

Brow tines varied from nubs to singles to multiples to pointing different directions.

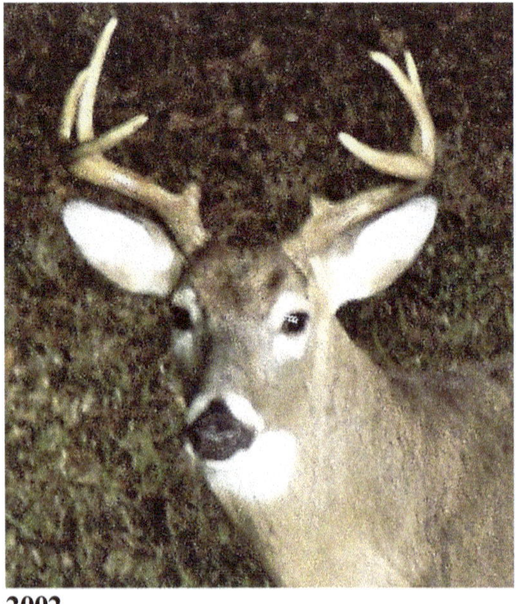
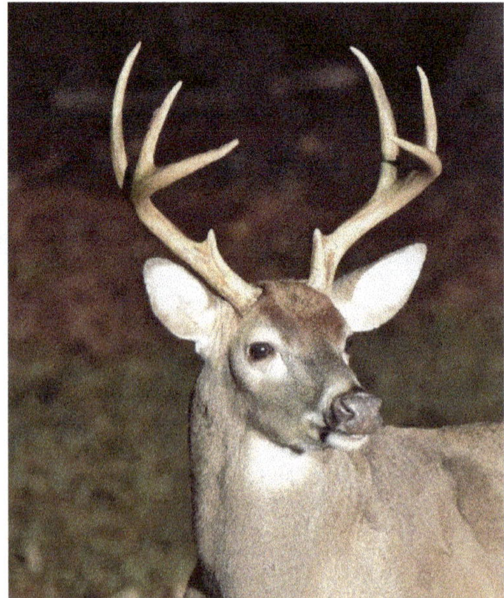

2002   **2018**

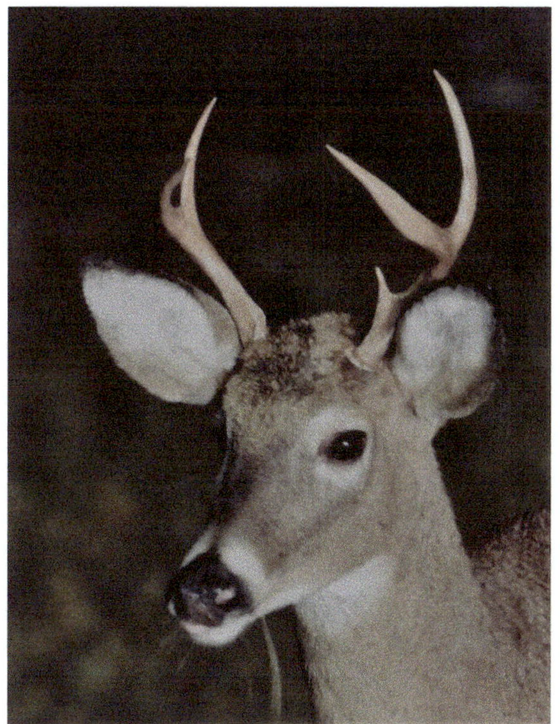

2018

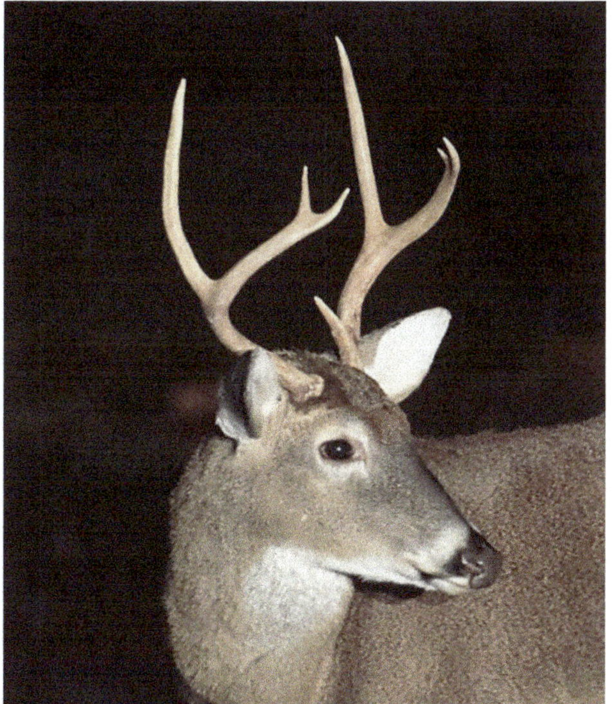

January 2015

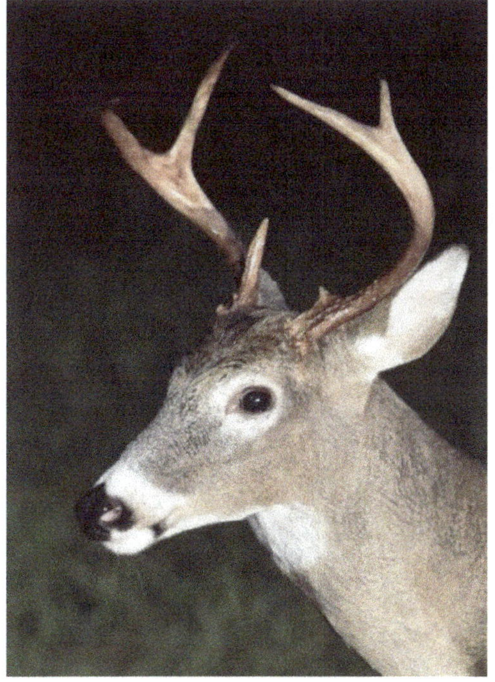

2018

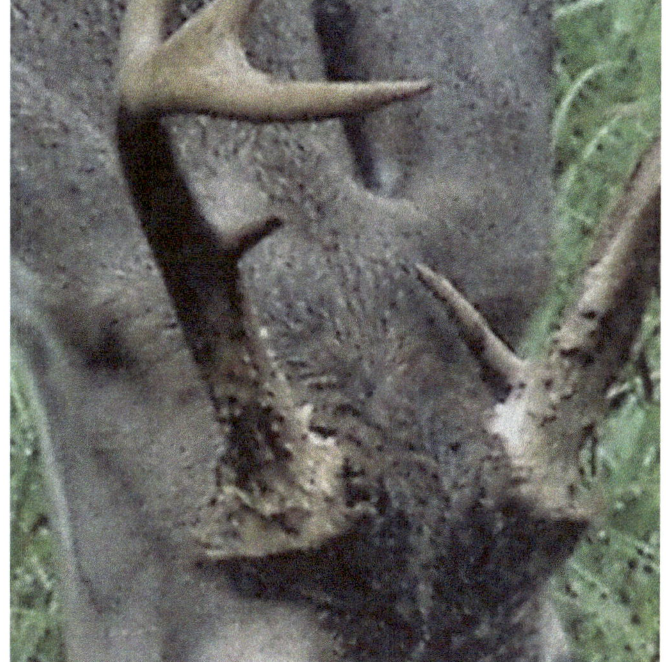

Early 2000s

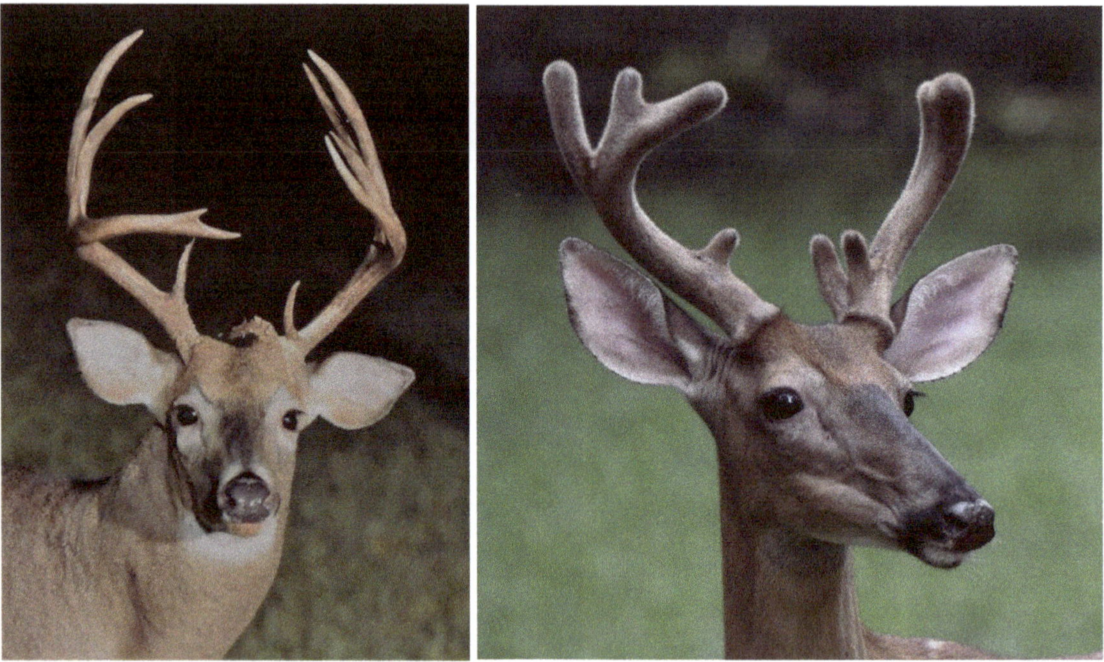

Some of the most interesting brow tines point all which-a-ways, to the front or to the side rather than upward. Some even lie almost flat. These appeared over a number of years.

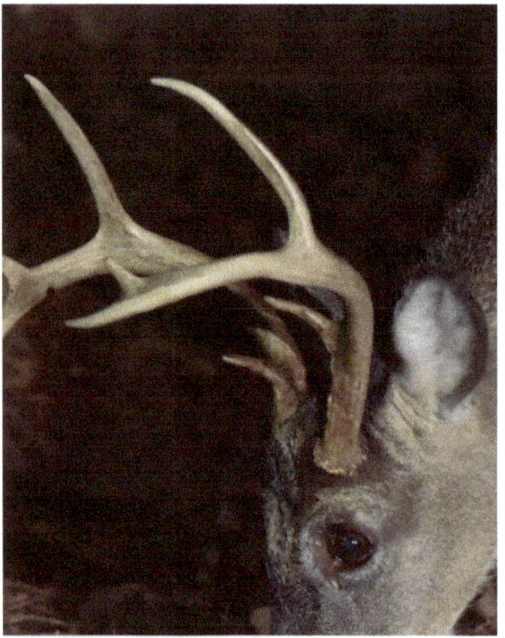

January   2020

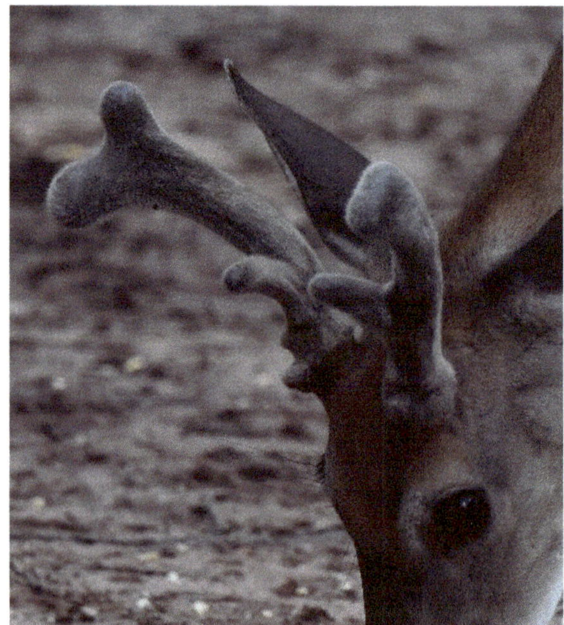

June 2021

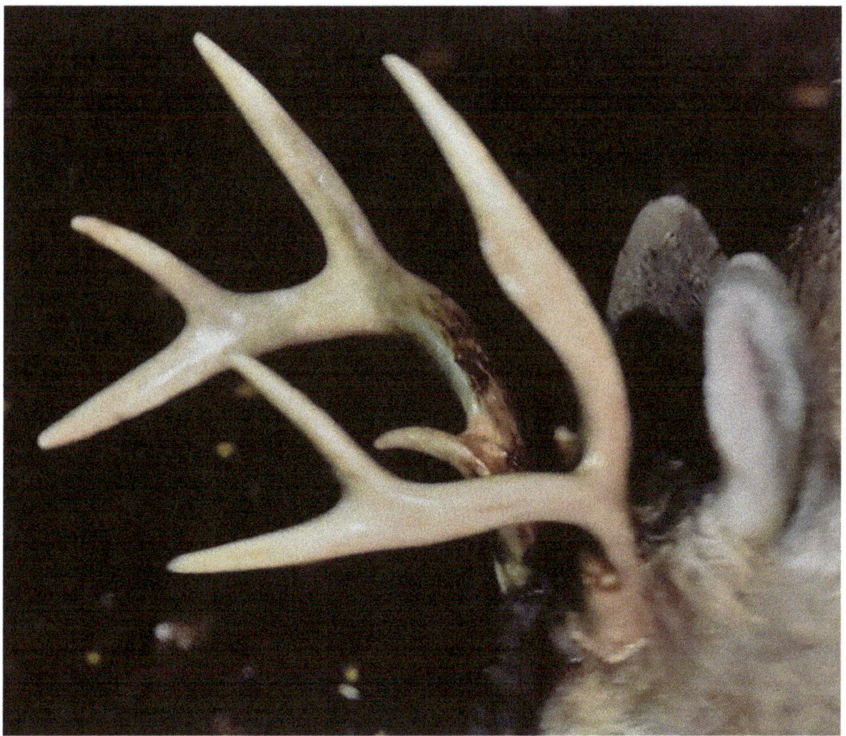

This beauty has one brow tine (just visible on his left) growing properly but his other on his right points forward like a rapier in the hand of a fencer. He also has a wave on the near tall tine, which might indicate the tine was about to fork.

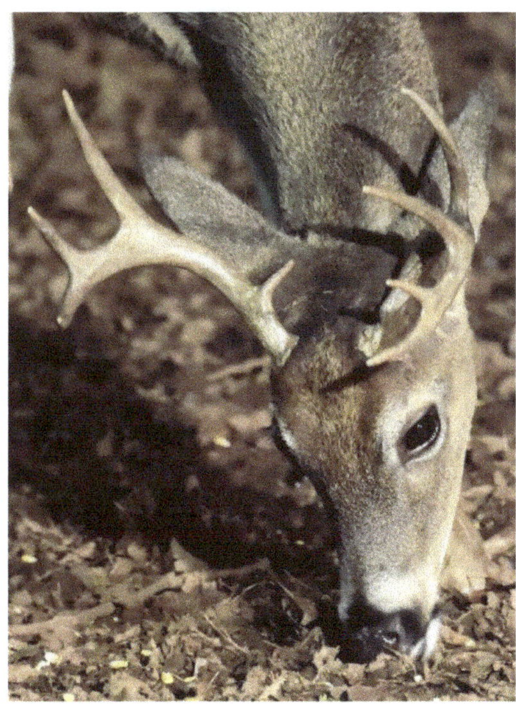

2020 Crossways

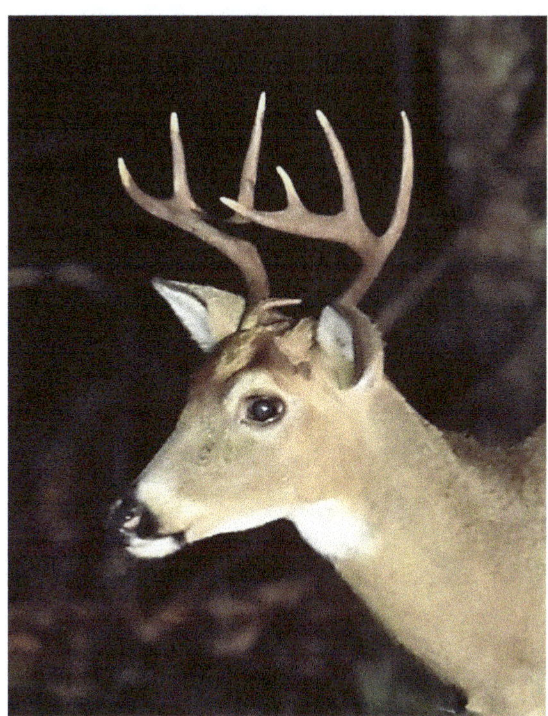

2020 Backwards

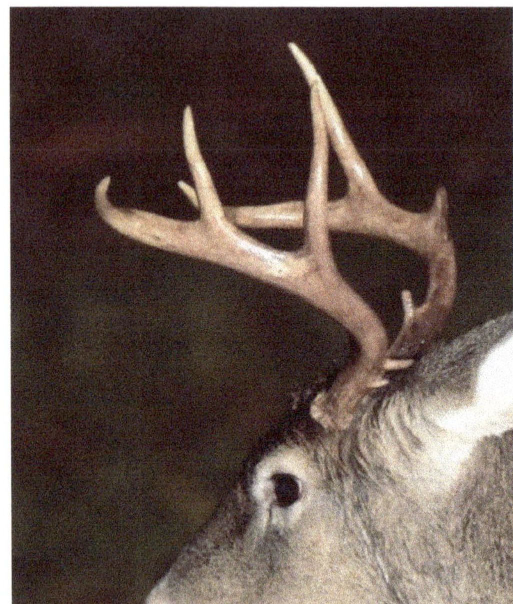

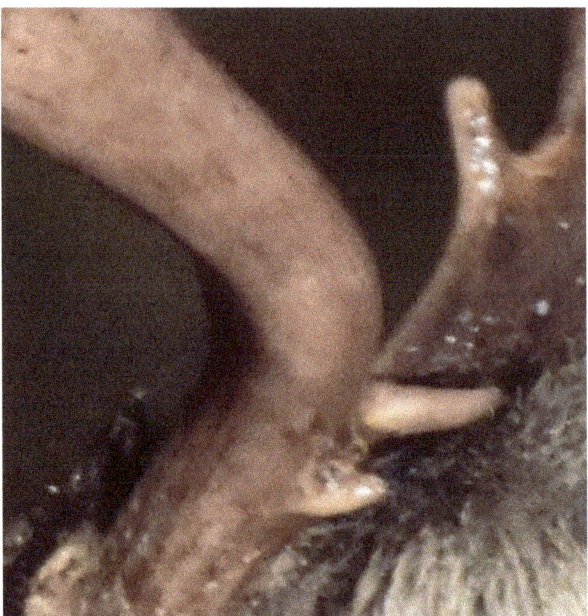

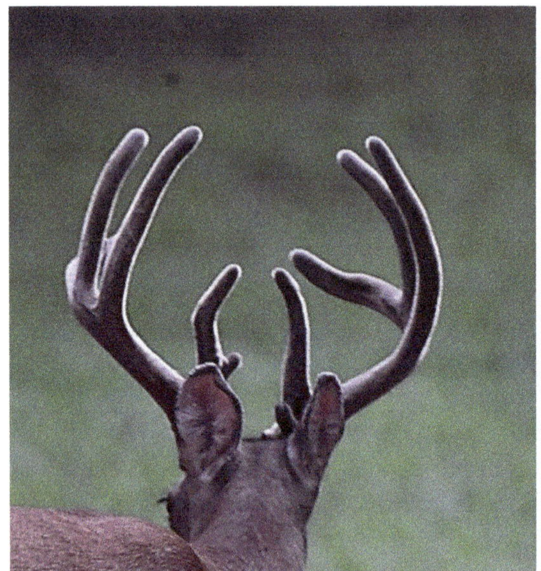

Another year, another buck with a
back-pointing nub.

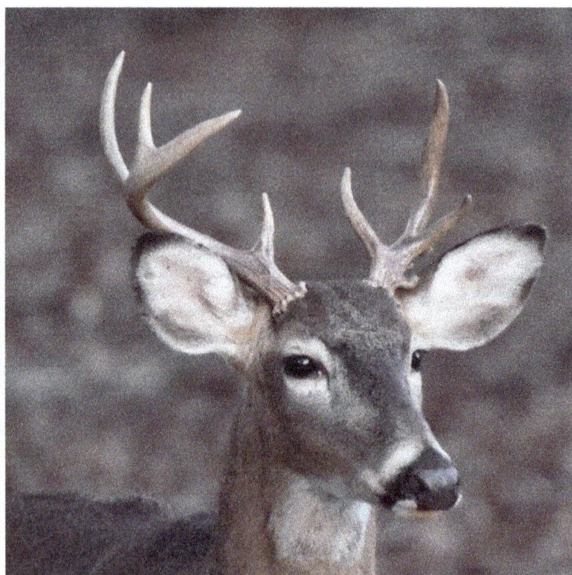

And one with a turkey-claw like antler,
surely from an injury.

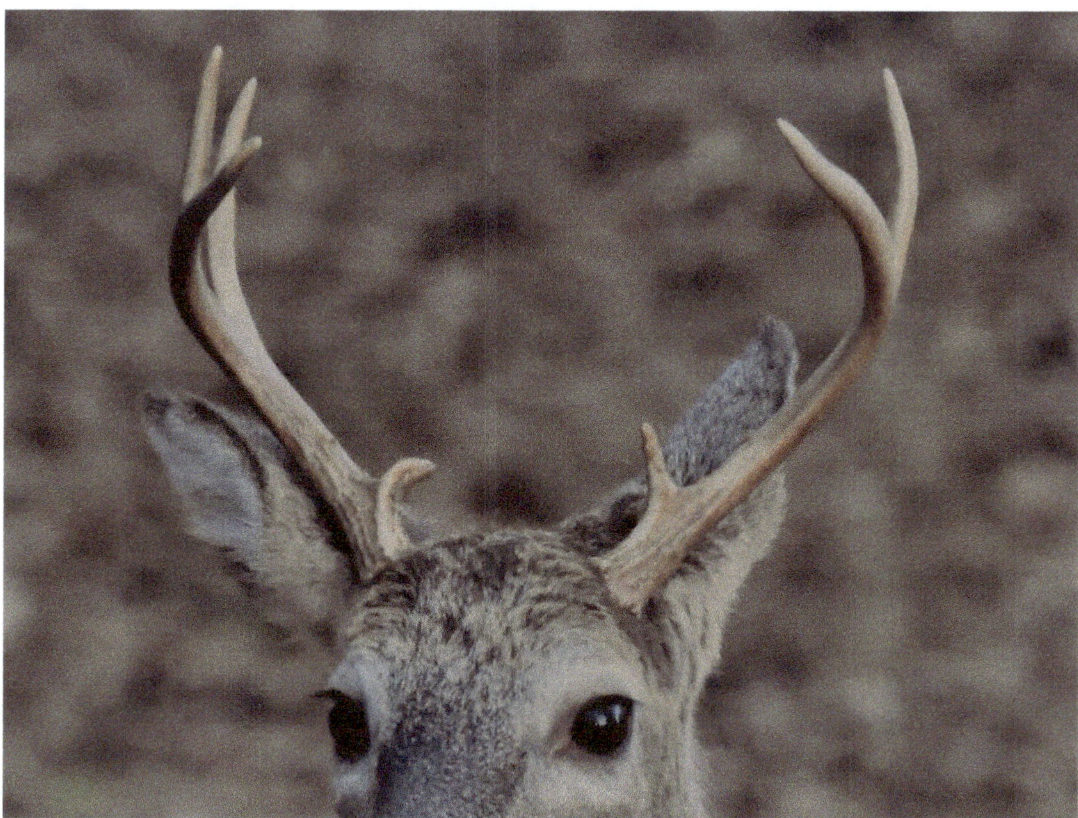

January 2020. He has both brow tines, one with a curl, but is a seven with a curve near the end of his left beam. Another tine that did not develop perhaps.

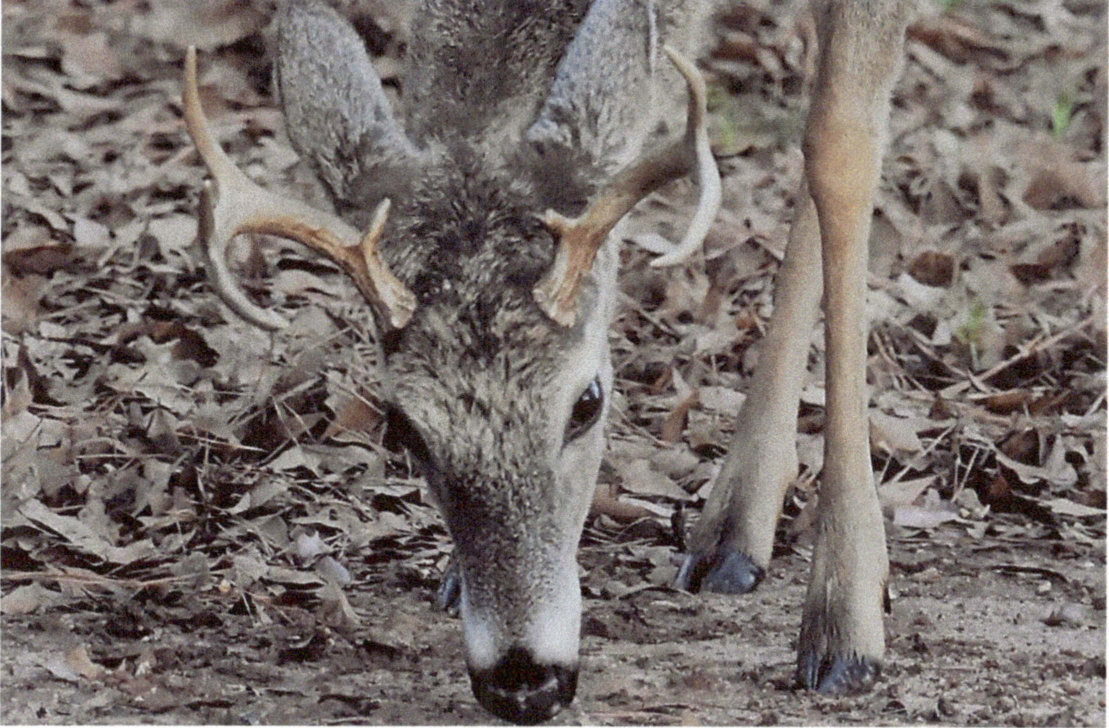

January 15, 2020.   They point across to each other.

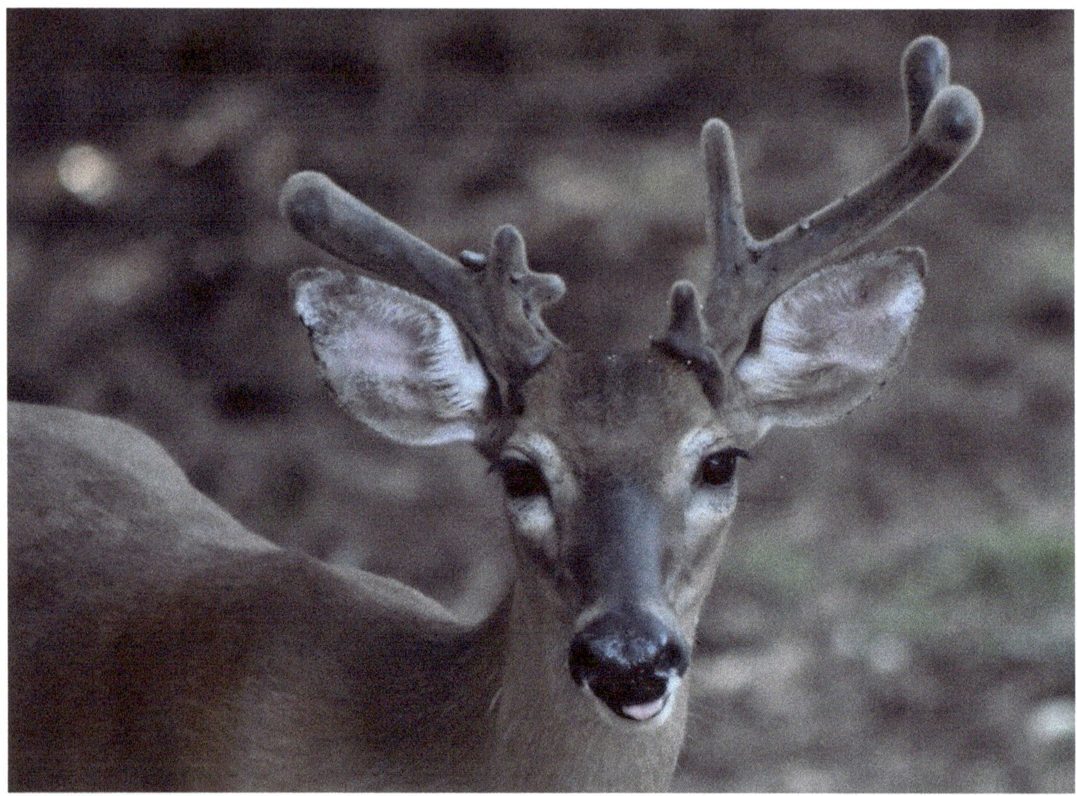

Another odd pattern, similar to the Bully's.

Numerous bucks with typical/normal/regular antlers came and went, with antlers ranging from spikes to eight pointers and a couple of ten pointers who both bit the dust at the hands of neighboring hunters. Only on rare occasions have I known what happened to or who collected one of the deer that came into my yard for a while and later disappeared.

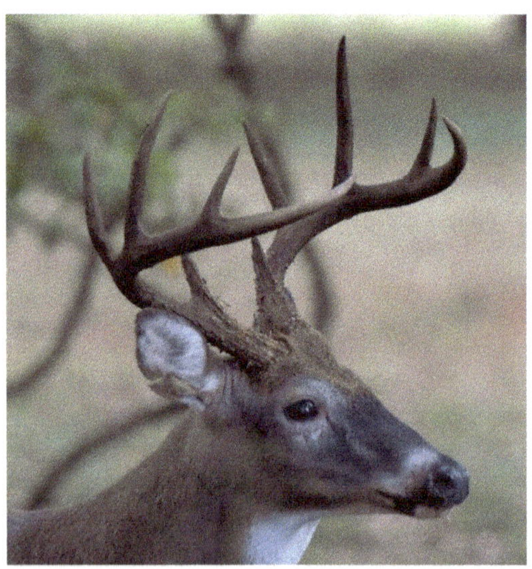

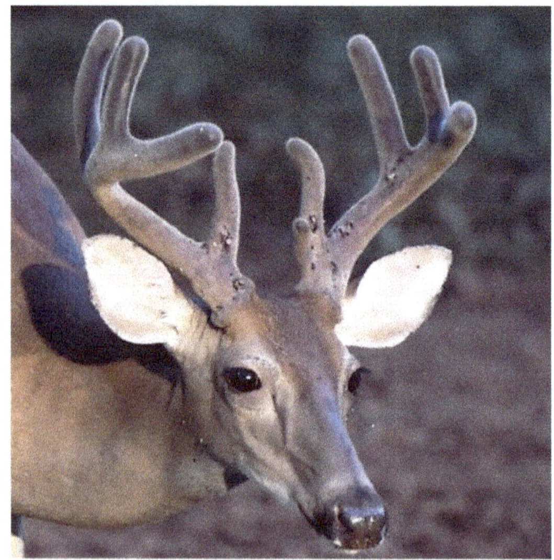

A few bucks with slightly atypical racks, that would keep any hunter happy, visited over the years. Most notable were the nine points (Pappy in 2019 and Pappy 2 in 2022) with a forked tine typical of the mule deer, not the whitetail, and also Wide Beams and the eight-plus-two.

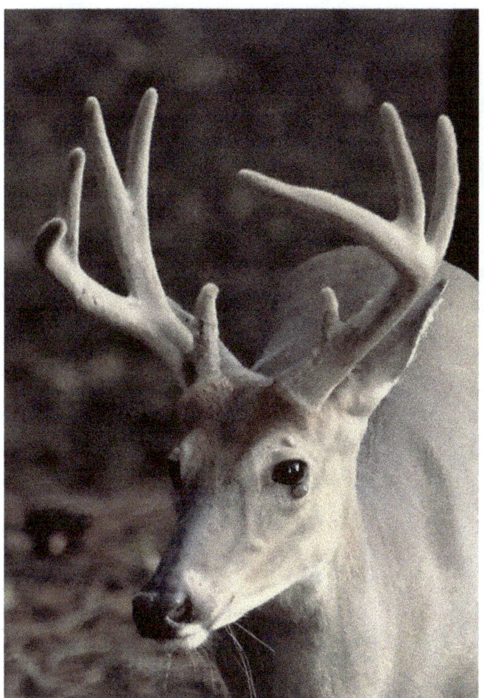
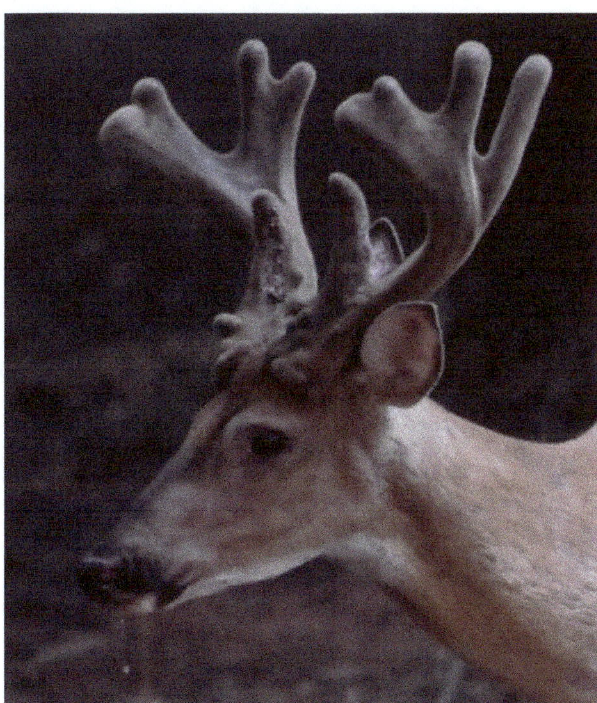
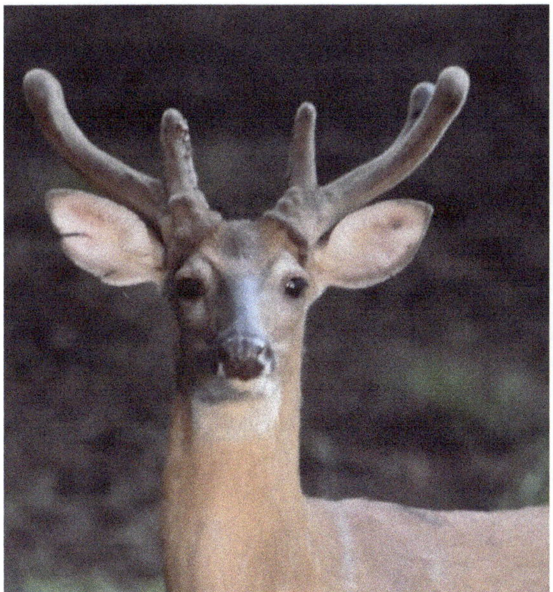
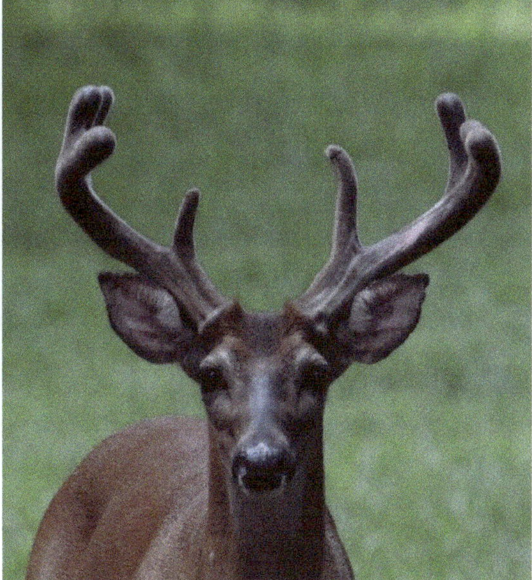

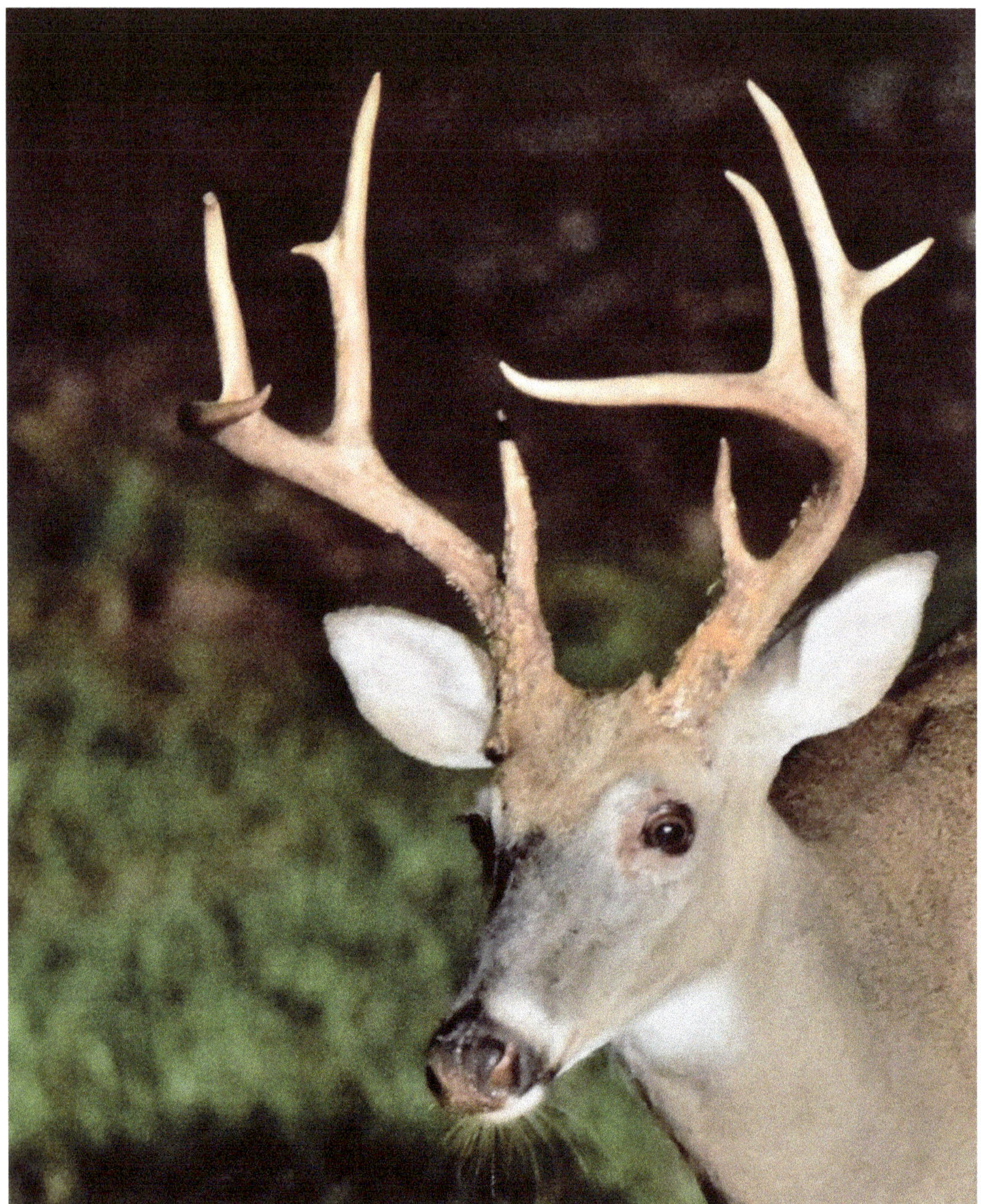

The residue on his antlers is from a cedar tree he has horned.

I called this odd ten pointer *eight-plus-two* because of the tiny points that projected to the side from the same tine on opposite beams. He was unique; I never saw a similar rack but have seen pictures of bucks with such horizonal points on their tines. Be interesting to see what shows up in the next few years that show his paternity.

ANTLER GROWTH IN TWO BUCKS IN THE WILD

Many penned bucks have been followed from spring buttons to full racks, but I found it somewhat difficult to follow a dozen wild deer from first regrowth or from buttons to antlers. No yellow tags on an ear to give me a number or code. I had to search for some individual variation—patterns of injuries in ears that remained consistent from month to month, or scars or any infestation. One buck had what looked like two ticks, but turned out to be papilloma, a type of wart (thanks to Dr. Karl Miller for the identification), one above and one below his left eye that I could see from the time he grew his spring buttons into nine points and he shed his velvet. He disappeared in October. He not only carried the papilloma around his left eye but bore a scar on his right side.

So I changed his original name from Tickeye to Pappy. Turned out he was a big enough fellow to deserve the name.

Another buck had no brow tines, and some had distinct ear markings which remained long enough for me to follow them until their racks became individualized.

PAPPY

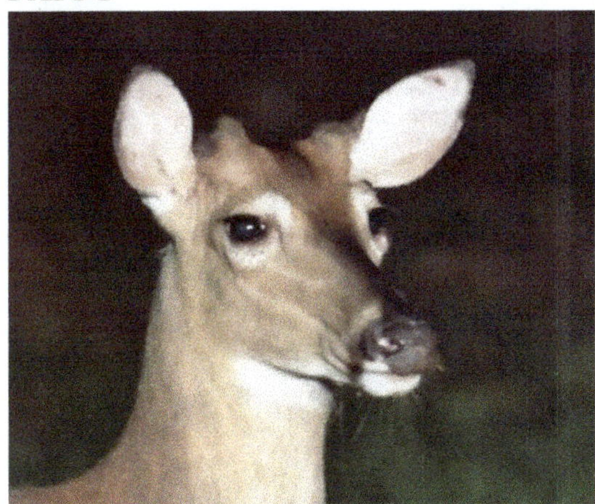

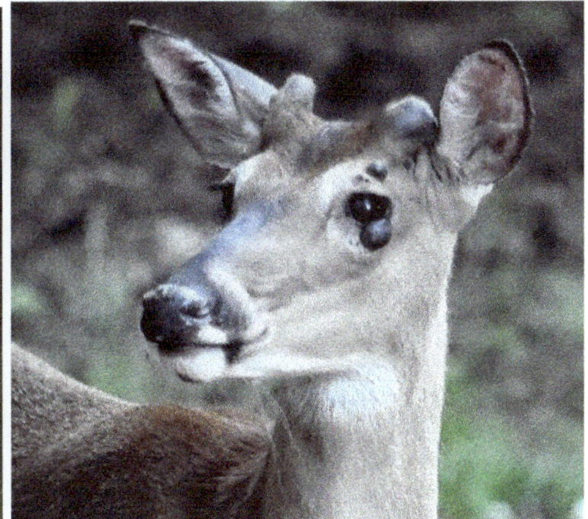

April 24. The warts are barely visible.   **April 30.**

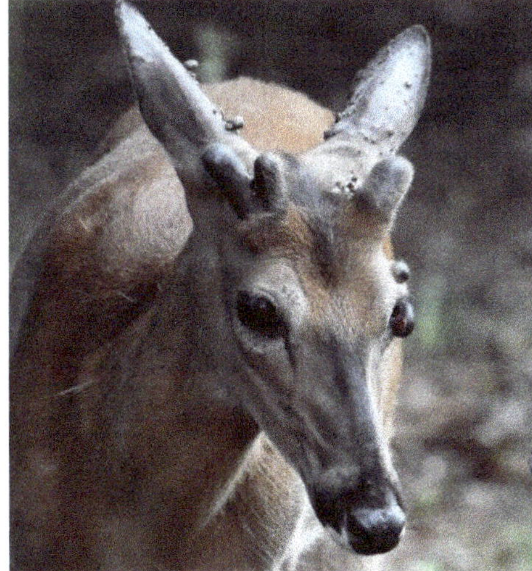

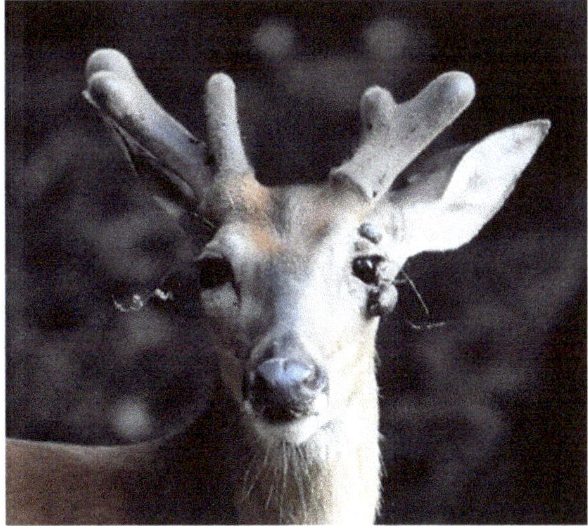

May 8   **May 31**

 Susan Lindsley

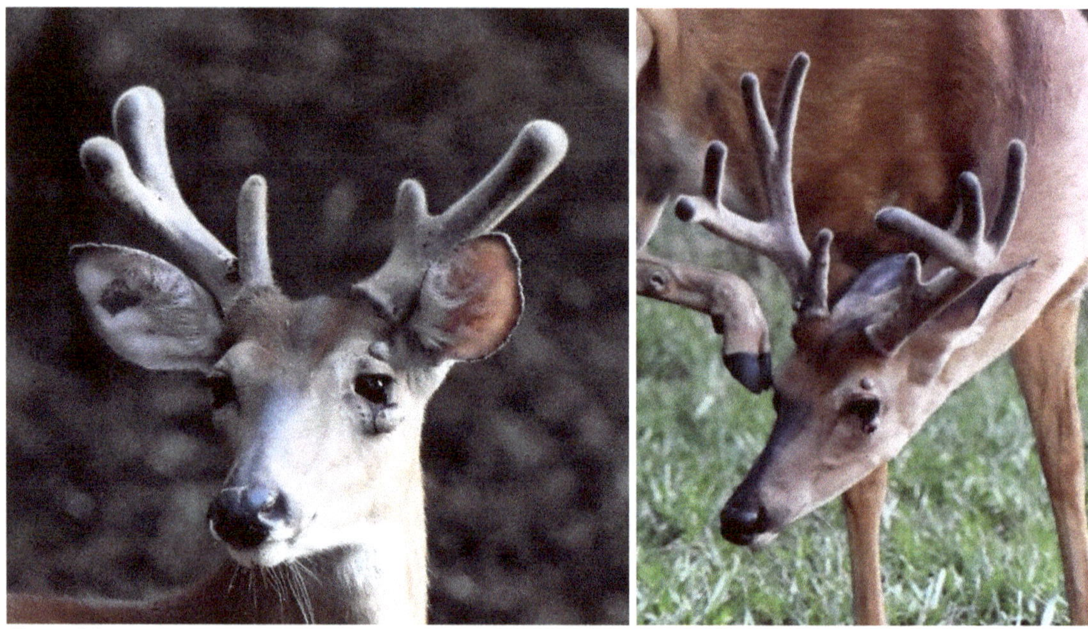

June 14

July 15

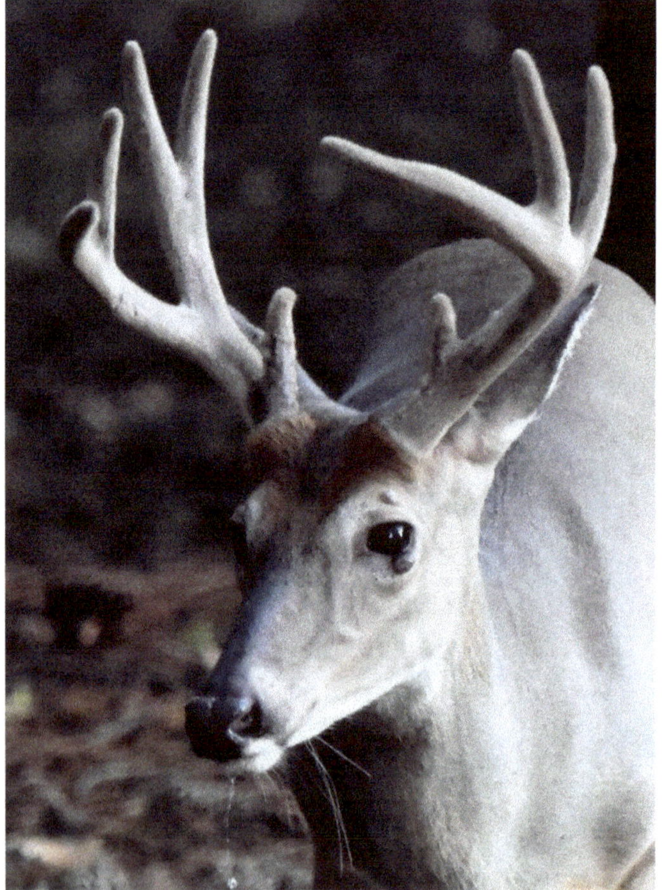

August 31

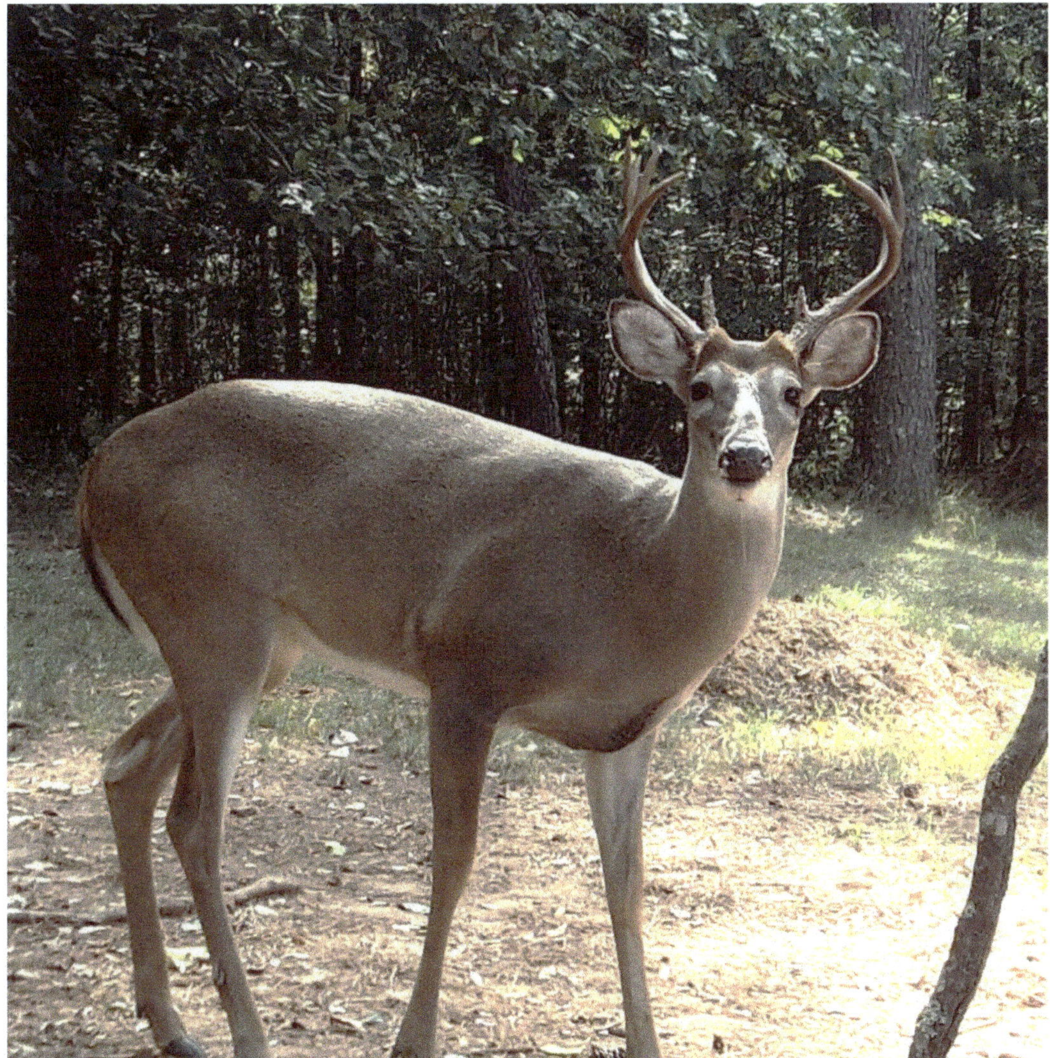

October 14, his last visit. Somewhere nearby a hunter got very lucky.

THE KNOB BUCK

Another buck I followed was a youngster, probably only carrying his first antlers. He ran buddies with Pappy for a few visits and changed buddies to a doe I called Clip Ear, who had a papilloma on her left hindquarter. They ran together for the rest of the summer and into the early rut. I was able to identify his early pictures from patterns of scaring and scabs in his ears.

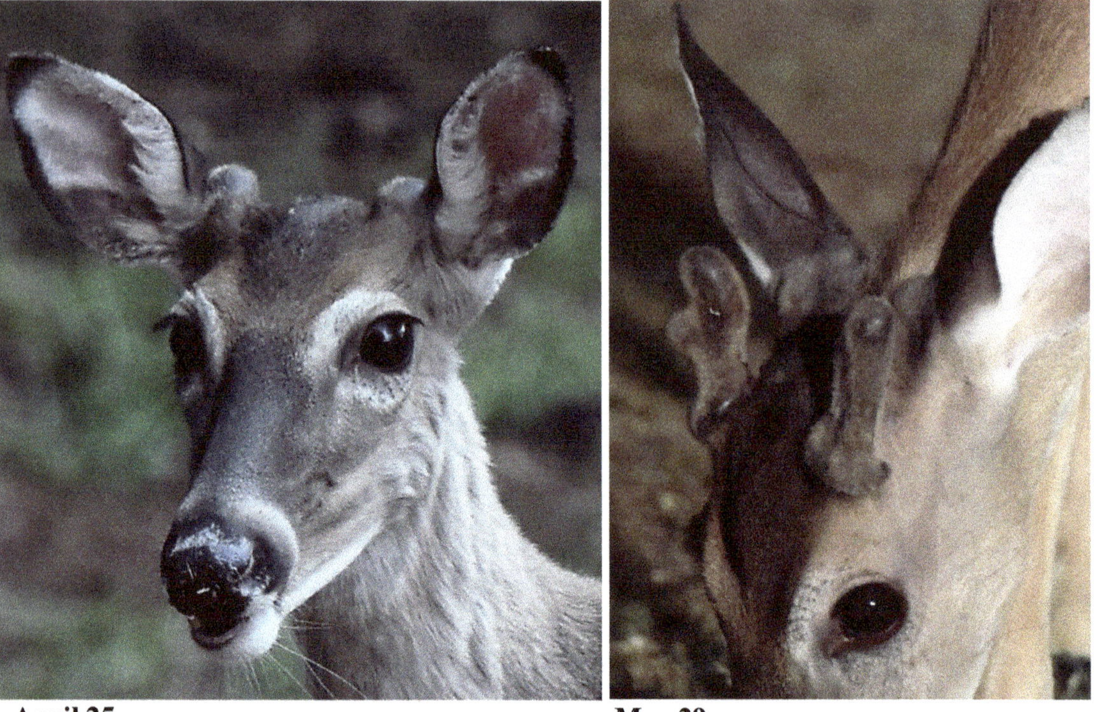

April 25

May 29

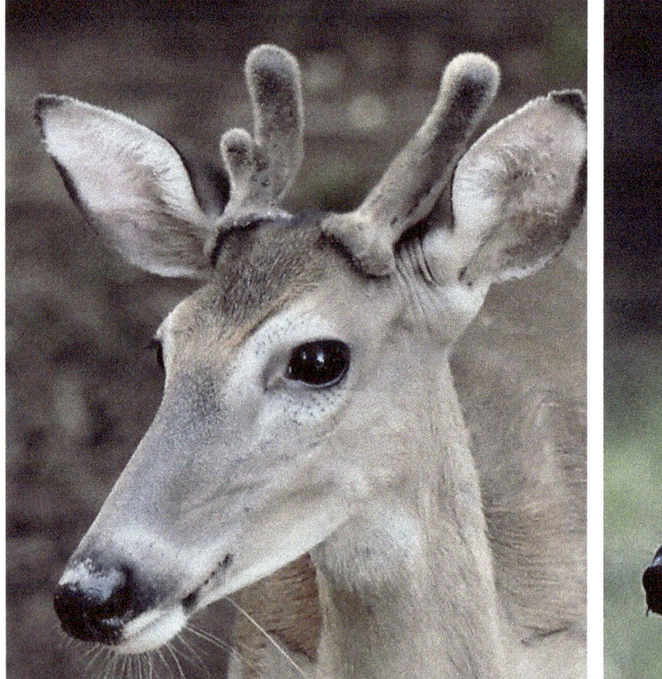

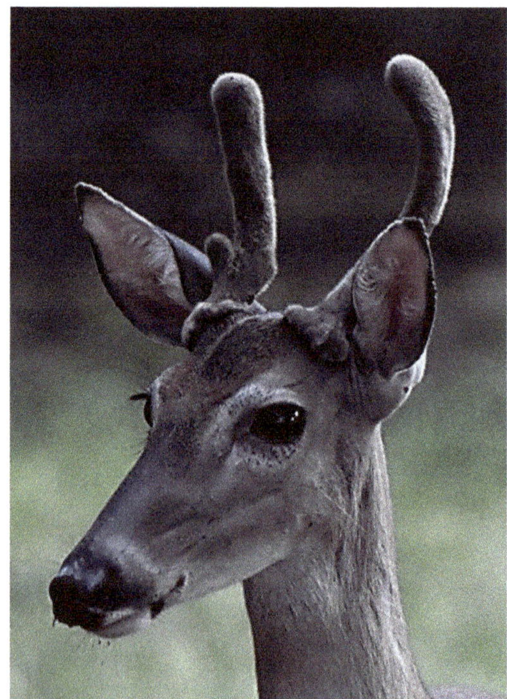

June 14

July 17

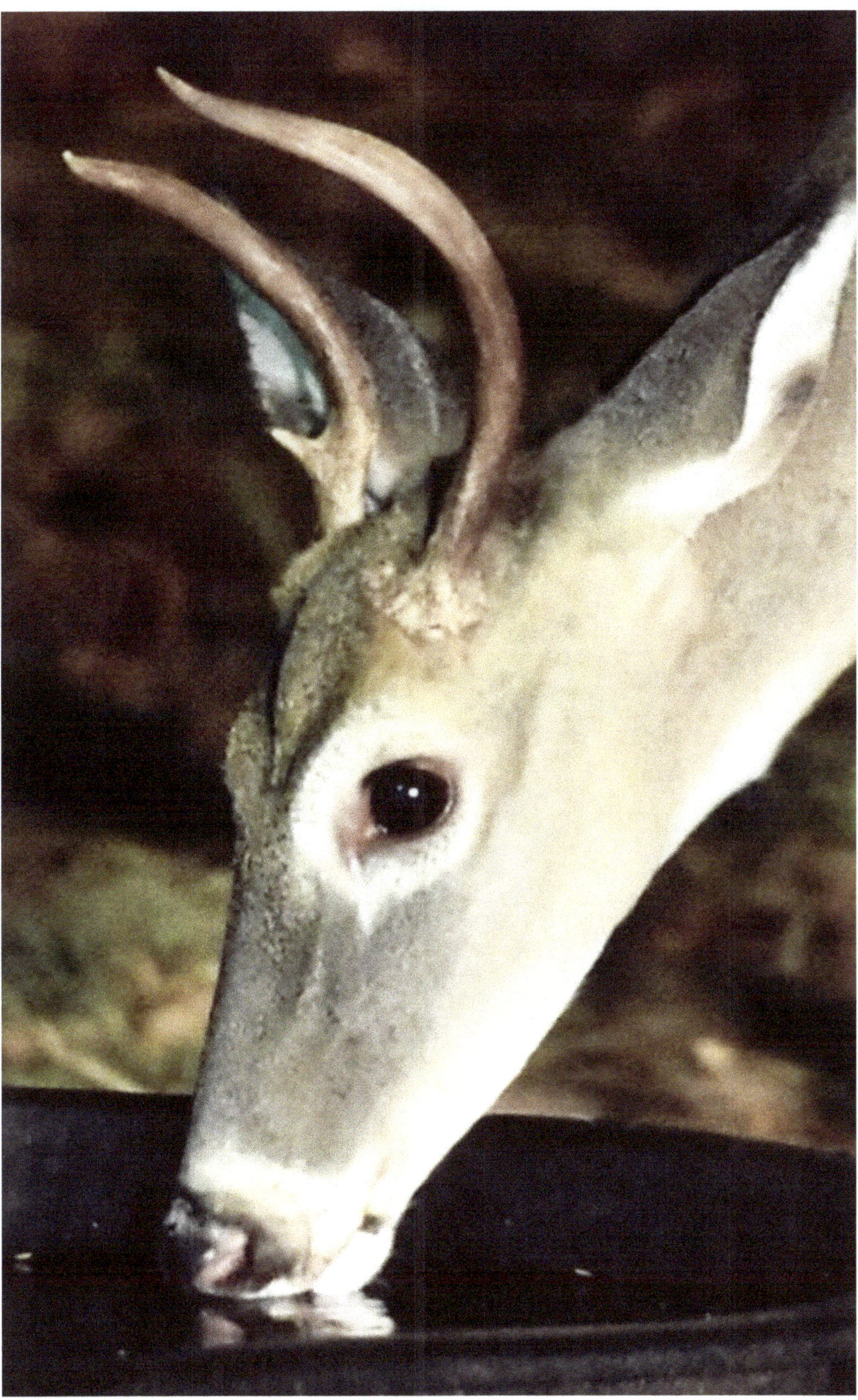

September

SHEDDING VELVET

In middle Georgia, the bucks shed velvet in early late summer and early fall. The earliest I have seen is August 27 and the latest September 14.

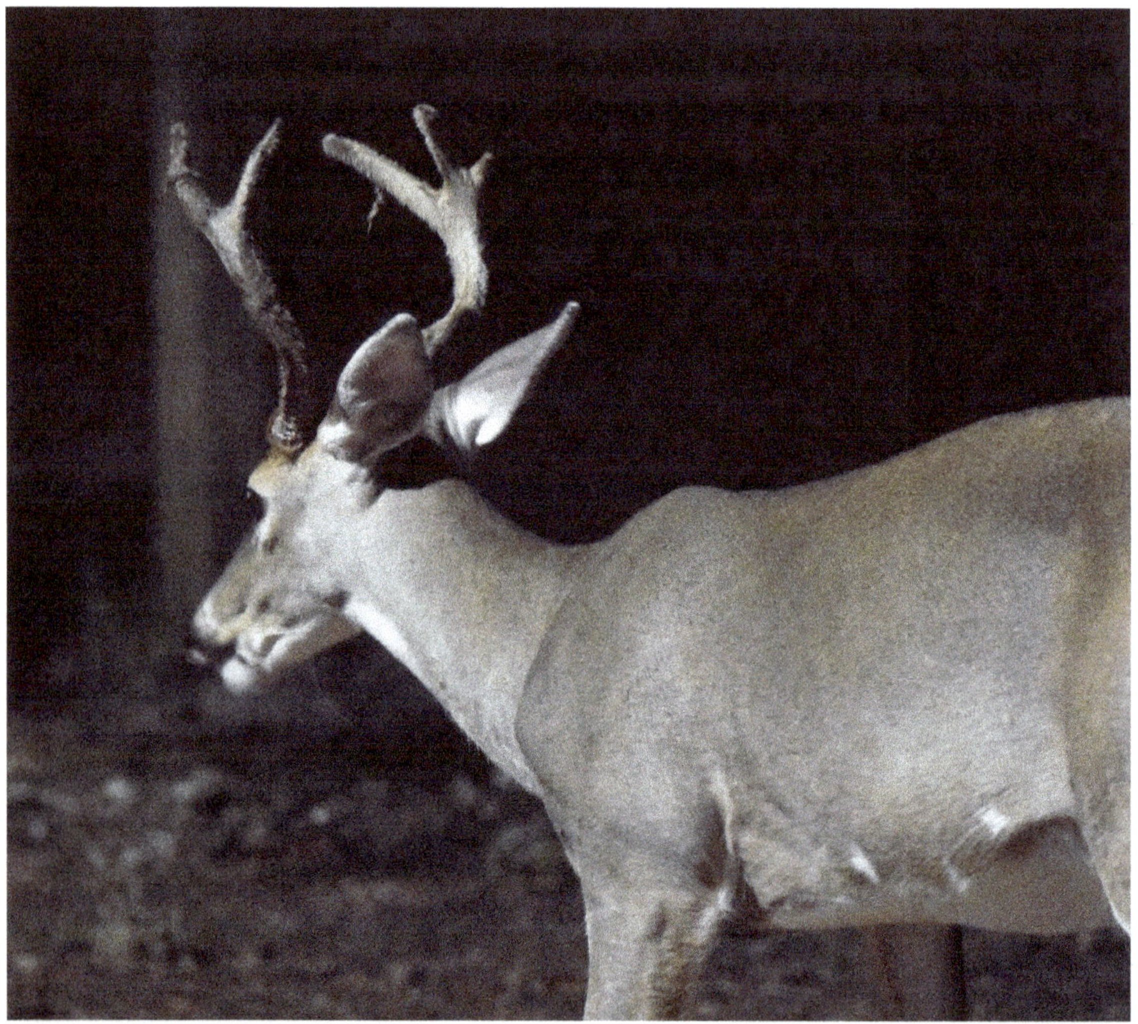

August 27. I called him *Two Spot*.

Shedding velvet is the most visible signal that the rut is approaching. Some bucks seem to pay no heed to the changes, whereas some find the streams hanging over their eyes a terrific bother.

One fellow ran around with his head shaking for three days to try to get rid of that streamer that flopped over his eye. Took me a while to realize what was going on because most of my pictures just showed his head in a swivel and a total blur. He finally stopped long enough for me to realize a strand of velvet was in his eye and he thought he could outrun it. He eventually managed to flip it over his neck.

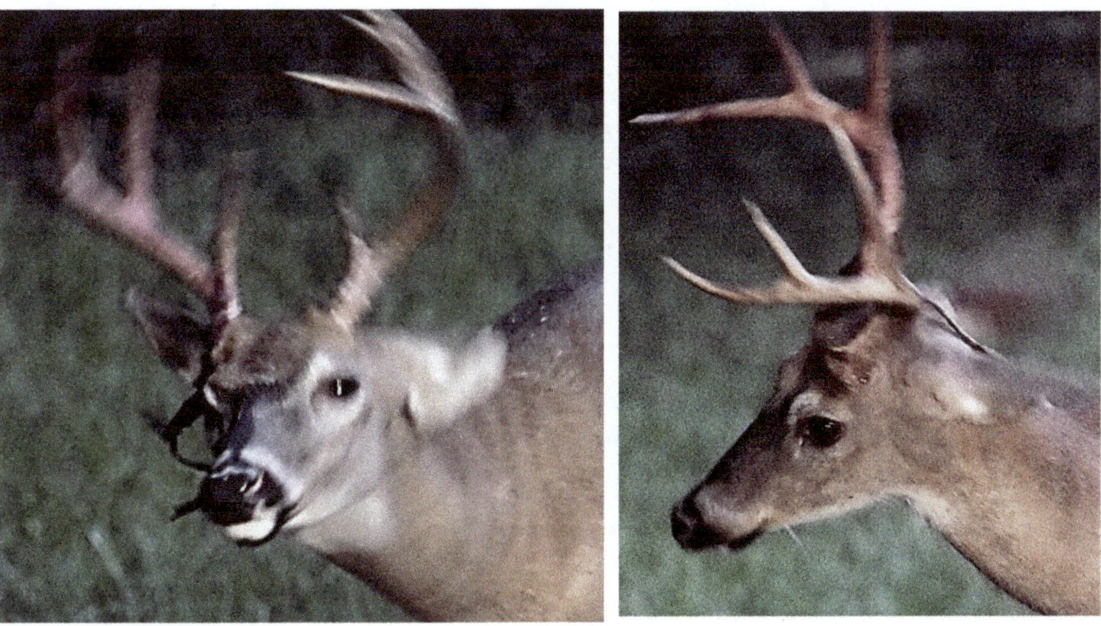

Several threw a hissy fit to tear off the velvet.

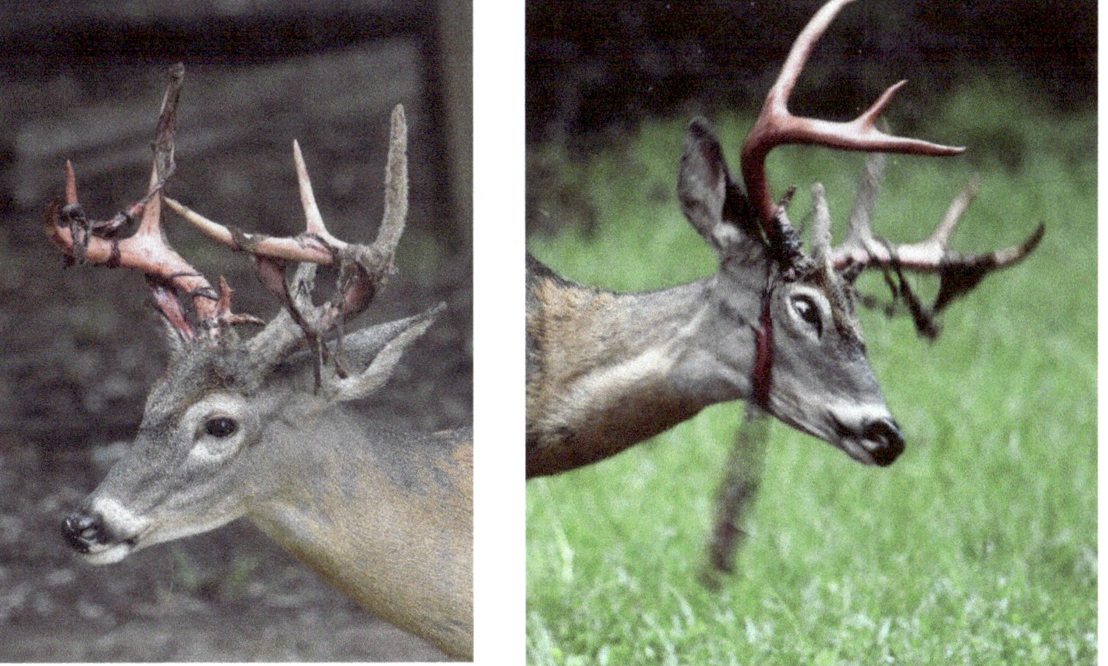

They look like comedians or clowns getting ready for the circus with the velvet hanging down like weeds and their trying to shake it off.

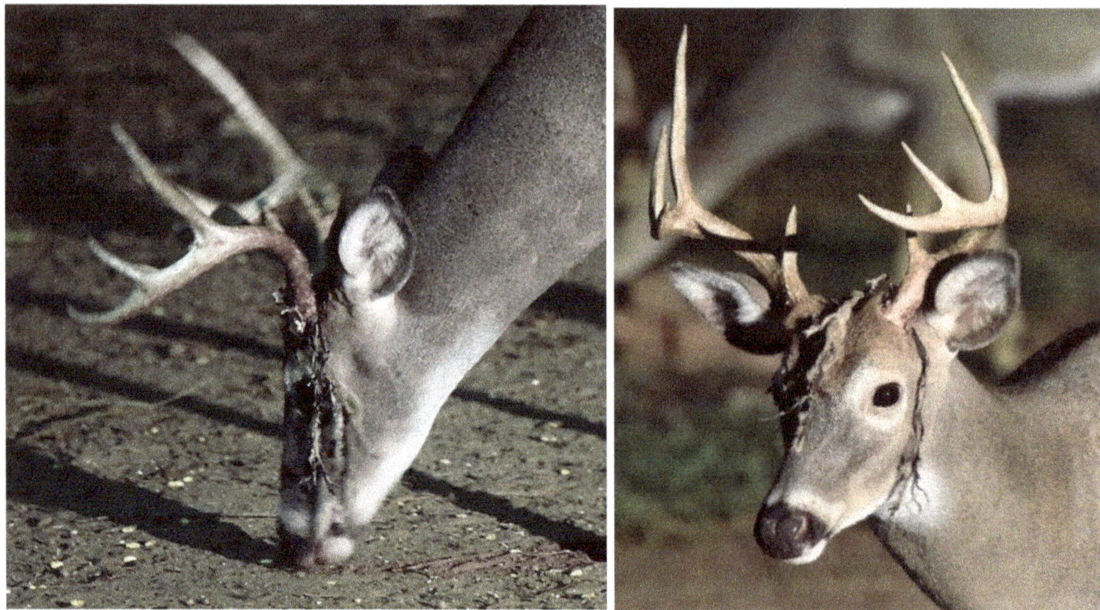

The boss of 2019 had velvet hanging every which-a-way for several days.

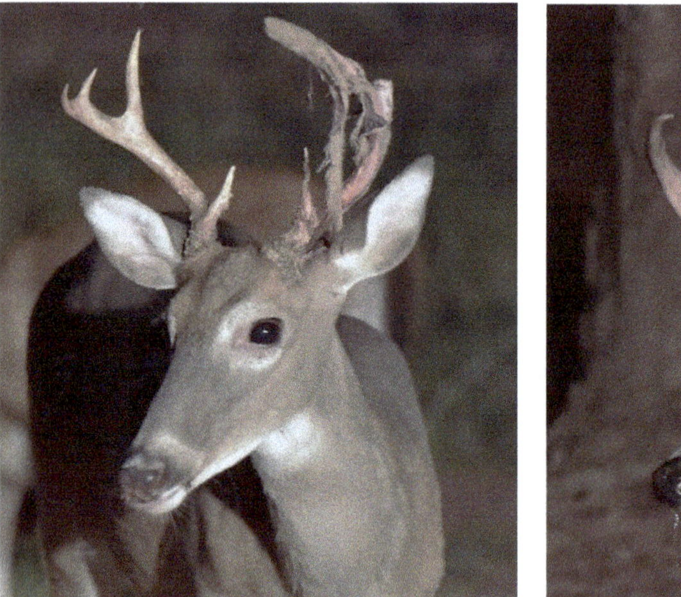

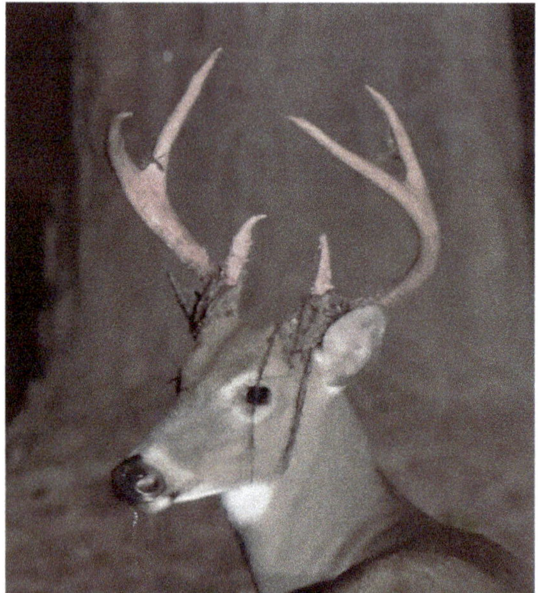

Sometimes the velvet dries, cracks and sheds almost like human blistered skin rather than in streamers. No matter the size of the rack, however, blood shows at some point in the shedding and often the antlers themselves show red as the velvet cracks.

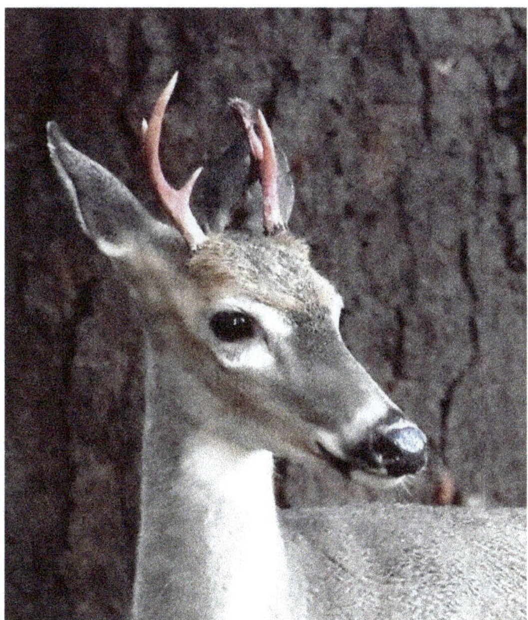 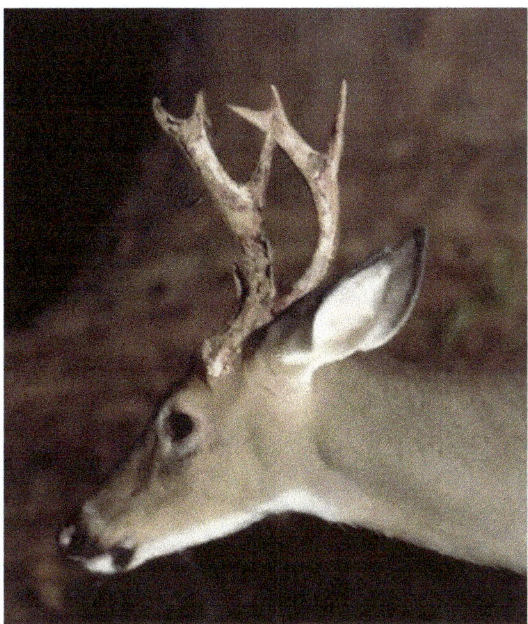

Antlers look much larger before the velvet dries and is sluffed off. A good example is Pappy. He is in full velvet and about full growth on July 14. The hard-antler picture was taken on October 2. I did not see him during September when he was shedding velvet.

In 2022, another buck appeared with a similar rack, which I named Pappy 2.

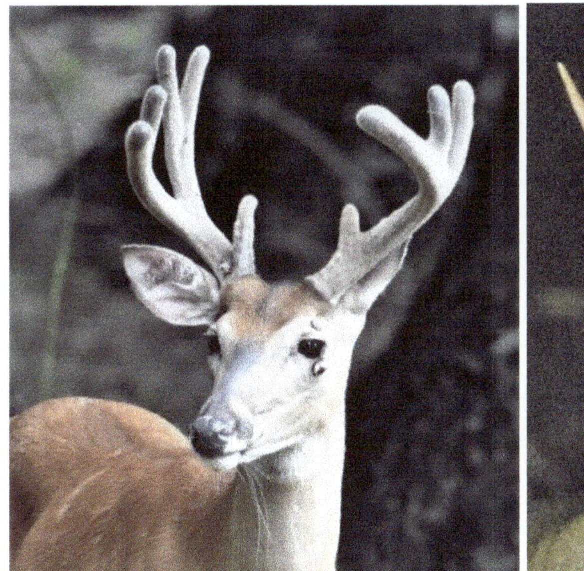 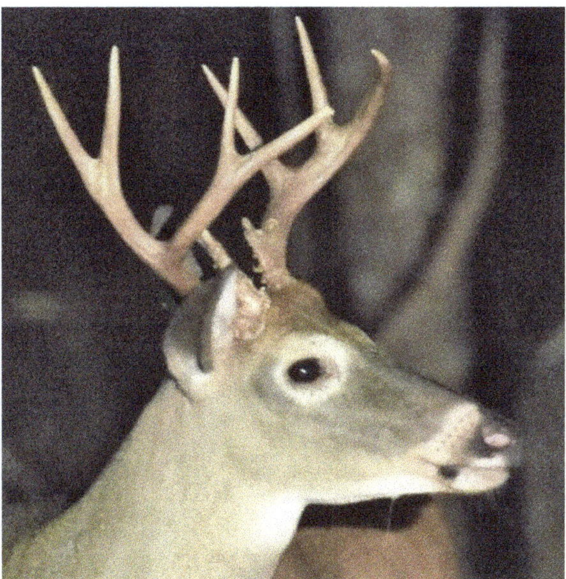

Pappy, July 14   **Pappy, October 2**

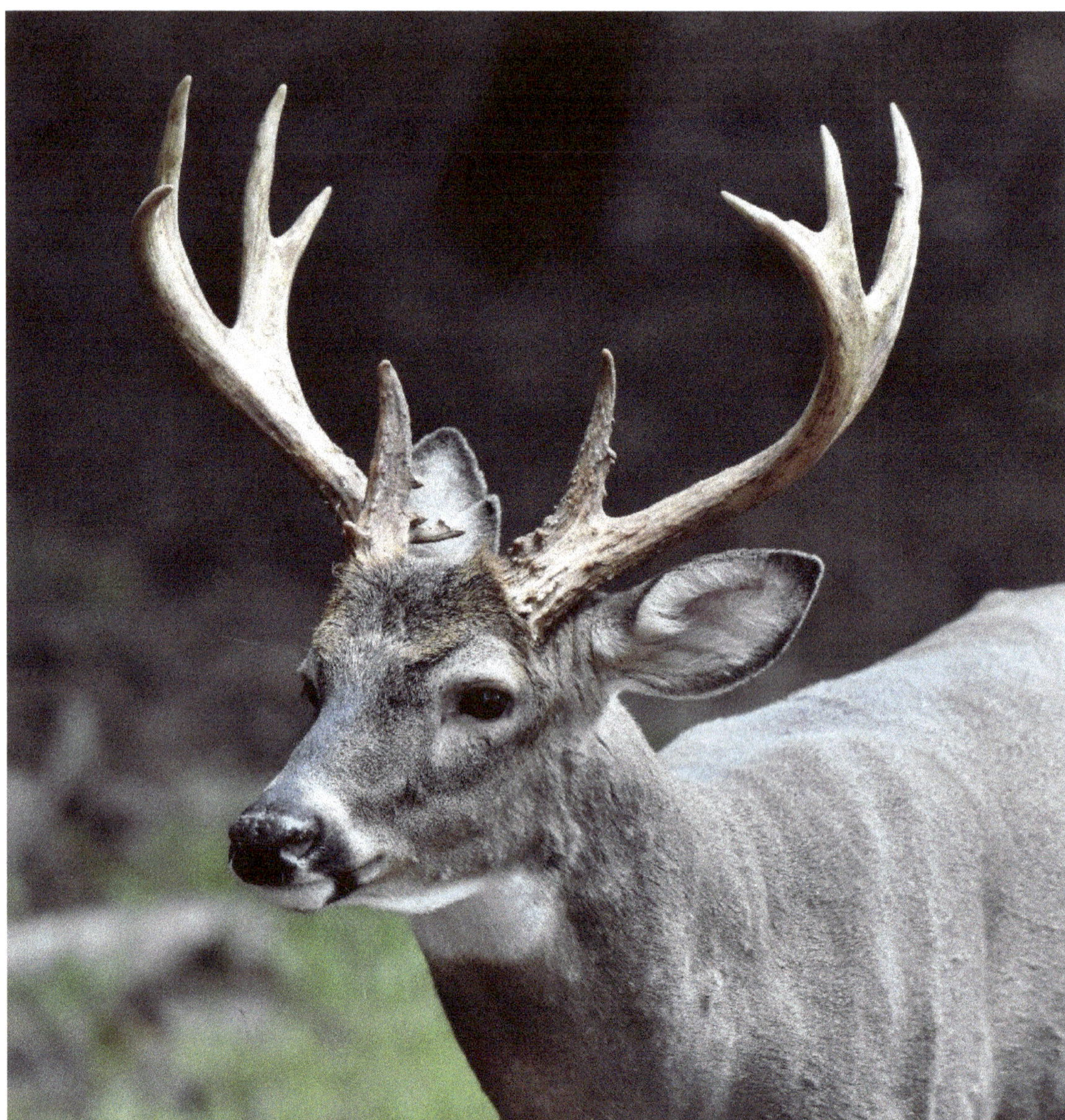

Pappy 2

"HORNING" TREES

As the velvet sheds, it often bleeds and leaves the antlers with a reddish bloody hue. With time and enough brush and tree tackling, the bucks rub off this blood and the antlers gleam.

These attacks on trees are not to scratch an itch from the shedding velvet—there is no longer any feeling in the antlers/velvet. The thrashing is an instinctive behavior that results in strengthening the body and neck muscles for the approaching rut and shoving matches with other bucks. It also marks the tree with the buck's scent from glands in his forehead so others will know who has been by.

Bucks look like teenage boys in late summer and begin to look like heavy-weight wrestlers as they fight the trees.

Even the biggest of the guys look small in late summer. For example in August Pappy 2 has not begun to bulk up for the annual disputes over the ladies.

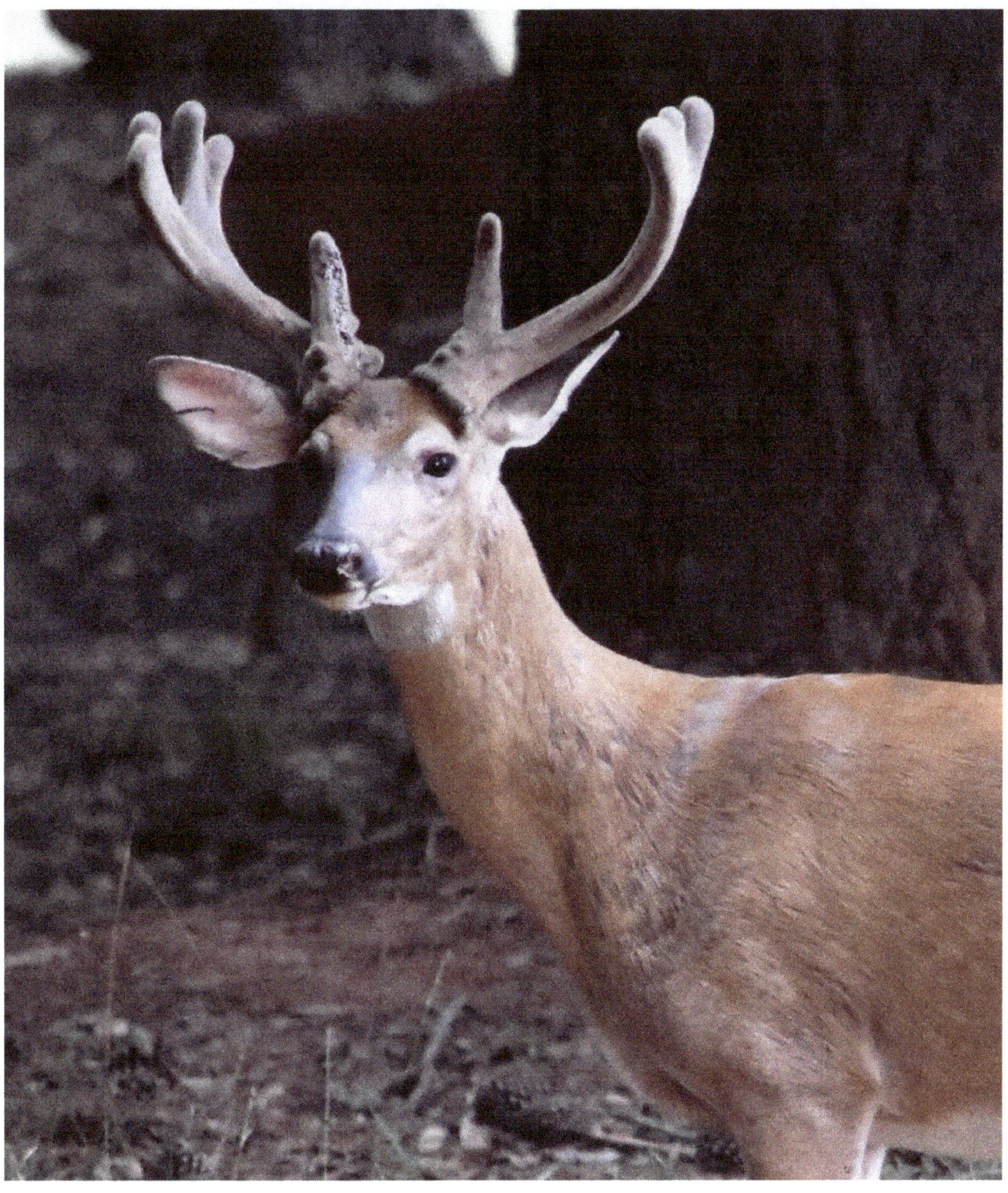

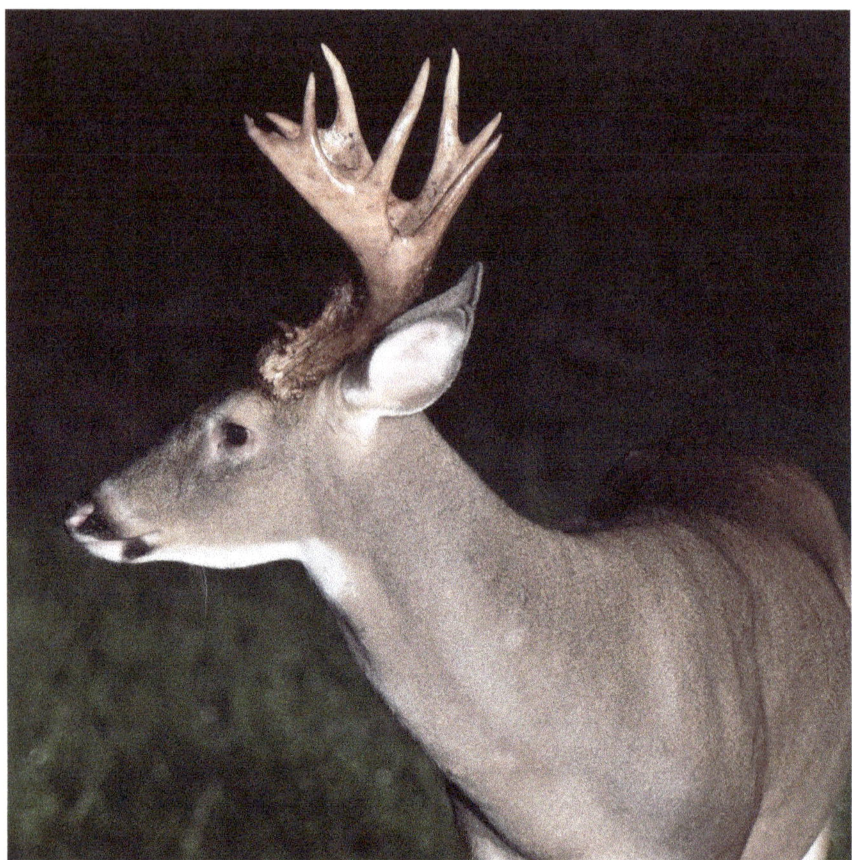

**In September, in his winter coat and with his velvet shed, he looks
ready to take on the other boys and court the ladies.**

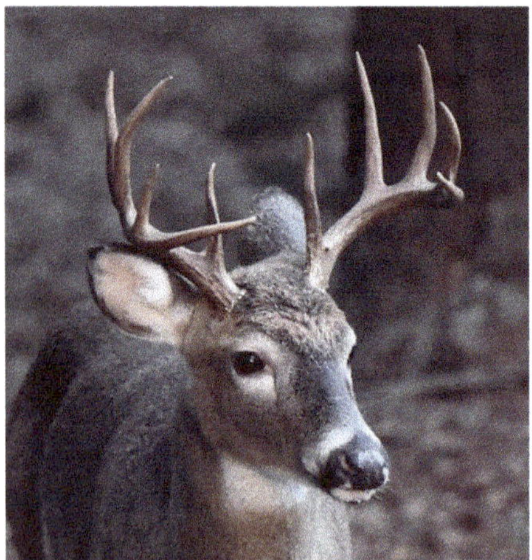

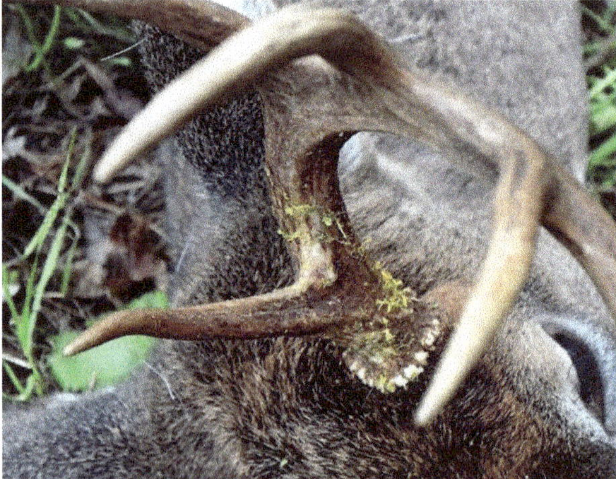

**This ten visited my pool on October 31. The next morning, he visited adjacent land where
he hit a scrape, horned a tree and walked in front of a hunter. Next stop, the freezer.**

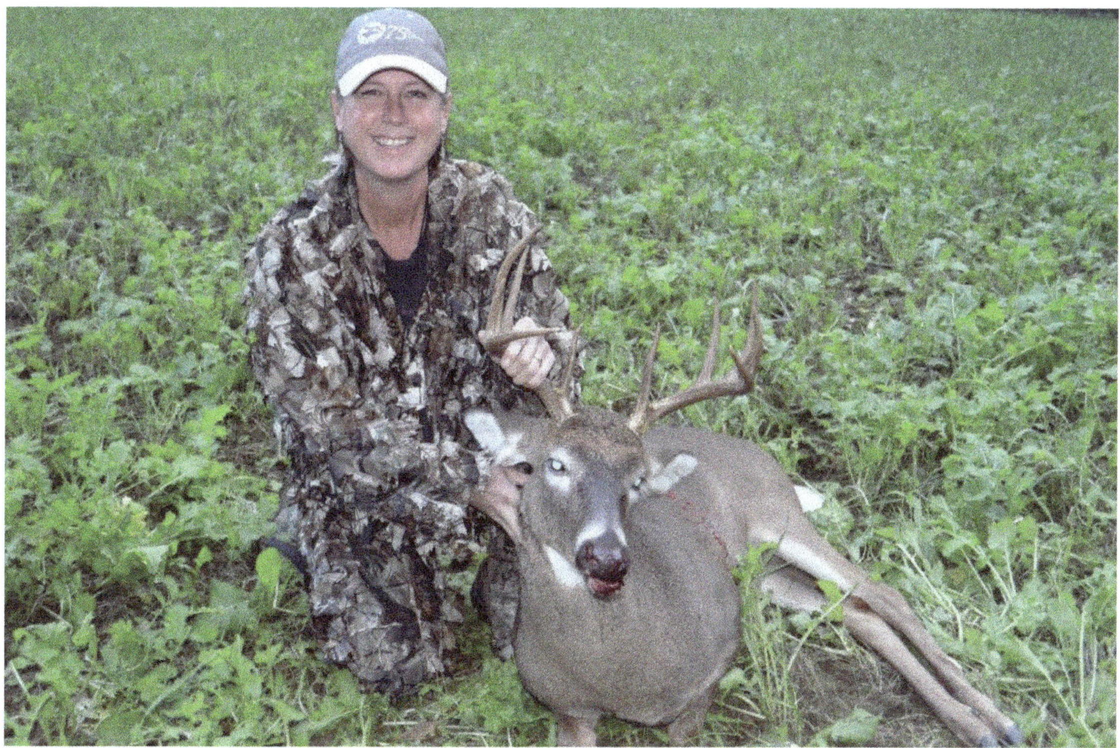

Congratulations, Cindy!

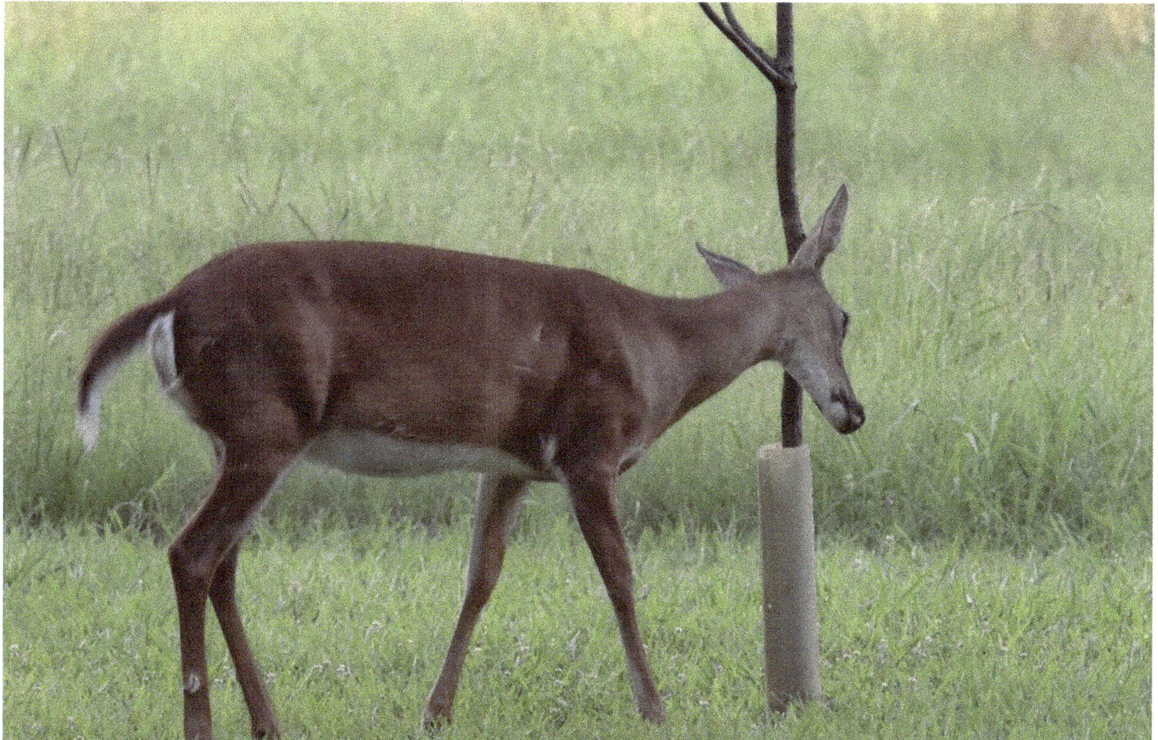

This doe must have had an itch on her forehead to be rubbing it against the tree. It's one of the persimmons that a raccoon planted in the yard and I have protected with that sleeve from the deer for several years.

Pappy and another buck managed to fight over one of the three and demolish it. As of summer 2022, two have survived, and, if female, these trees will probably offer my yard deer persimmons for years to come.

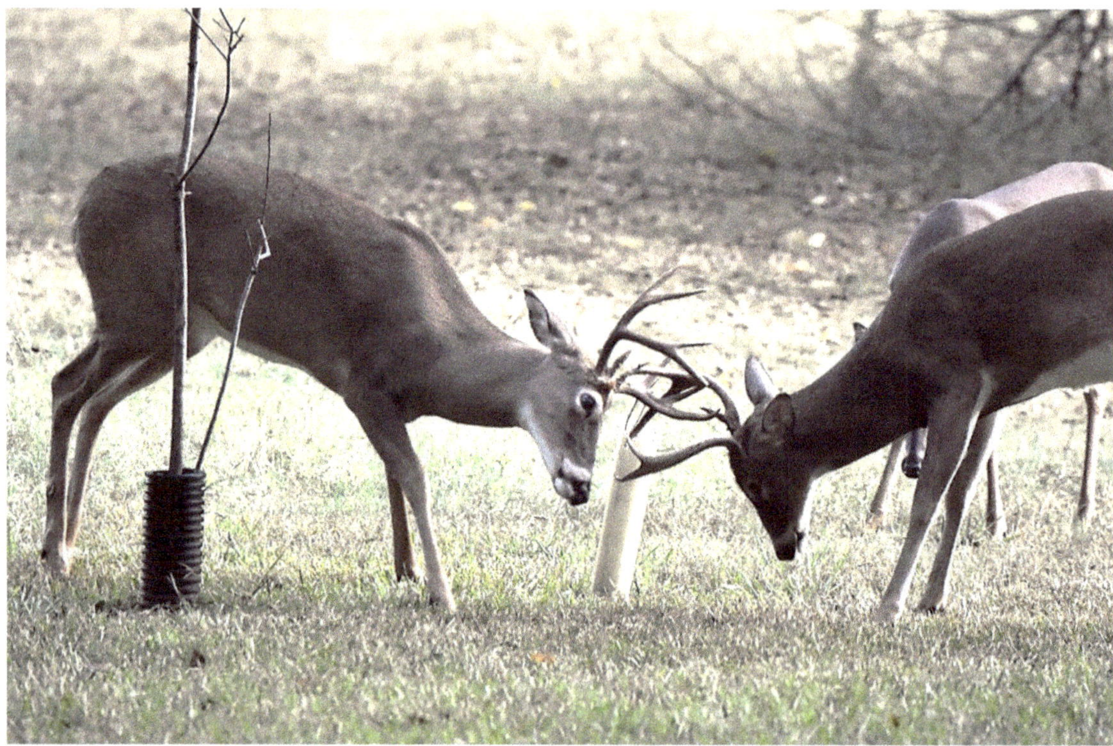

A buck does not think of establishing a hierarchy of offspring. All of his preparation for the rut and his rut behaviors are instinct, not rational thought. His only "rational thought" concerns finding a receptive doe and his moment of pleasure.

The size of the tree selected to rub holds no relationship to the size of the antlers. A large buck with a massive rack and long main beams that almost touch has to lower his head almost to the ground to get his antlers around the trunk, whereas a spike can just lean onto the tree and rub. Close Tips is a good example of a buck that has to duck, but he got his antlers polished.

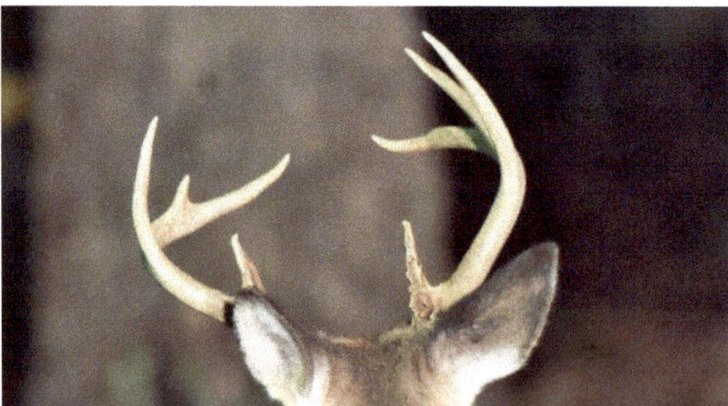

I see more small trees, less than three inches in diameter, with bark rubbed off, than larger trees. Bucks like heavily scented trees. Perhaps they think (if they think!) that the scent of cedar is pleasing to the ladies.

Anyhow, they showed me their love of cedars by hitting only cedars in my neighborhood. These were alongside Jeep roads in my woods, all about five to ten feet from the road or alongside a heavily used deer path.

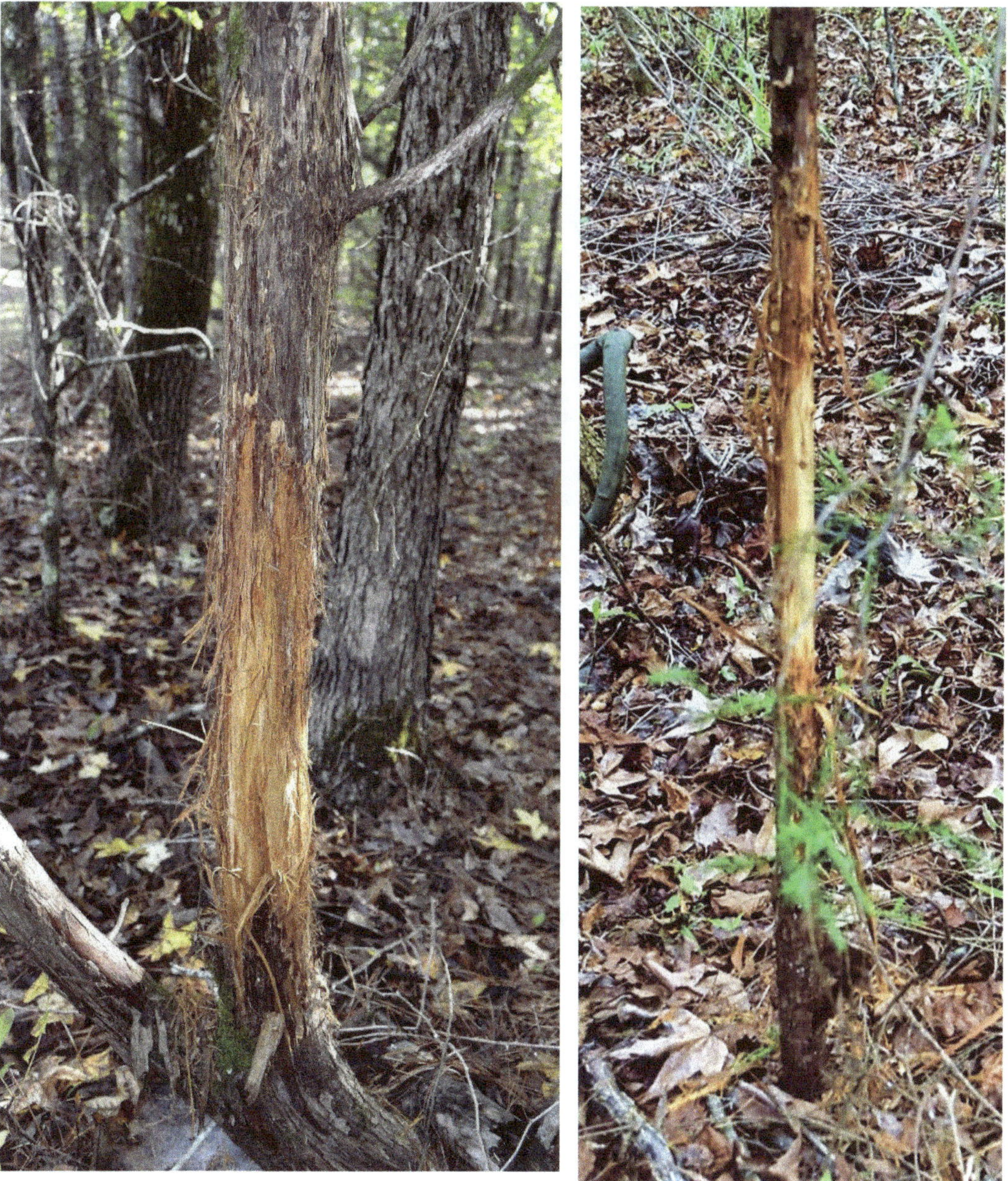

These two small trees could have been hit by a wide-beamed fella, such as Big Ten, in one attack. The uneven level of the damage, however, indicates it also could have been a youngster showing off, either alone, or after the larger buck to add his own scent to the rubs.

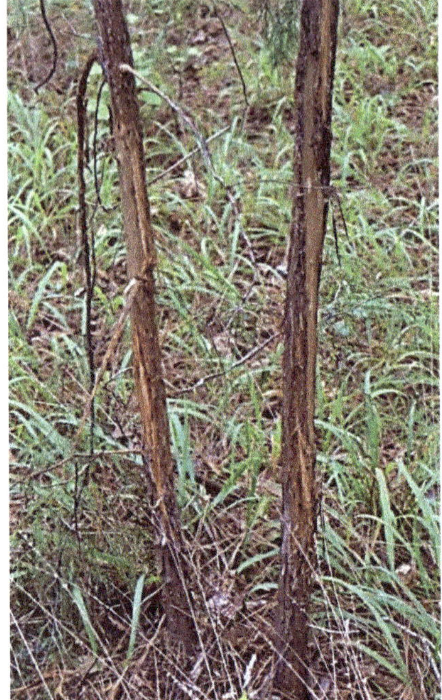
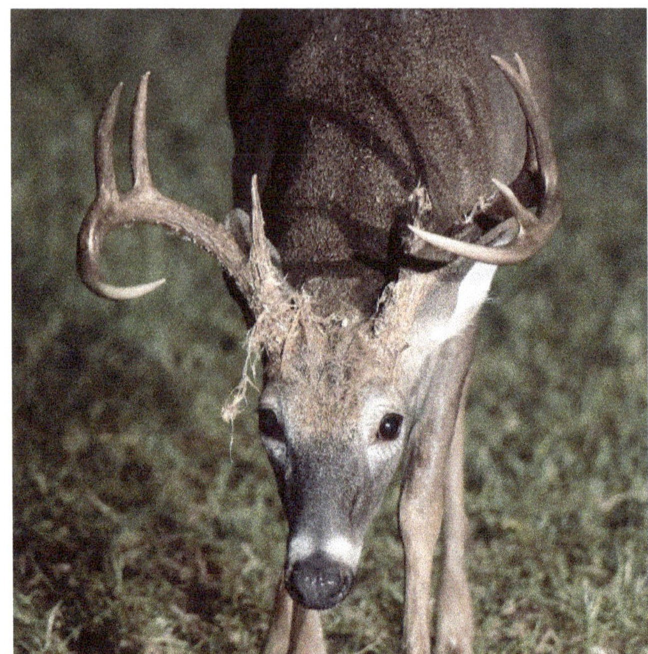

**In a few weeks, a rub looks
as if it were made a year ago**.

I could almost tract buck movement by rubs from the persimmon cluster to the land line where they had also rubbed a Chinaberry tree raw.

Bucks lay down scents from glands in their foreheads when they thrash brush and rub tree trunks. Other deer, both bucks and does, recognize the scent and know just who came by.

In the fall of 2020, cedar seemed to be the choice for bucks, but in 2021, they preferred the sapling persimmons, sweetgum and Chinaberry. A pine sapling in my yard fooled me into thinking it had been killed by buck antlers, but on closer view I realized it was just dead.

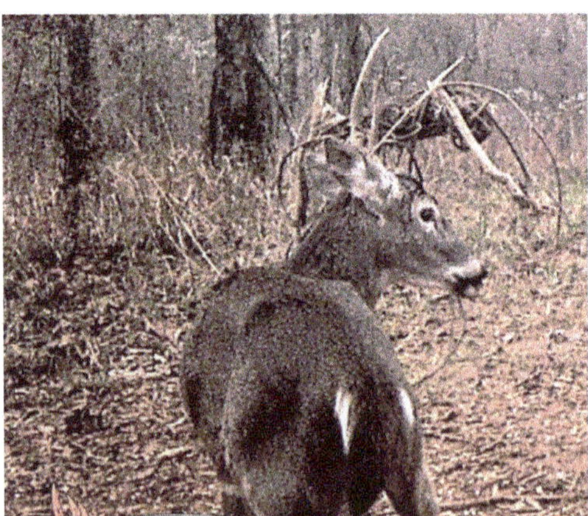
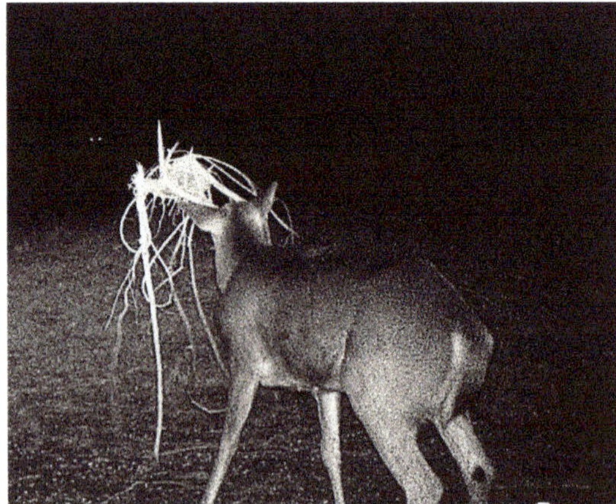

This fella walked in front of Chuck Beaty's trail camera several times.

One of my favorite pictures of a buck is this guy looking silly and proud, with a turkey leading him into fame and glory. He wore his trophy for about five minutes before he managed to dump it.

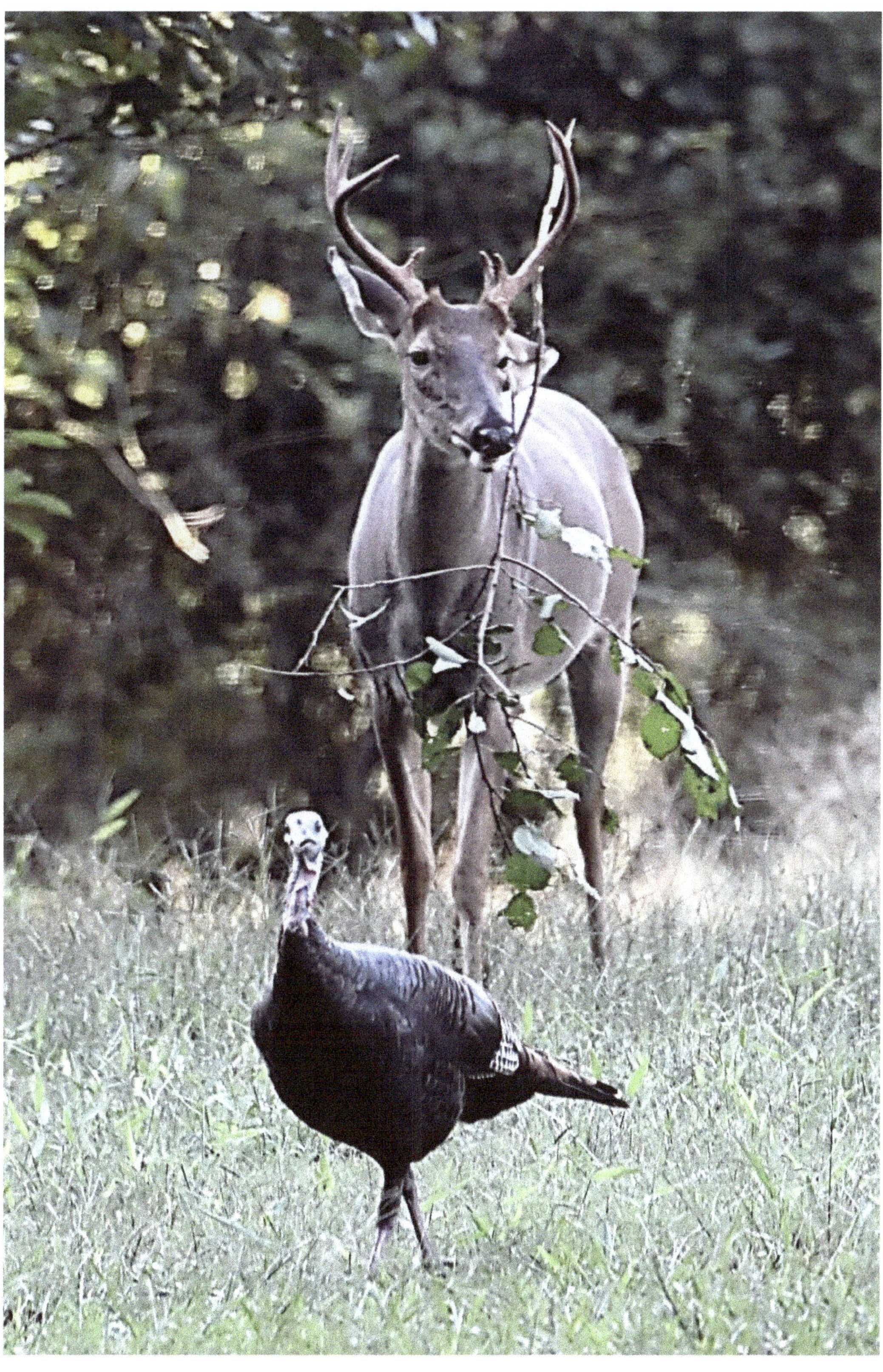

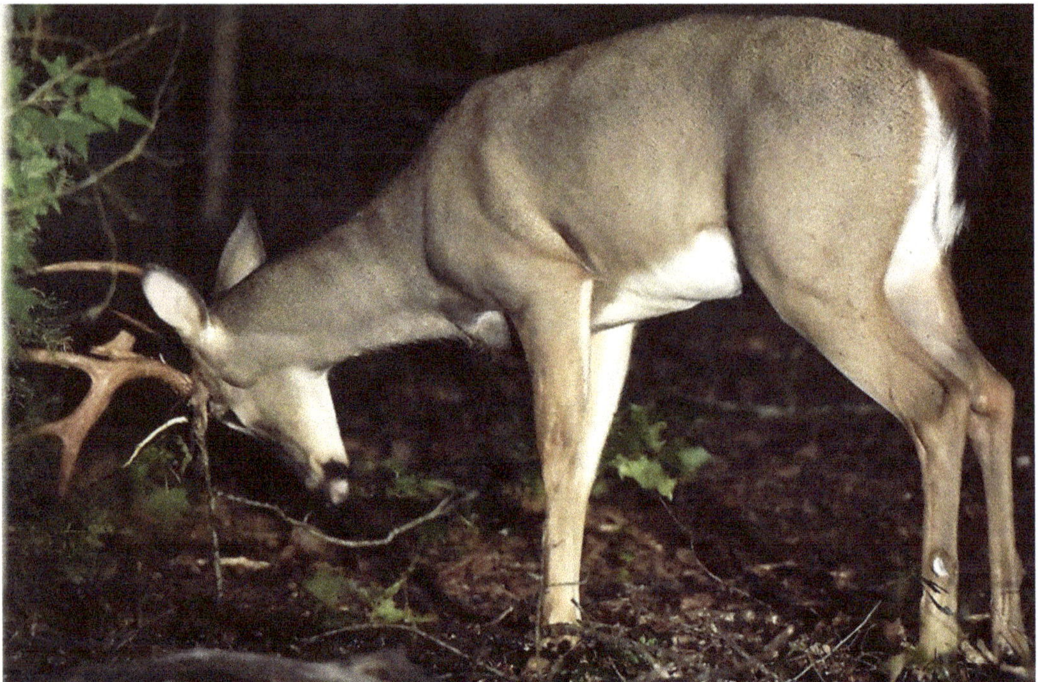

August 31. Sometimes they simply thrash brush to remove velvet that is aggravating them; the stream of velvet swung back and forth over his eye.

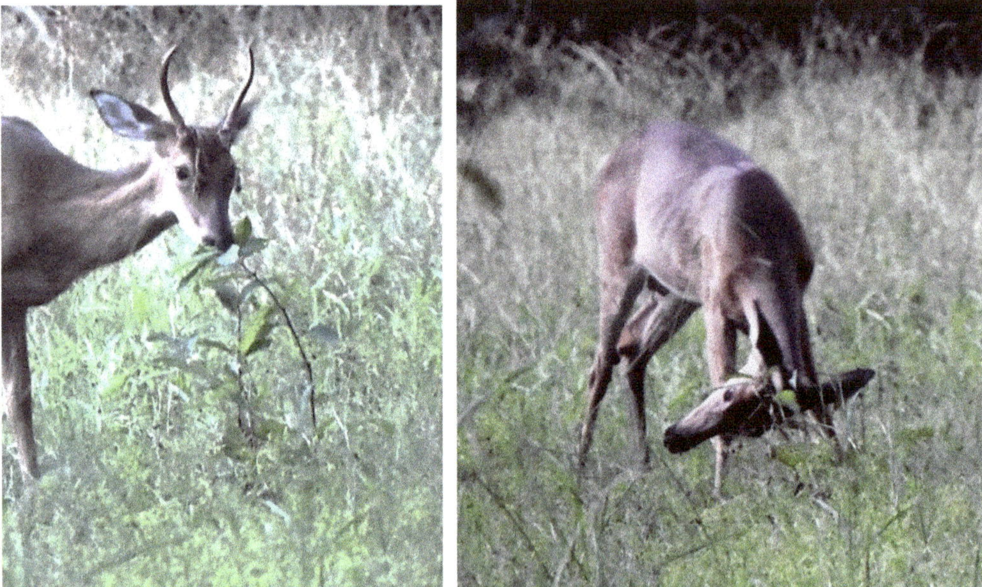

Only once have I seen a buck eat leaves from a bush and then thrash it, as this youngster did. He too had a velvet streamer flapping his face.

"Horning" trees and thrashing bushes are rut-related behaviors occurring when the buck is preparing for battle over mating rights and scraping to lure the ladies. These rituals begin in mid-Georgia in late August with shedding velvet and extend through the rut, ending as antlers drop.

SCRAPES: A BUCK'S INVITATION TO LOVE

A buck tells the world he is seeking love by making a series of scrapes around his territory, and sometimes even far beyond his normal living area.

Back in the 1960s, before most hunters had heard the word "scrape," a friend of mine found a large area that had been pawed. The hoof marks were fresh, and he decided the deer was trying to find salt. He dumped ten pounds of salt on the scrape.

I was fortunate. I knew he had demolished a scrape, a spot usually under a limb where a buck paws the ground and urinates to leave his scent to inform all passing ladies he is eager for loving and to inform all bucks he is in the neighborhood.

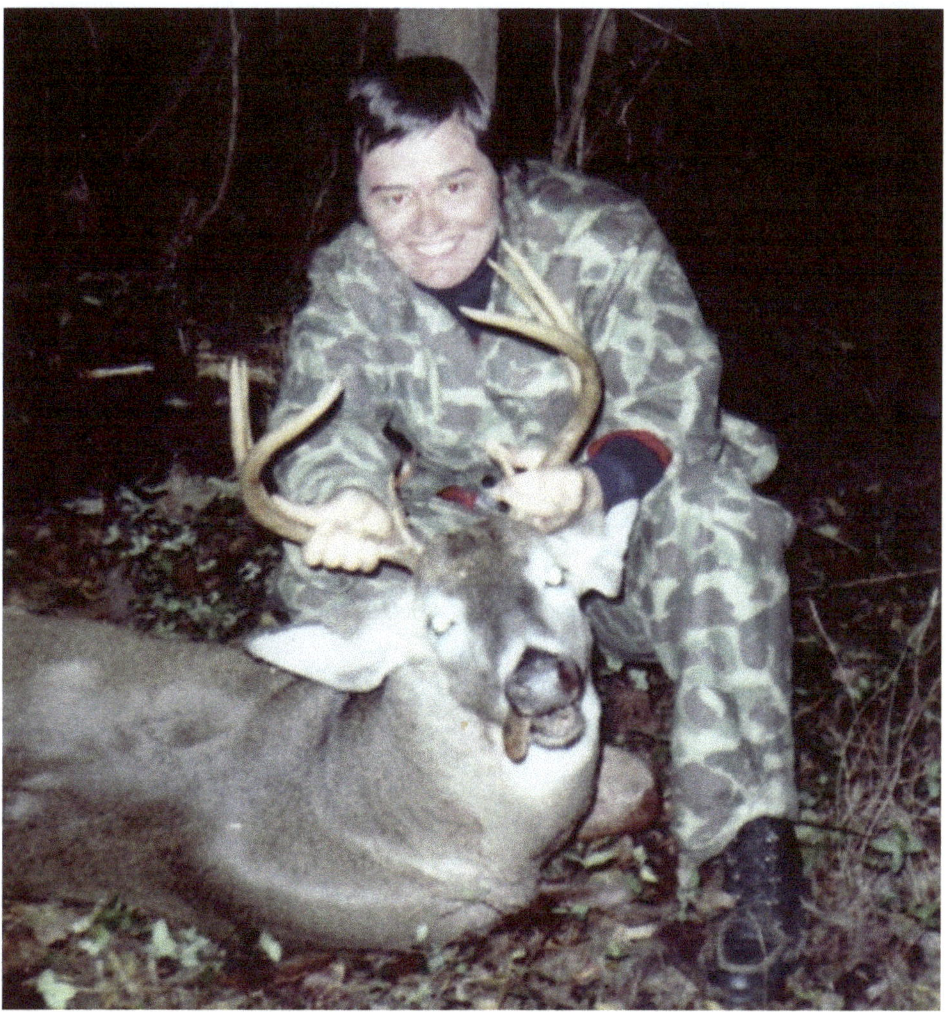

Jack Benford, a local wildlife ranger, told me about scrapes, and one day when I found a spot with only three pawed swipes on it, I asked if it could be a scrape. Jack said to hunt it. I did. November 1968, I collected my third deer, and my first one over a scrape.

Making a scrape is an instinctual ritual and locations are predictable. Scrapes will be located beneath a limb, often a hardwood or cedar, rarely a pine. The buck nibbles or thrashes the overhanging limb and deposits scents on the limb from glands on his head. He is putting out information to other deer about who he is. Peak scraping occurs about two weeks before the peak of the rut.

He paws the ground and then urinates or even defecates on the spot. Sometimes he will urinate on the tarsal glands, those white patches on his hind legs. (More on them later.)

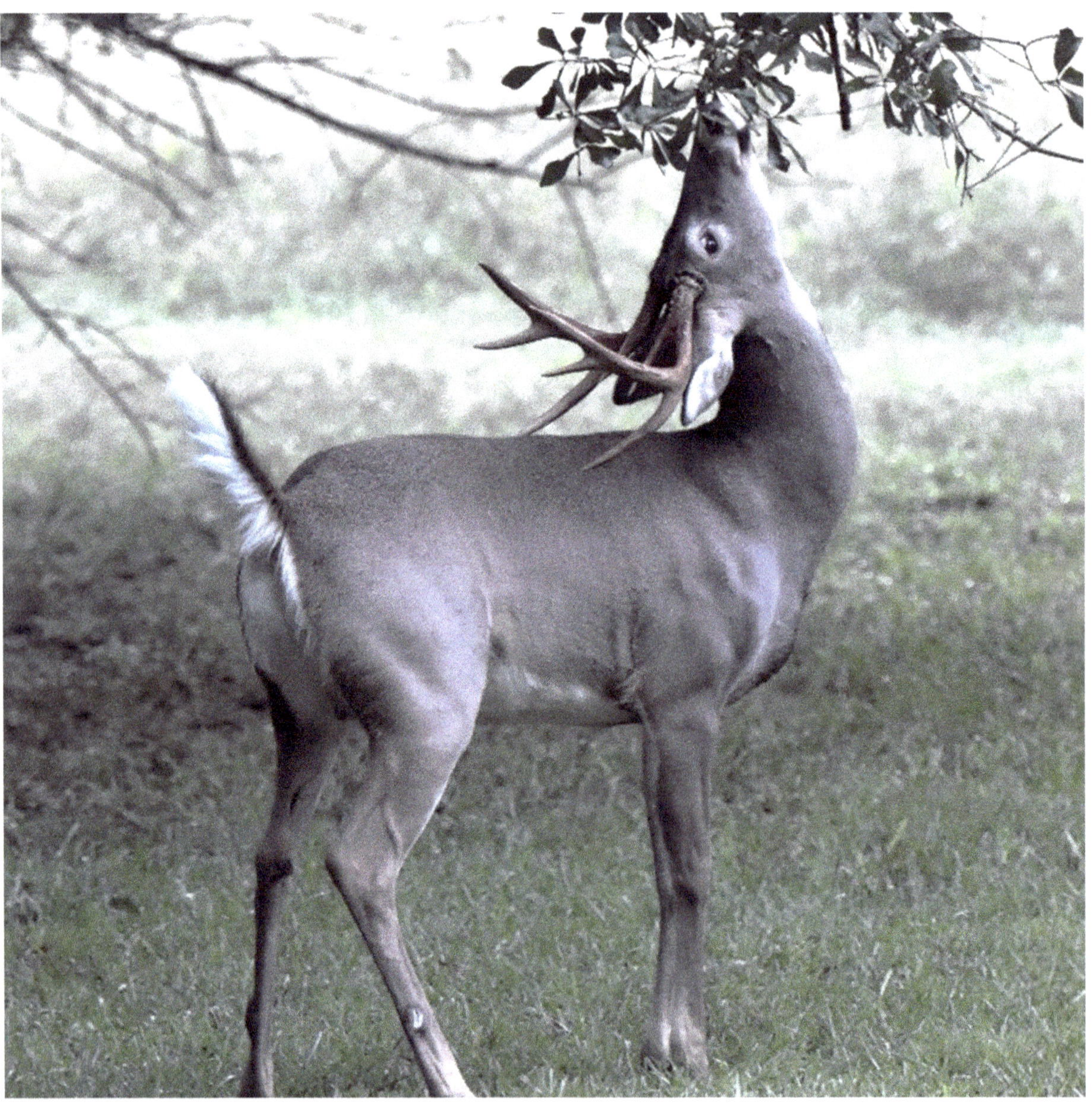

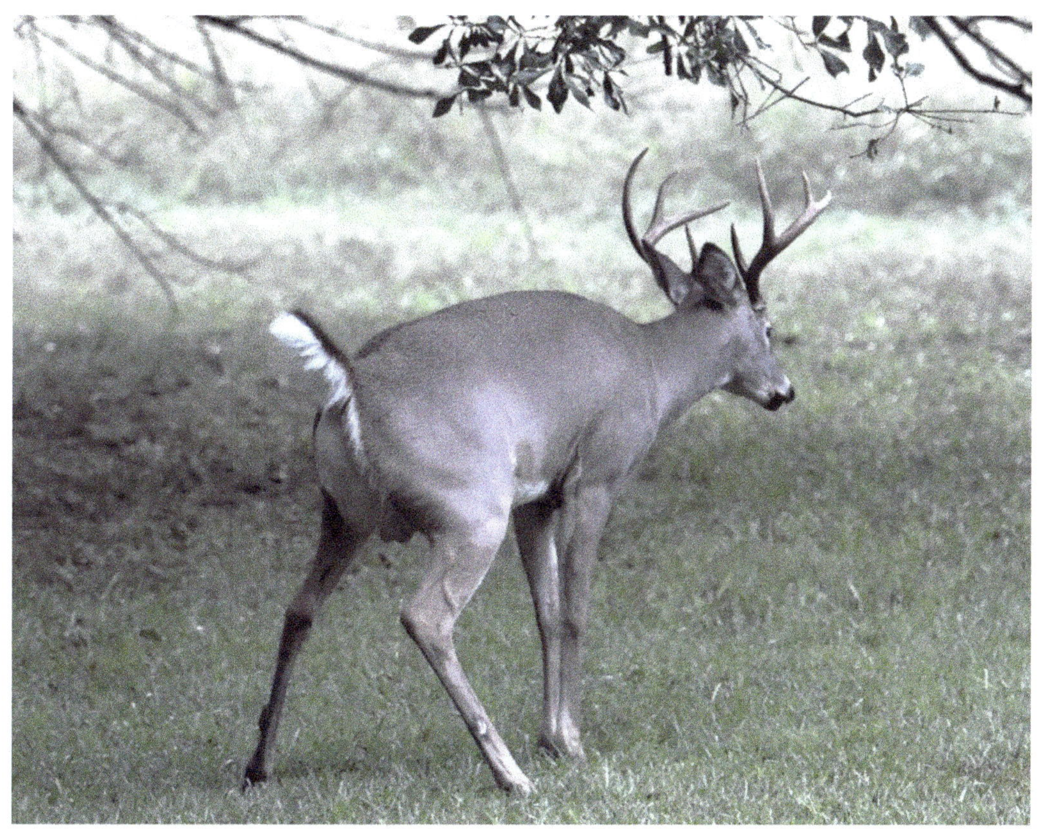

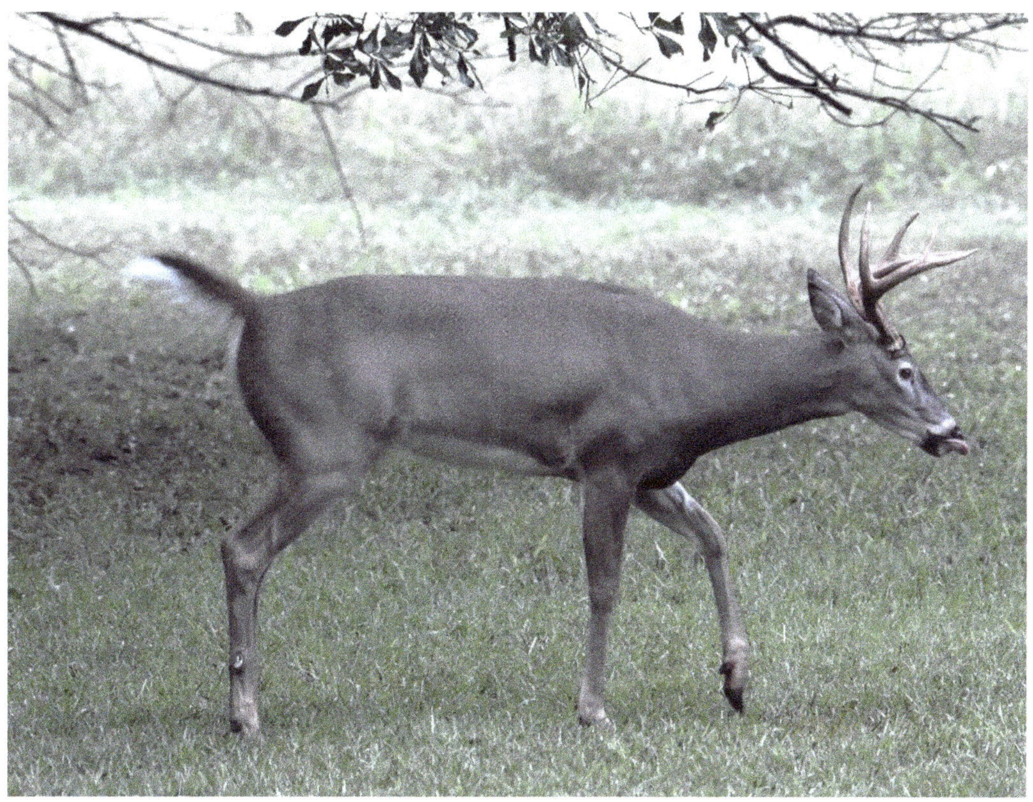

The buck trails the doe as soon as he whiffs her readiness to mate, whether or not she visited a scrape.

I have heard hunters state that a buck will "send a doe out front" when they travel, for her to detect any danger. In fact, he is simply trailing her in hopes of consummating their relationship.

He may paw again. Many of the scrapes I have seen contain a hoofprint as if the buck stomped his hoof to say, "I am here; bucks beware." Other bucks don't necessarily *beware*, for some will share the scrape.

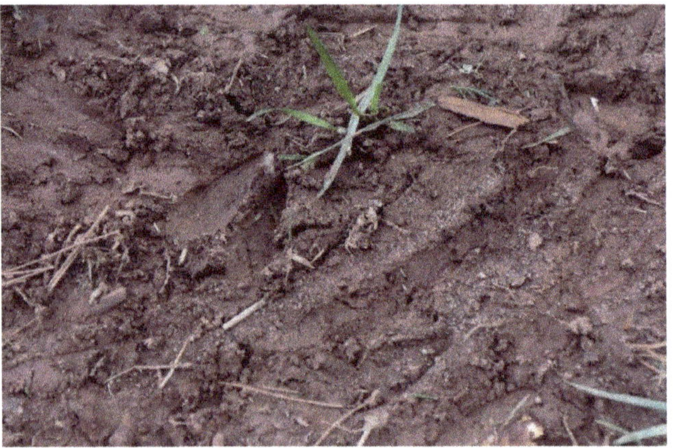

A scrape can be as small as a few hoof slashes or as large as a pickup bed in a heavily buck-populated area. Bucks scrape along trails or drives and in areas where they know does congregate such as near food plots and feeders and food sources such as persimmons or crabapples.

Some scrapes are easy to spot and well defined. This one was under a cedar limb, the picture taken the day after rain in mid-January. The buck had high hopes of a New Year's romance.

Others, like the next one, are only a few slashes and not easily spotted.

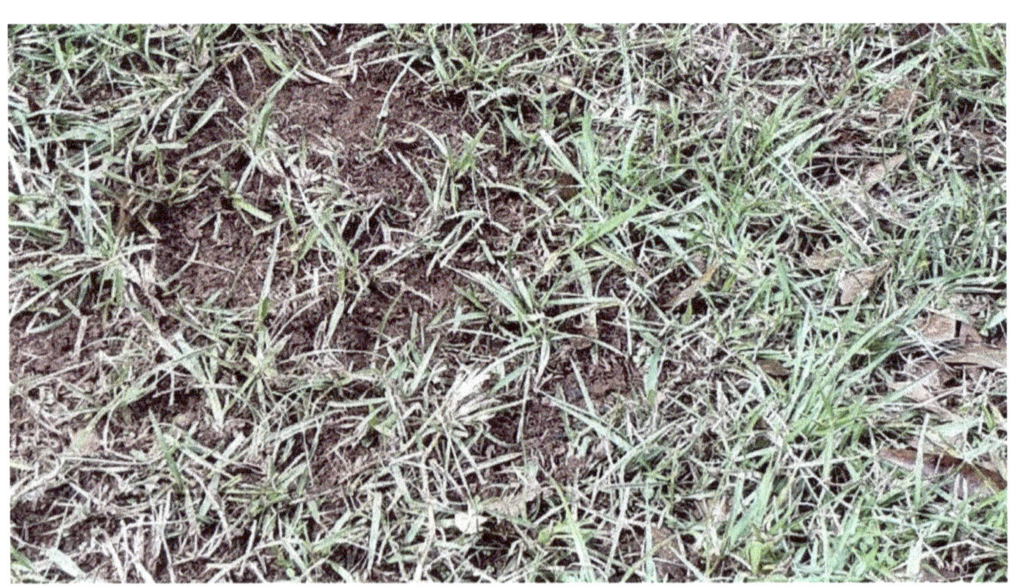

A doe in heat might wait at the scape for him to return, but she won't wait long. Her "wait" might be only to eat nearby food. My hunting buddy Norman talked about watching a doe wait for a buck one morning. Norman perched in a small oak in a hanging stand, in the days before ladders and towers were in use, and he looked over a truck road and a persimmon/oak cluster. And most important, a scrape beside the road and beneath an oak limb. Soon after dawn, several does came uphill from the other side of the oaks and began to feed on acorns. One came to the scrape, pawed it and urinated in it, and stood looking around for a few minutes. She then rejoined the others and fed. About a half-hour passed and a buck ambled up the roadway where Norman had walked in. The buck never lowered his head to sniff the ground; Norman had dropped some pine scent on his boots, so there was little or no human odor to alarm the buck. The buck reached the scrape, dropped his nose to the ground, jerked his head up, and looked over at the does. Norman shot.

Norman explained *at least the fella died happy*. Norman was also happy to fill his first tag of the season.

Bucks are attuned to the sounds in the woods. When they are in rut, every sound is sexually related. I had several visiting hunters, and when I found a series of scrapes, I placed each hunter overlooking a scrape in a hidey-hole. Back in the 1960s hunting was *sit on the ground or on a half-rotten red-bug-infested pine stump*, so they sat on the ground and overlooked the trail. I went on down the hollow to the landline to be out of the way.

Only it turned out I was IN the way. I was kicking leaves to clear a place to sit against a tree when I heard something coming my way. Yep, a buck, I thought. It was hitting one of his scrapes. But he leaped the landline fence and trotted directly to me. *Sorry, visitors, but I wasn't going to pass up my chance at a buck, so I took him.*

In later years, I used other sounds to attract deer when I hunted. I used a couple of shed antlers to rattle and thrash against a tree trunk, and bucks answered by coming to see and perhaps join the fight. I also used a bleat call, which imitated the sound of a doe or fawn, and managed to call in several bucks with it.

When a buck smells a doe in heat, he pursues. She is in heat for about 72 hours and receptive for about the middle 36 hours, or a little longer. If he tries to mate before she is ready, she flees and snorts her "no." Emphatically. He may have to pursue her for a day before she will accept his advances.

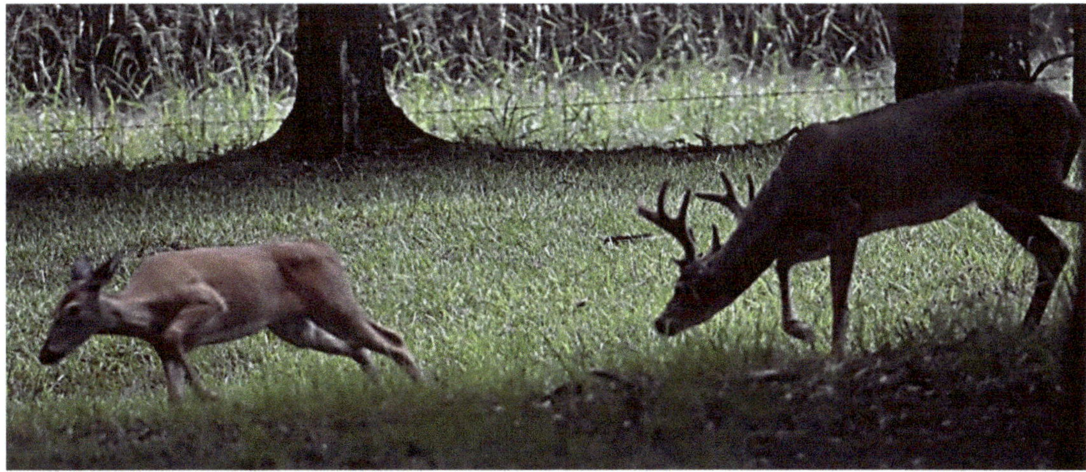

One morning when I was hunting, I heard a doe snort and blow for about a half-hour from before daylight until the sun was well up. I eventually heard the buck grunting as he pursued. I did not see the doe, but did see a buck, a handsome fellow any doe would be proud to marry, but the lady did not accept him that day. He ran behind my stand, stopped to grab a mouthful of browse (on my wrong side and behind me, so no humane shot) and he was off again. To my dismay a poacher on adjacent land, where hunting was not allowed, shot only moments after the buck crossed the fence.

Another day, I heard a buck grunting as he followed a doe. She kept up a steady pace, from my right to my left then behind me and after a half-hour or longer she came back on the same trail, the buck still behind her and begging with his "I love you" call. Without the sound effects, I would have thought they were out for an afternoon stroll together.

Another morning, I watched a buck and doe feeding and moseying along as if they were just companions. That had to have been her last hours in heat, because the next morning, he came alone to visit his scrape—his time with her was over.

The buck's grunt sounds a bit like a hog grunting, but his voice is soft and almost gentle. I have tried to imitate the sound with just my vocal cords, but could not convince a deer to respond. I learned that both bucks and does respond to a fake call if the human caller is good enough to duplicate the deer voice. During the rut, all bucks are in love with any doe, even with the unseen doe, and when he hears *her* bleat call, he will likely come looking. Testosterone speaks to him. If a buck is alone and hears another buck grunt or hears the clash of antlers, he is just as likely to come running to steal any nearby doe.

I grunted one afternoon and a spike came downhill from an oak hillside to the meadow I overlooked. Four times I called him back before I quit and let him walk.

Another morning I was in a climbing stand in a sweetgum, as high as I could go with a limb halting me. I had a pair of antlers, and a WoodsWise deer call. I bleated a couple of times, waited a couple of minutes, grunted, then raked an antler against the tree trunk and slammed it against the small branches. I did not have time to re-hang the antler on a limb before I was covered up in deer. A doe and buck came from my right along the ridge; two bucks also came along the ridge from the other side, and a buck came uphill from the swamp. It was quite an interesting event. The deer stared at each other, and the doe decided she wanted no part of a crowd of sex-crazed bucks; she fled downhill toward the swamp. Her courting buck dashed off behind her, and the other two hopefuls followed.

One mid-March when I was planning my turkey hunt and hoping to find a roosting area, I found a fresh scrape. I knew I had also found a great site for the fall deer hunt. If a buck were sexually active in March, I figured he'd be around the same area when the next rut came around. And he was.

Because deer are in my yard year-around, the most-used scrape site under an oak limb gets a dose of urine almost weekly and all year long. The overhead limb varies from a leafless licking limb in winter to a nibble limb in spring and into summer. Many deer stop at the site on their way in and/or out of the yard, both does and bucks.

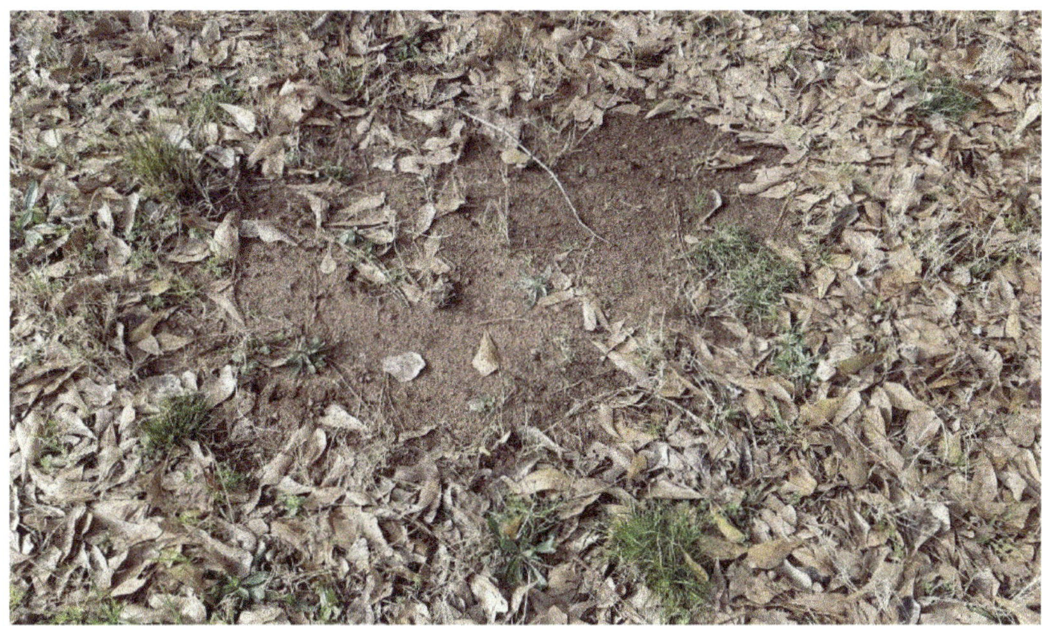

Visited on February 11 and still freshly wet in mid-June.

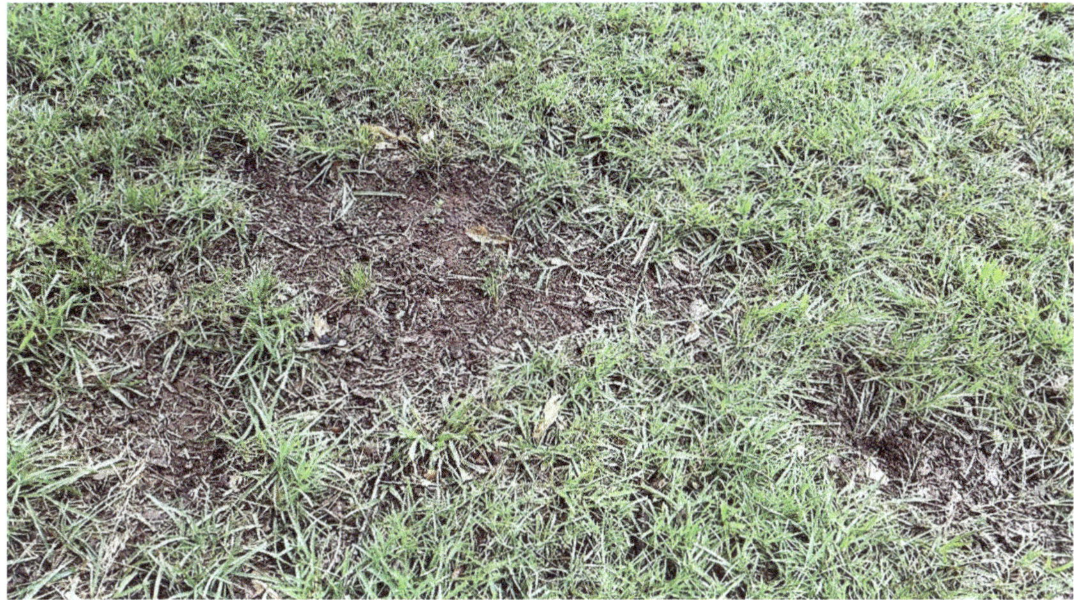

I have looked at other nearby scrape sites, but not found another one that stayed worked or urinated in for these long months. I think it becomes simply a buck hello-to-everybody site when the rut is over. I have seen bucks standing nearby while they groom each other.

These bucks simply use the site to urinate.

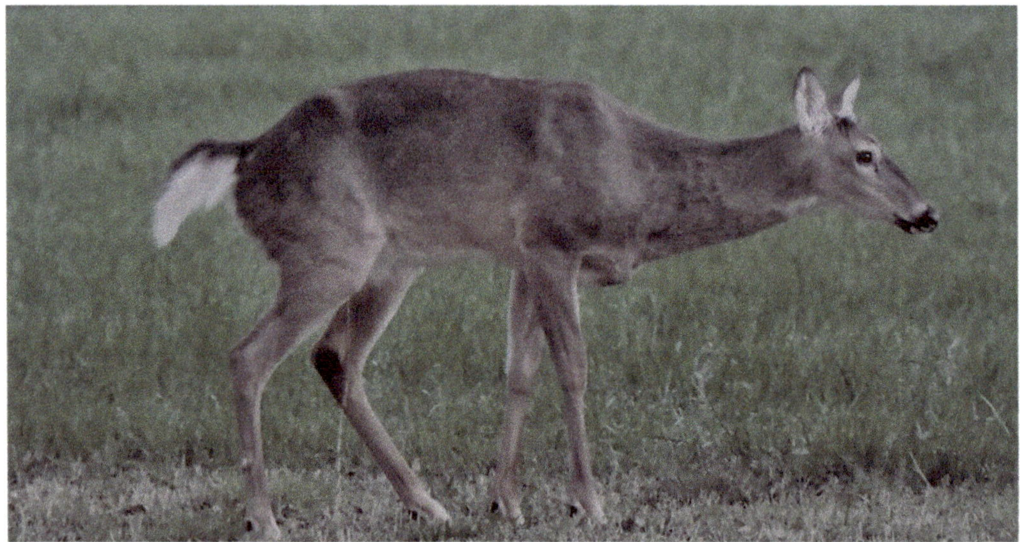

March 22

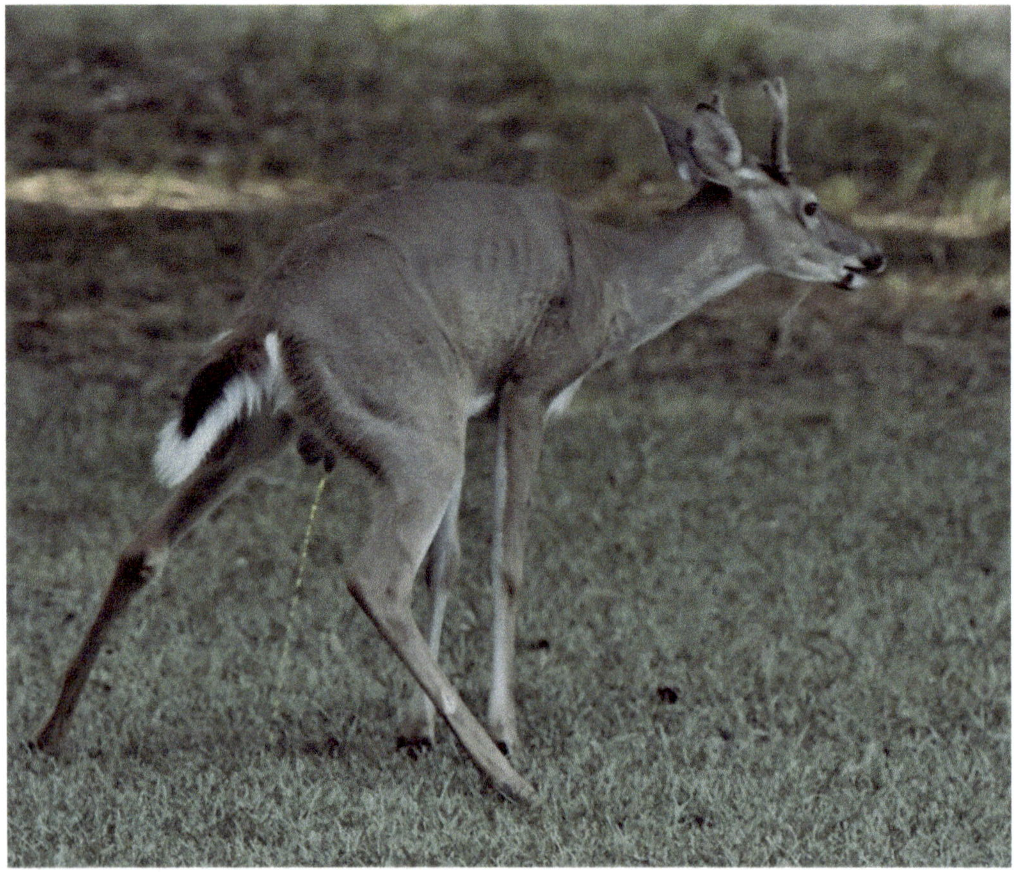

Late August, same old scrape site.

SHEDDING ANTLERS

Whitetails, like all deer, shed their antlers. As winter ends, their testicles shrink and testosterone levels drop. Bucks no longer fight for domination, although they may shove each other in play fight or over food.

Late February and early March, I have found antlers in thick woods and in the middle of the hay fields. The only time I found two together was under an elevated feeder where the antlers fell off when the buck lowered his head to grab a bite of corn. The antlers were prong-down in the dirt and side by side. Most bucks seem to shed them one at a time.

My neighbor found this pair dropped simultaneously in her yard.

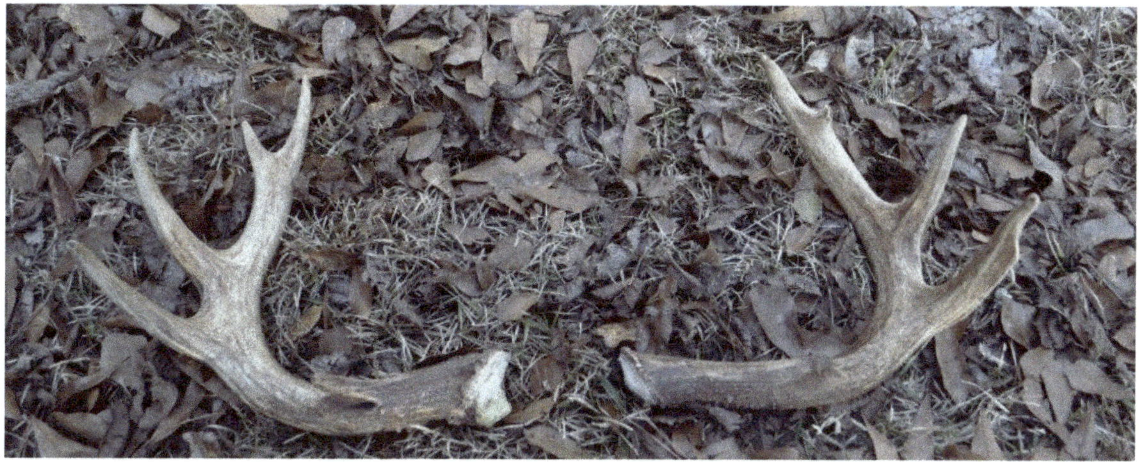

I have found a number of antlers in my hayfields, some with evidence of non-normal shedding, with part of the pedicle on the base of the shed, probably related to an abscess the buck developed as a result of a rut-related injury.

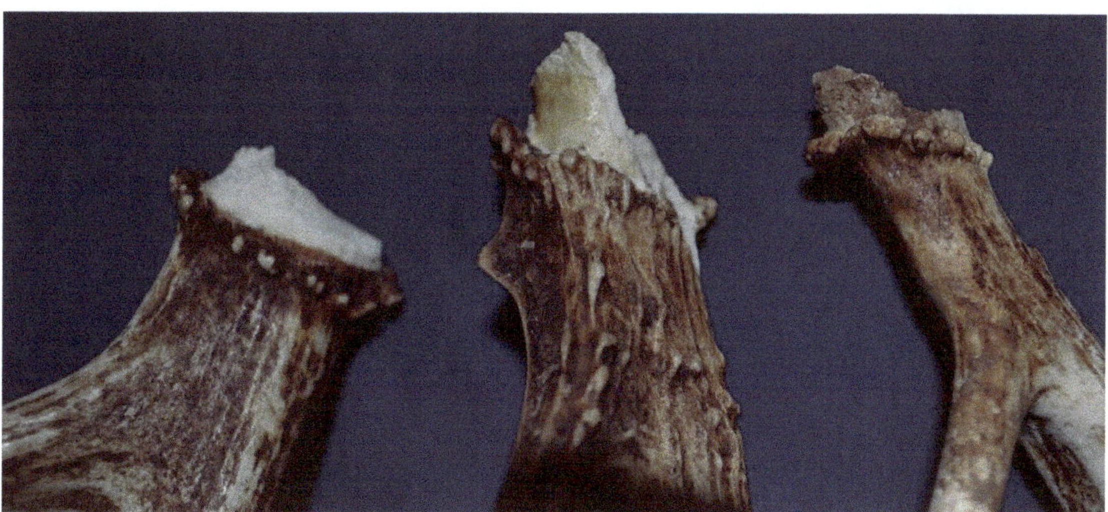

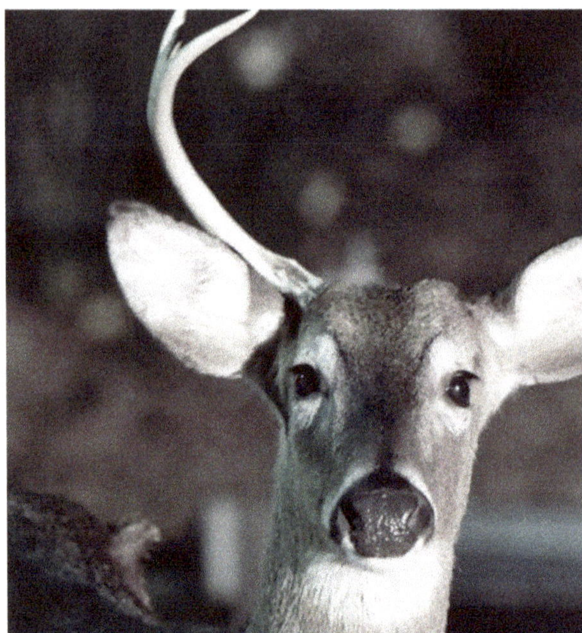

Having settled dominance as the rut began, the bucks don't forget who is boss, and the guy who ruled earlier remains boss buck, at least until all antlers have fallen. Even in March, everyone fled, including six and eight-point bucks still wearing their antlers, when One Horn approached.

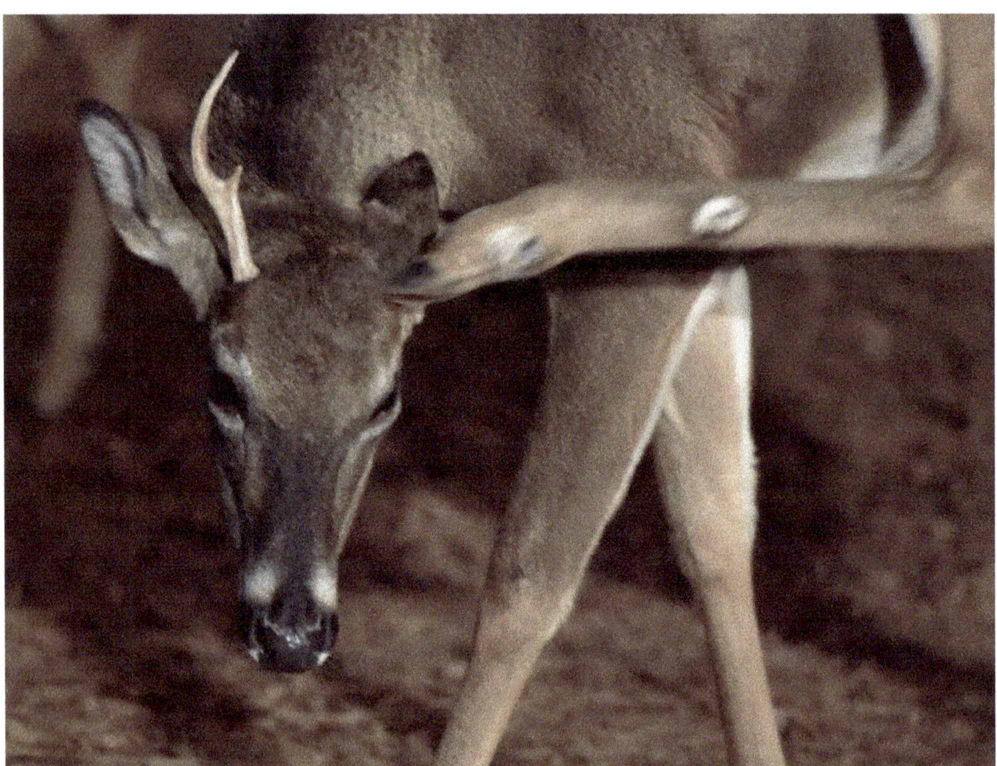

The pedicle may be itching to be scratched.

I've heard some hunters say the bucks are so ashamed to have no antlers that they hide from other deer until they begin to regrow antlers. Not true in my deer yard. Bucks show up continuously although they look like does until their budding antlers show.

The pedicle might or might not bleed if the antler simply drops off; if the antler is forced off, e.g., by the buck's trashing brush, the pedicle may be damaged and bleed.

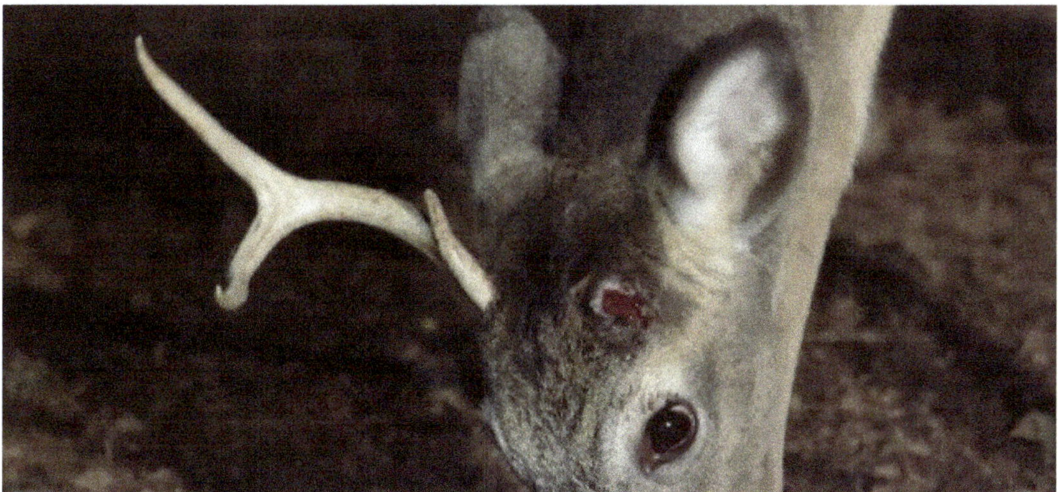

Blood does not necessarily indicate a damaged pedicle. This looks to be a normal shed.

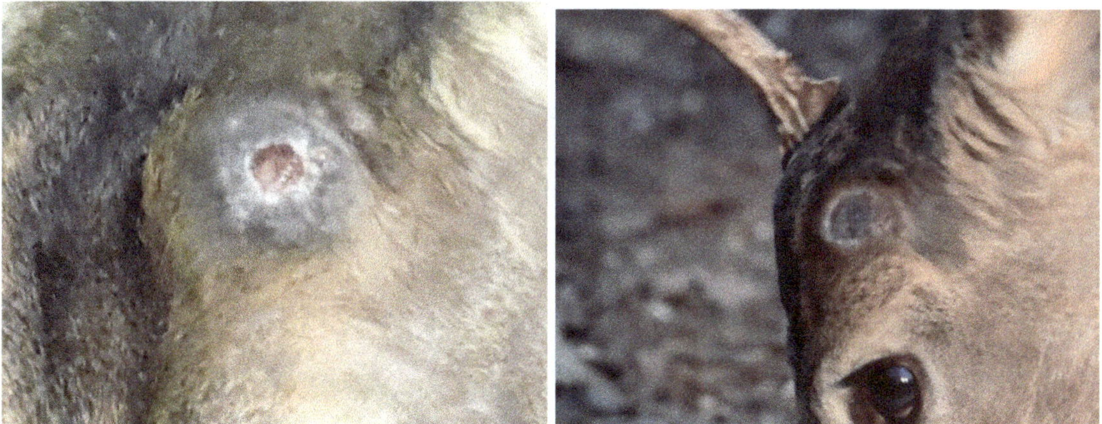

Pedicles from clean sheds.

For those of us who hunt for sheds, finding one is as exciting for us as finding a silver coin is for a treasure hunter. The shed carries information about the deer's health and diet and potential for future antler growth. Lindsay Thomas Jr. has documented these findings in "How to Read Shed Antlers for Health and Habitat Clues," National Deer Association, March 25, 2020. He reports on a study of antler bases and their relationship to deer health: Concave base indicates less healthy; convex base indicates a healthy deer.

Matching a shed to a picture is the height of excitement when I find a shed, especially when the pattern is unique. I have found very few large sheds; I think most of those deer fall to nearby hunters.

For me the pleasure is finding one and being able to match it with a deer I photographed. My best and most exciting match was the Claw buck's shed.

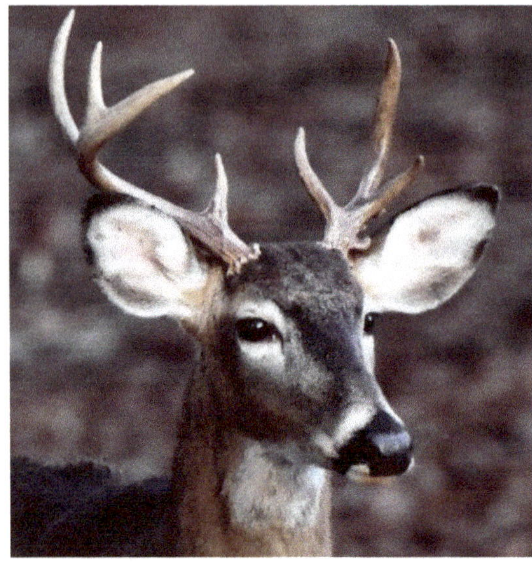

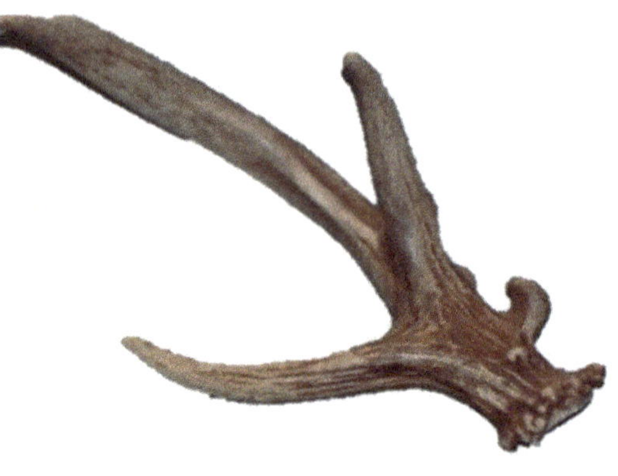

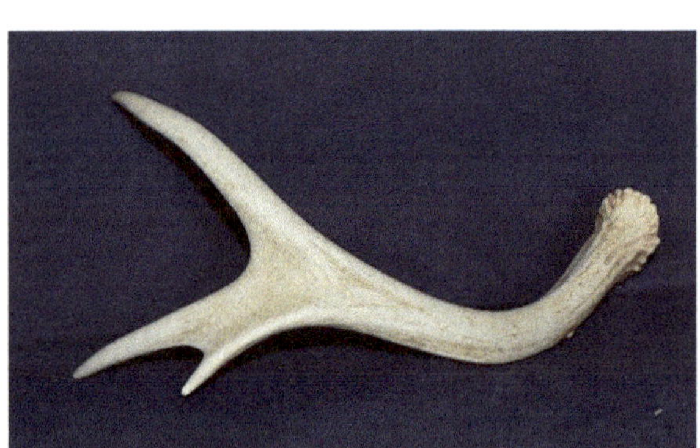

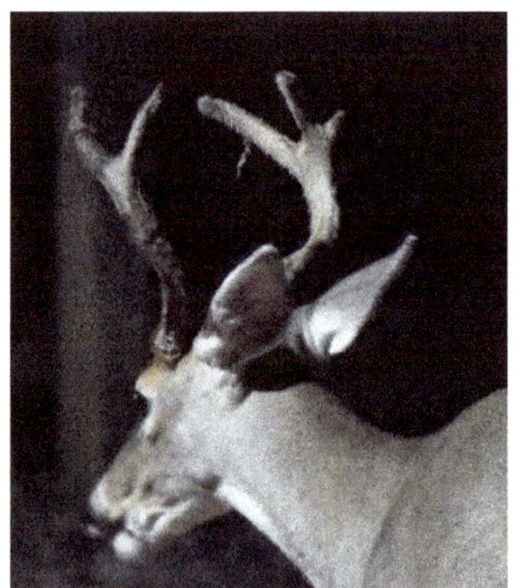

It was easy to match the shed to the two-spot buck.

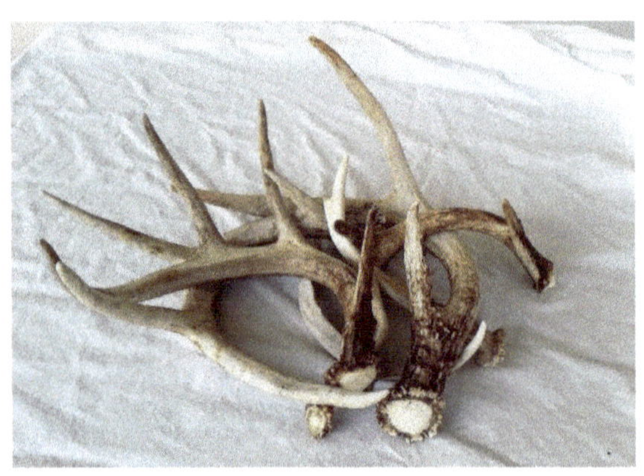

A neighbor whose yard is an ideal flower garden of heavily fertilized plants and includes a variety of fruit trees yields a shed collector's dream each spring.

ILLUSIONS

These antlers were not shed cleanly, but some of them created visual illusions that fascinated me. When shed hunters find an antler, I wonder if they look it over as I do. I find images on antlers and other bones.

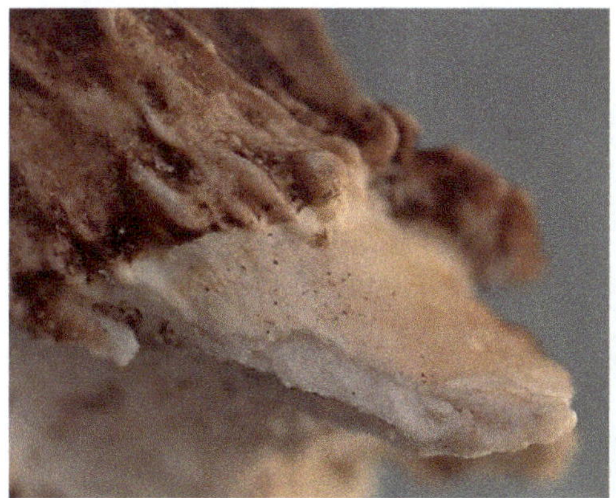

Alligator

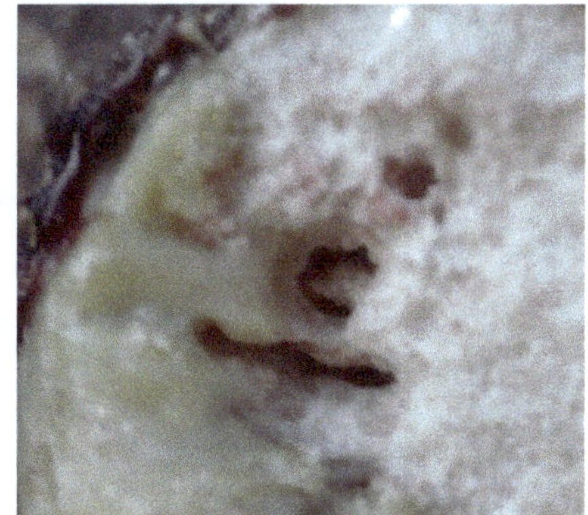

Creature of nightmares

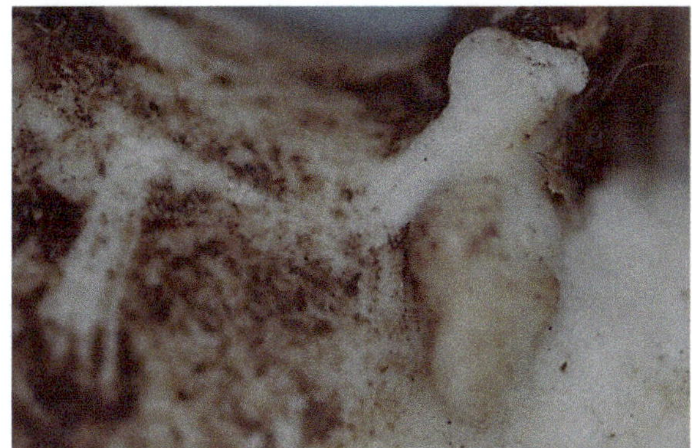

Monster from the grave

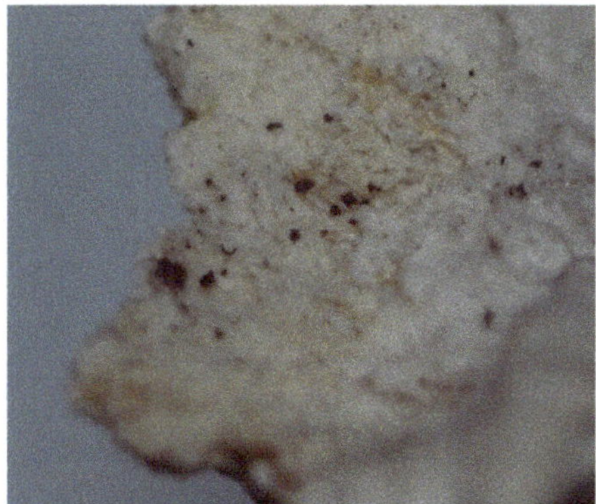

One-eyed monster grinning

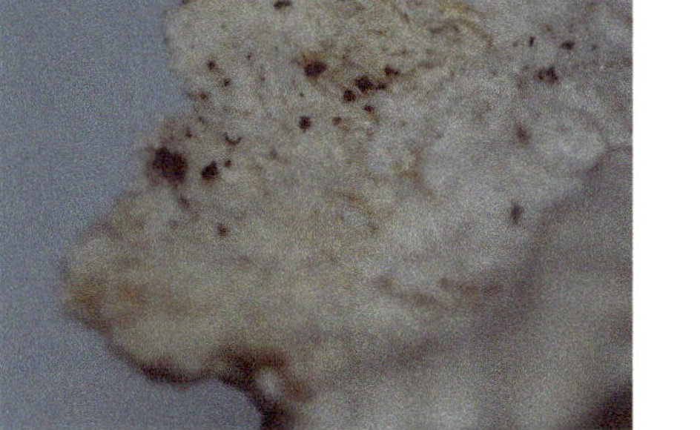

Old man's ghost

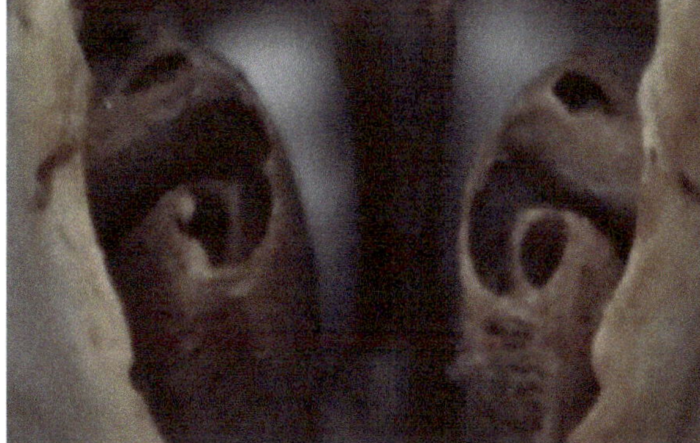

Watchbird watching you

NOT ALL SEXUAL BEHAVIORS LEAD TO REPRODUCTION

At birth, the only interest in a buck's life is food. While he still bears spots, before he is six months old, however, his other, greater, interest develops: Sex.

Fawns dream big, especially the baby bucks who try to become sexually active. The baby doe is happy just to be, but baby bucks still wearing spots begin experimenting with sex by mounting their mamas. Mamas just walk out from under them. Deer have no concept of incest.

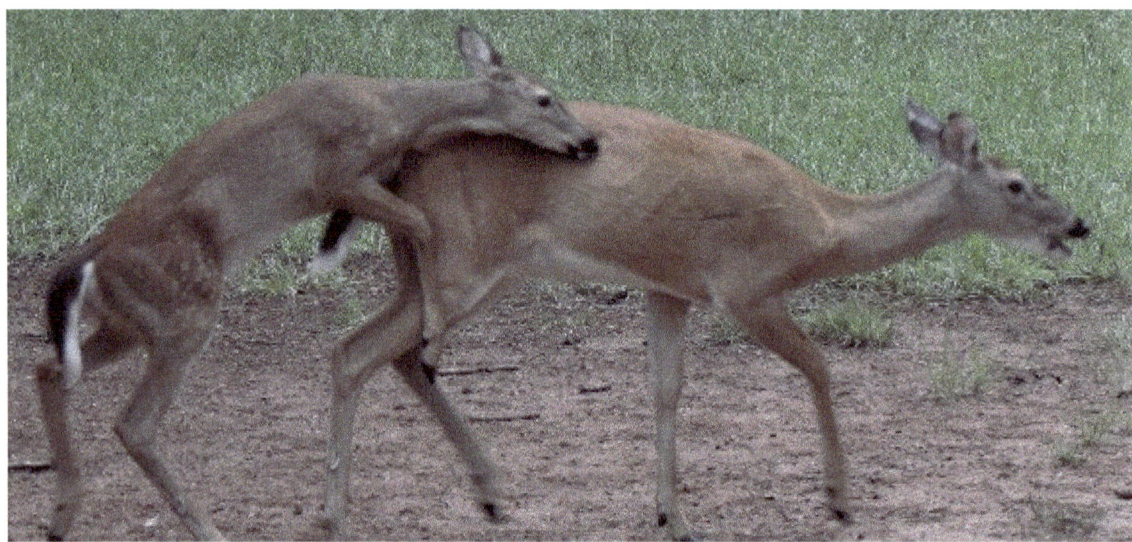

Buck fawn, September 2020, still with spots. Doe is his mother.

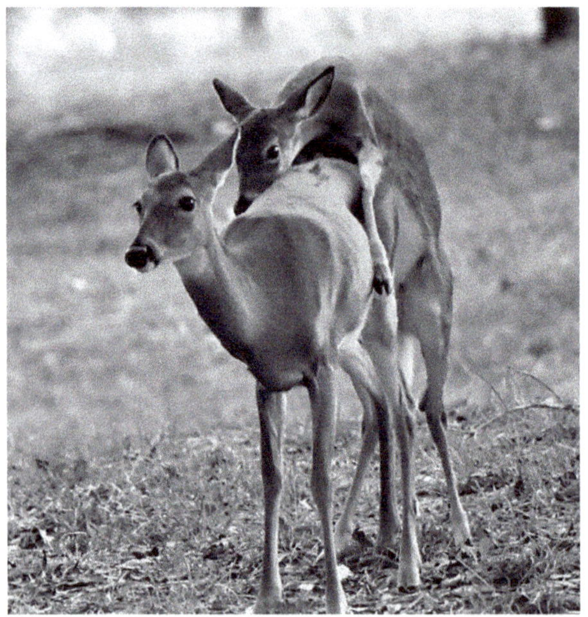

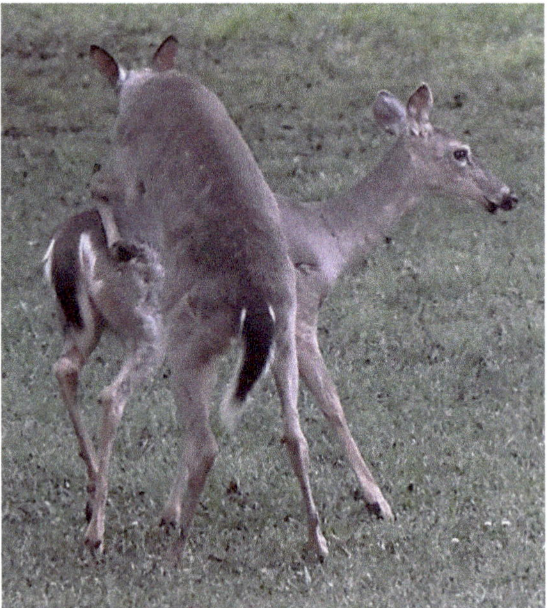

Other autumns, other fawns with their mothers.

The does usually pay no mind to the youngsters and just walk off, as this mama walked out of the camera view and away from her offspring.

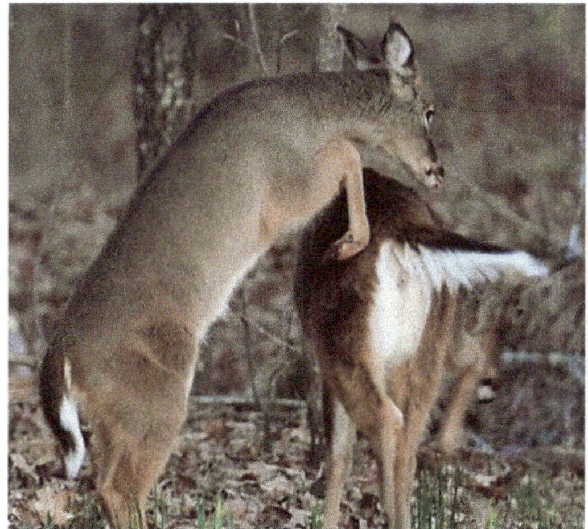 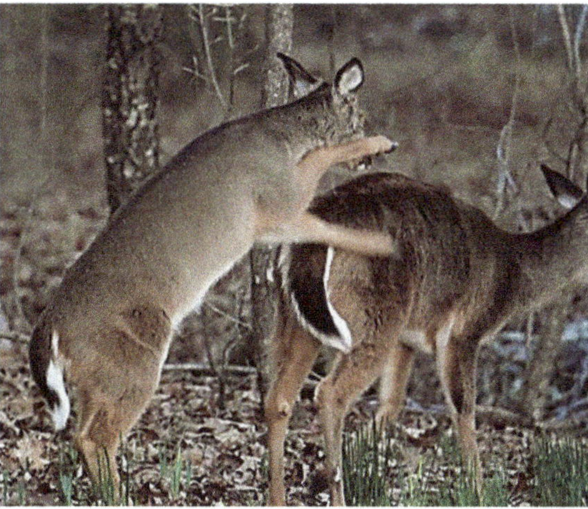

Deer perform a ritual called *rub-urination*: They urinate down their back legs onto the tarsal glands and rub the glands together. The behavior is more common in bucks than in does, and is also more common during the rut. Even day-old fawns have been reported as performing this behavior. I call it the "sex dance" because I have seen it mostly during the rut and the deer shifts weight from side to side as if doing the Texas two-step.

This fawn was the first one born that spring, and he bullied all the other fawns who visited the feeding area. His bullying behavior continued into the next year.

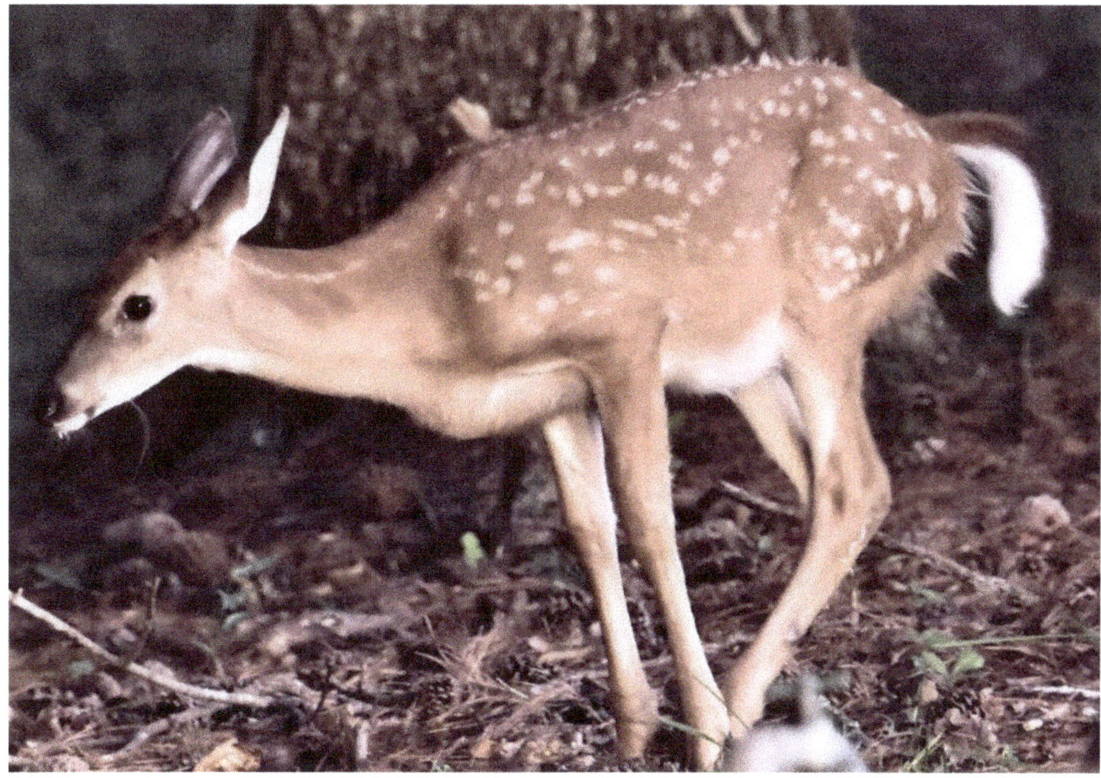

When bucks are older but denied mating rights by more dominant bucks, they release their frustration by masturbating. This buck rubs his penis against his side and then cleans himself. His musk glands are clean. The rut has begun but not yet reached high intensity. It is only October 1.

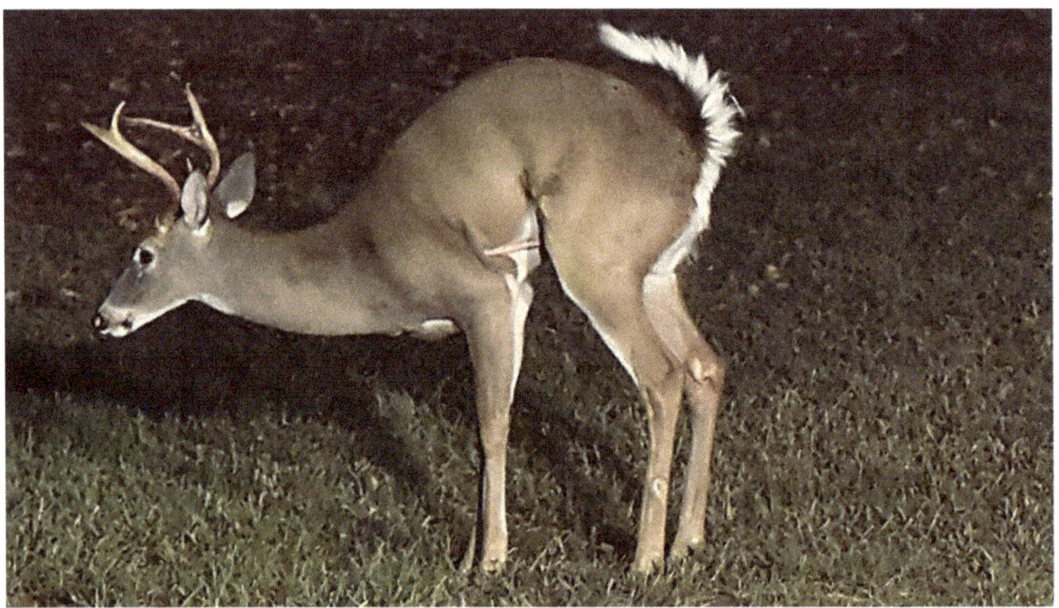

October 1, 2019

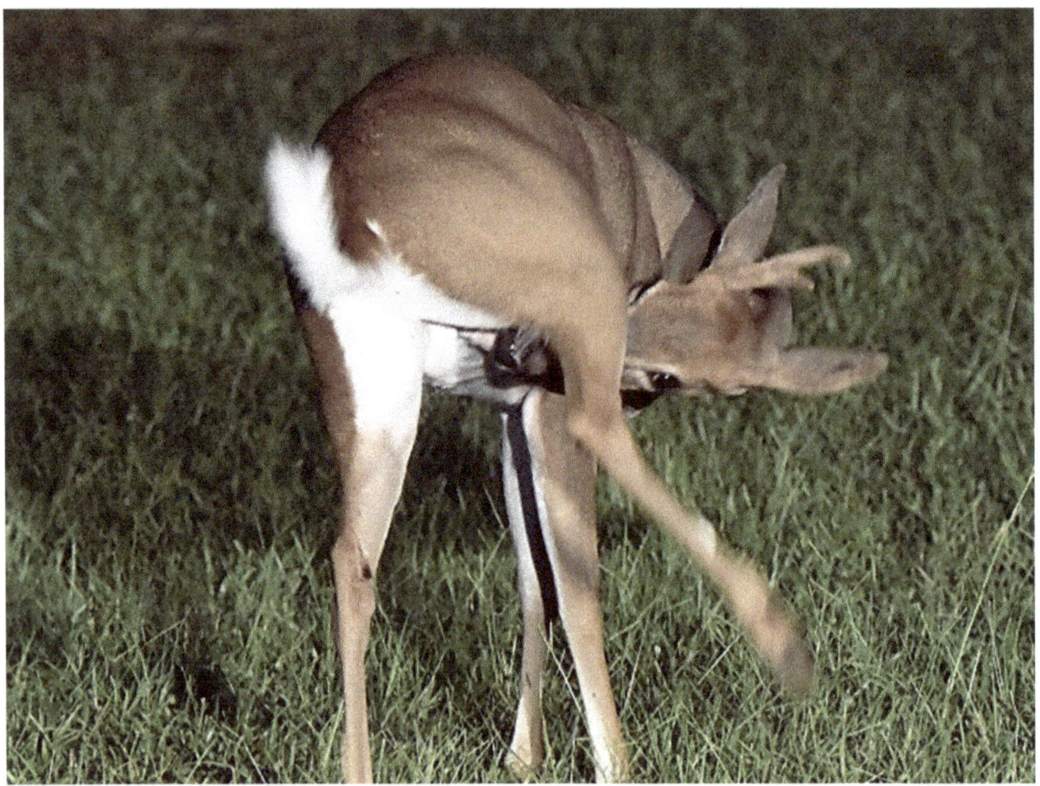

September 2, he seems to be either orally masturbating or grooming himself.

Other pre-rut activities serve to release sexual frustration. The buck on the left (Two Spot) appears to be sexually aroused as the fight began. This rumble lasted more than five minutes and covered about 20 yards.

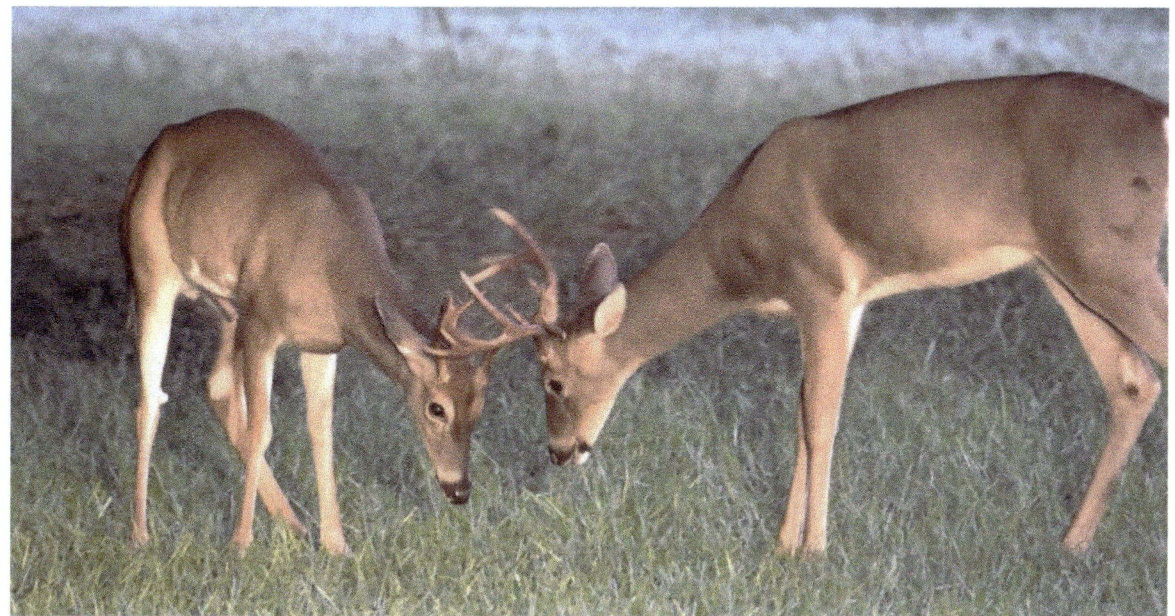

After their battle, they appeared to hug each other, antler style, as if they were buddies.

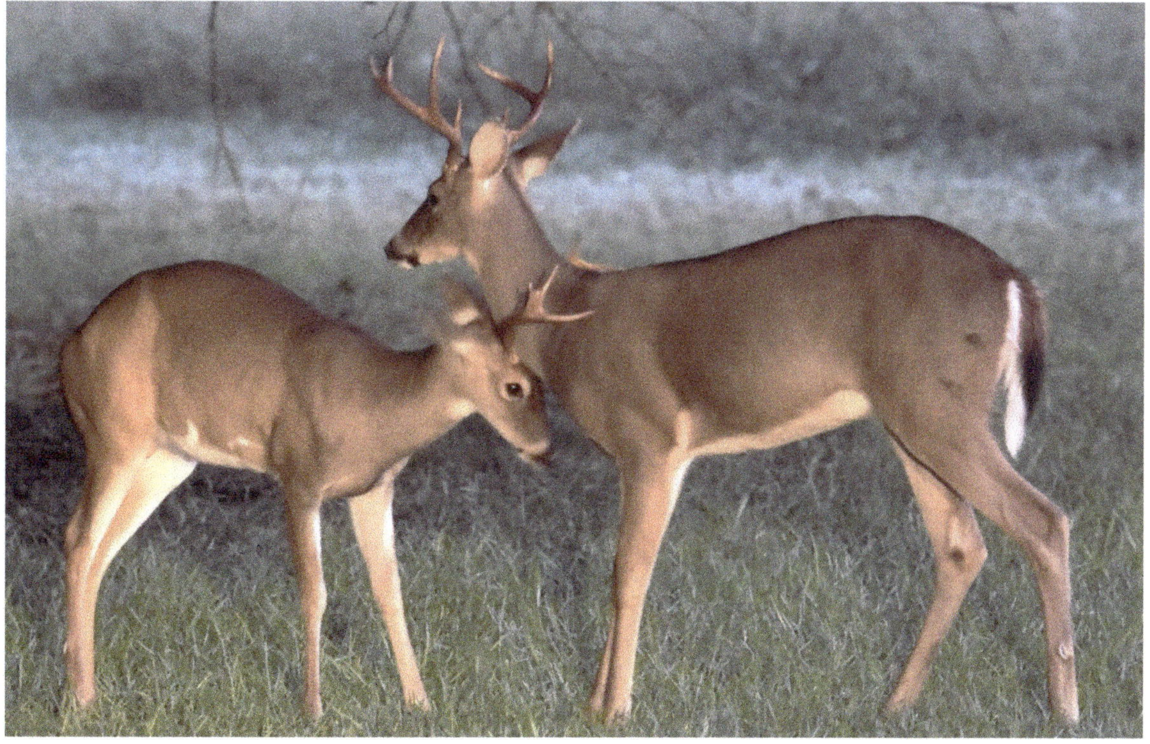

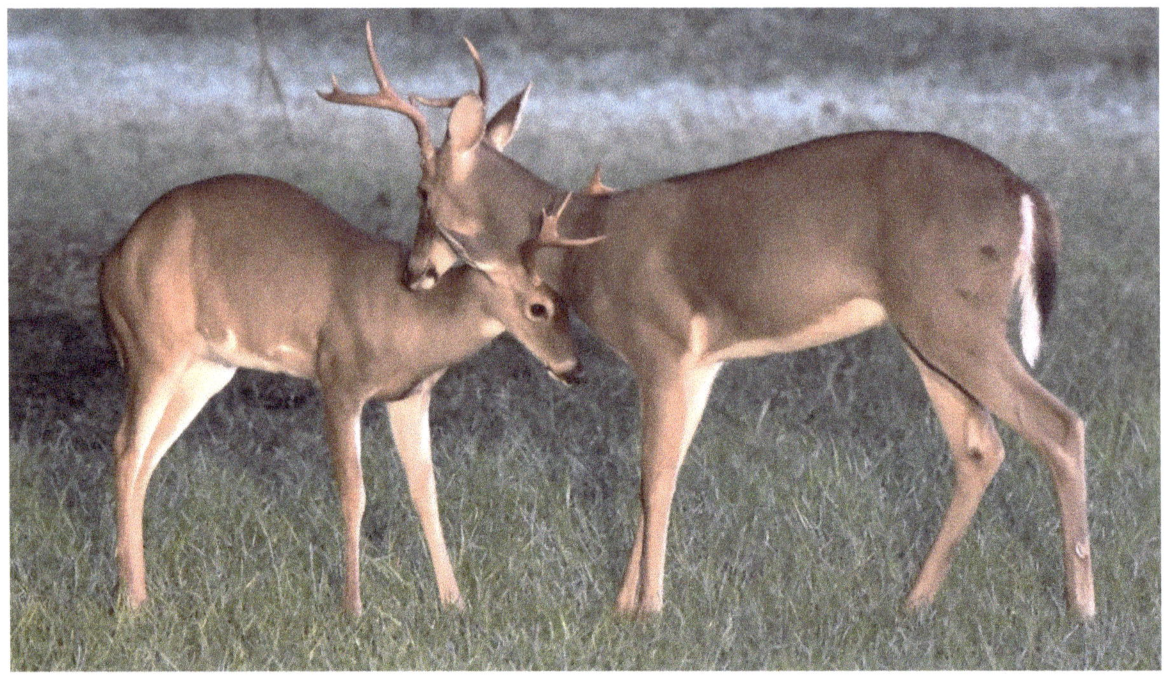

They continued the shoving match again, pushed around the house and eventually reappeared with positions reversed, with Two Spots showing on his other side.

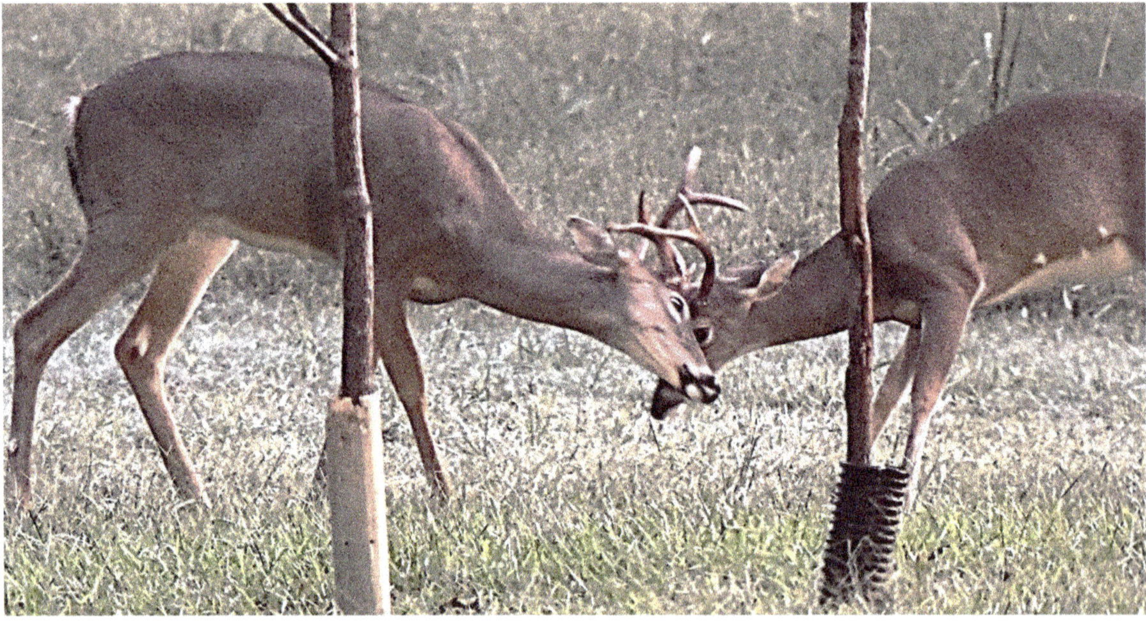

The buck in the foreground has just completed the scrape behaviors and he seems to be sexually excited. The fella in the background (Swayback) showed up often.

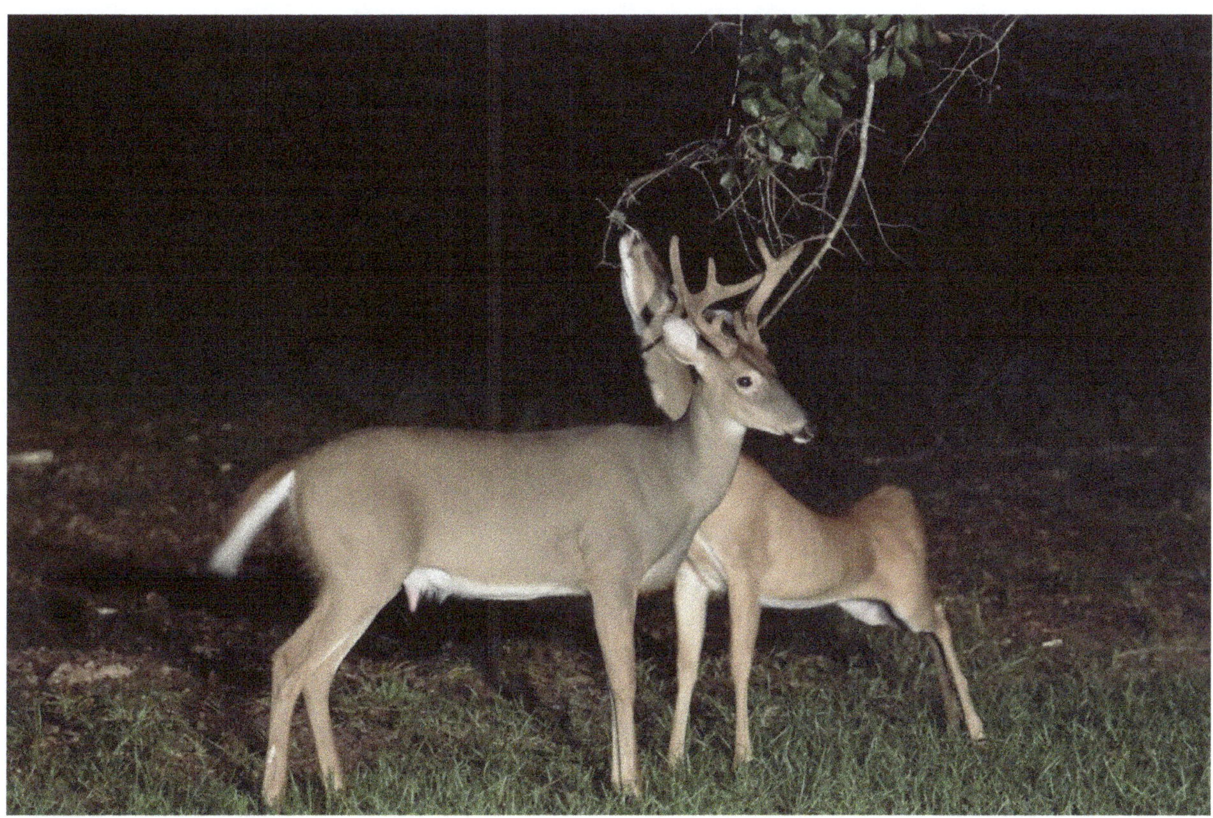

A doe will lick another's tarsal glands to gather information about the other one through her scent. This doe urinated immediately after her "get to know you."

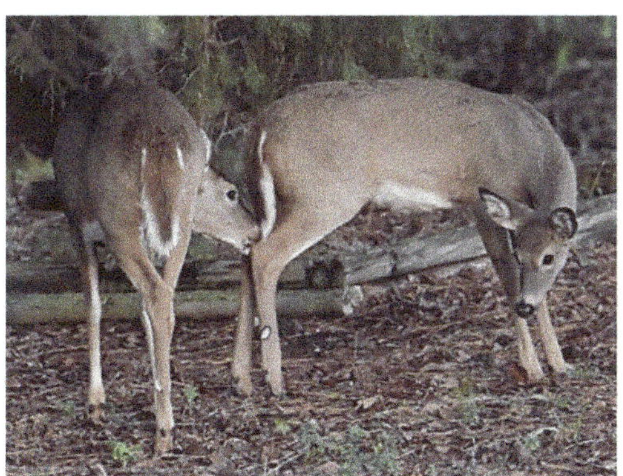

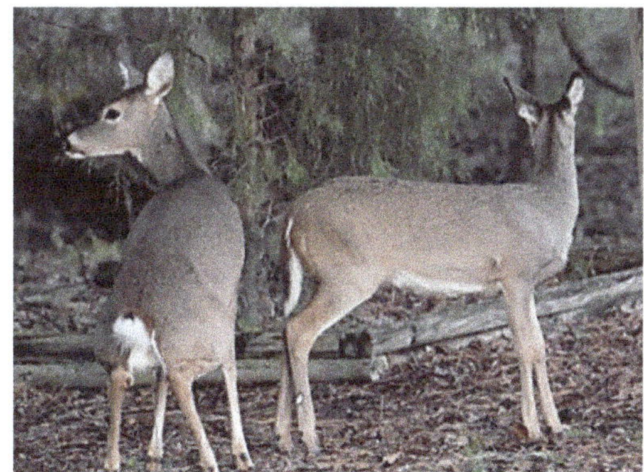

On several occasions I have seen antlered bucks mount other antlered bucks. Perhaps a show of sexual frustration or dominance. A yearling mounted his travel buddy in my yard September 7, 2021, while another youngster watched. The event lased two minutes, longer than the buck-to-doe mating I photographed in 2018. The dominant buck remounted four times when the subjected one walked out from under.

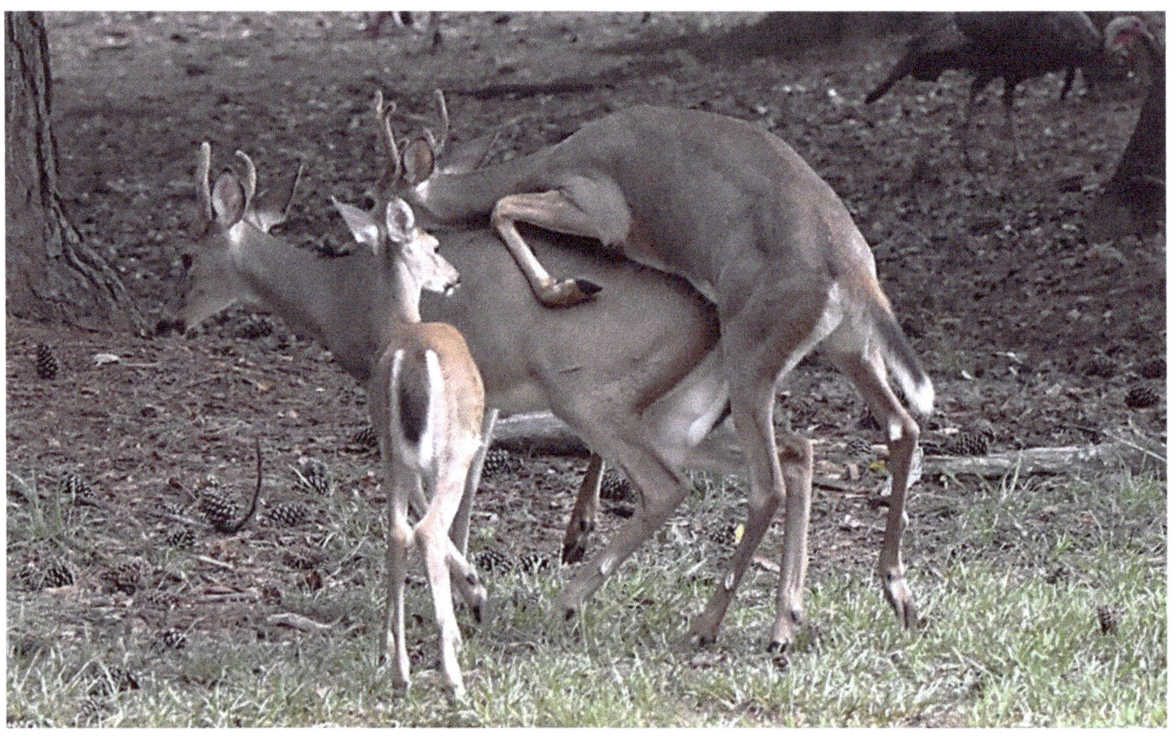

In spring 2022, a six-point buck groomed Two Spot and then attempted to mount him from the side, as I had seen fawn-age bucks do with their mothers.

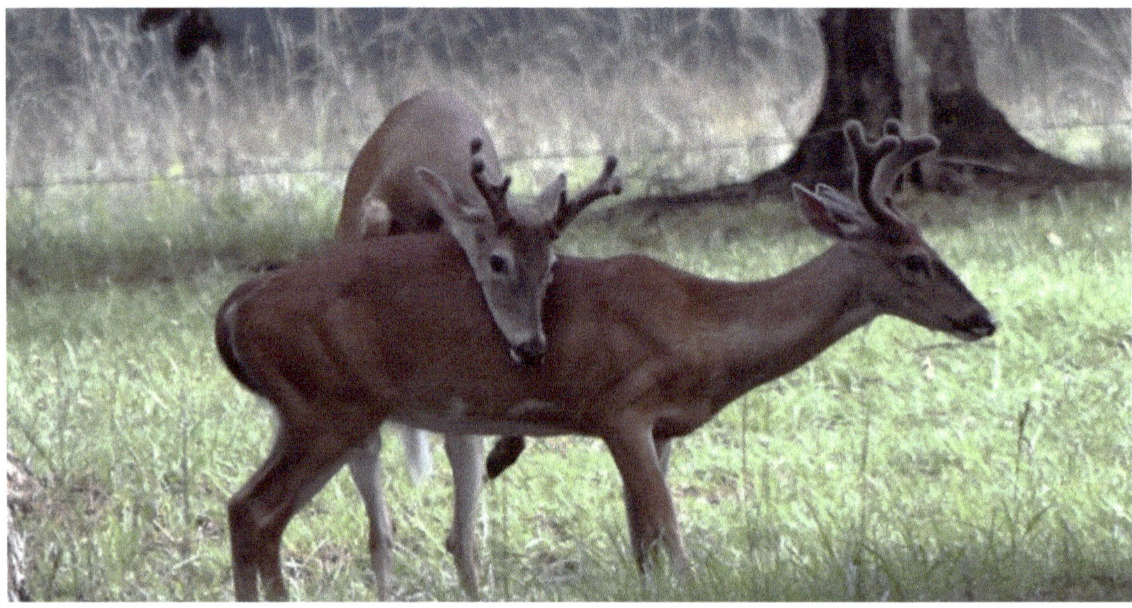

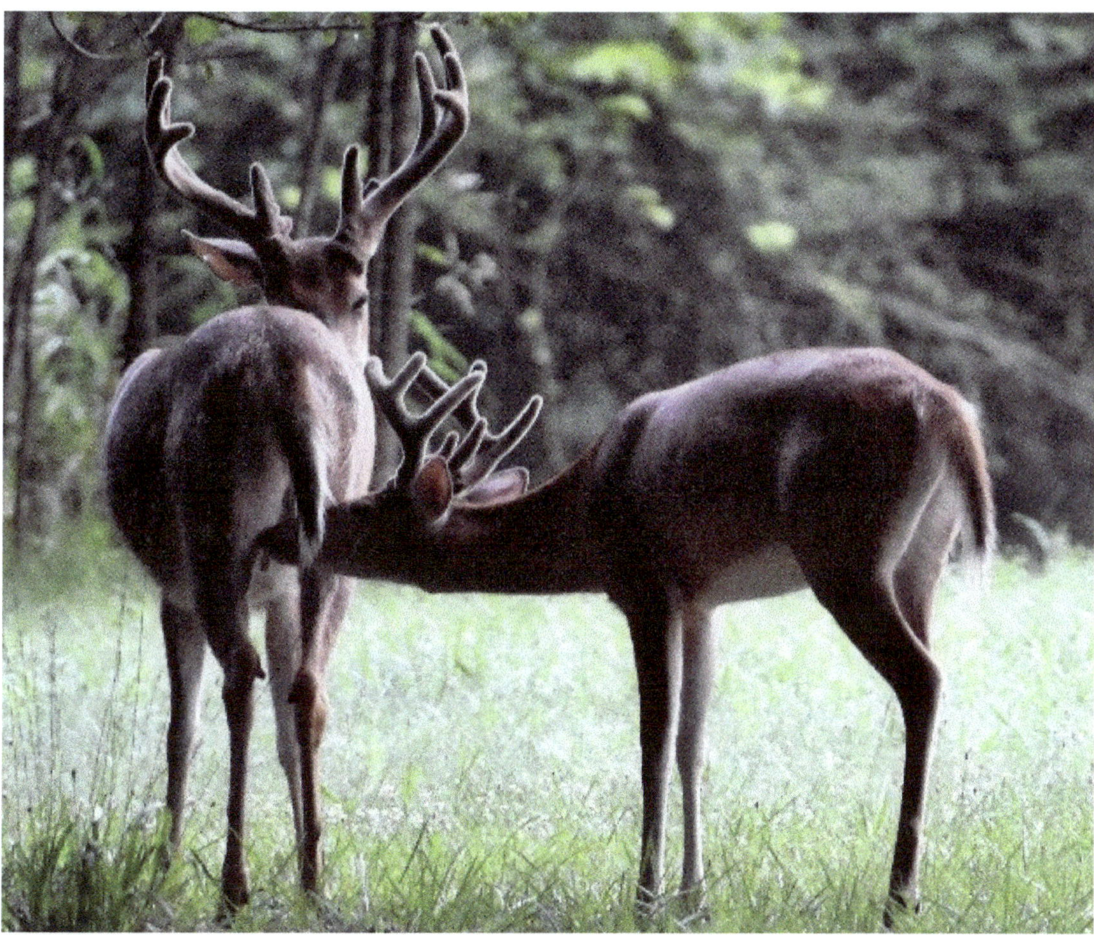

Sometimes a sniff is necessary to know who the other fellow is.

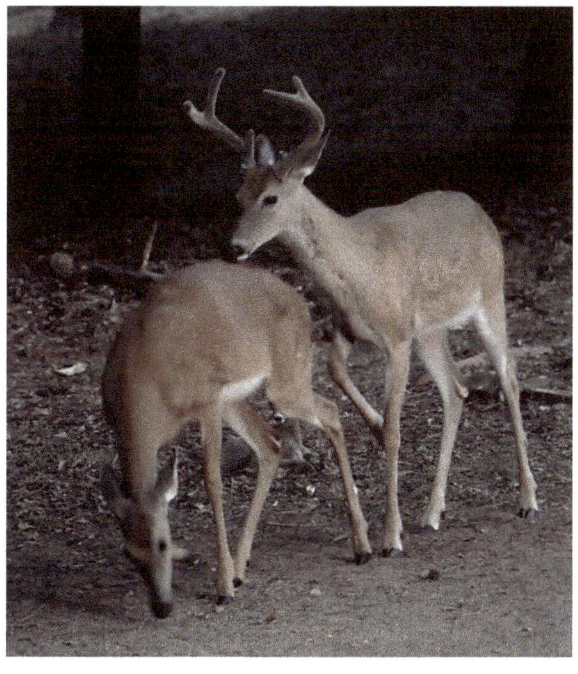

There is always a dreamer, even in July, but this doe walked away before the buck could mount. The fellas would most likely not have sufficient sperm to become daddies anyway.

When bucks are not competing for food or ladies, they can be cordial and often groom each other while waiting for the feeders to spin.

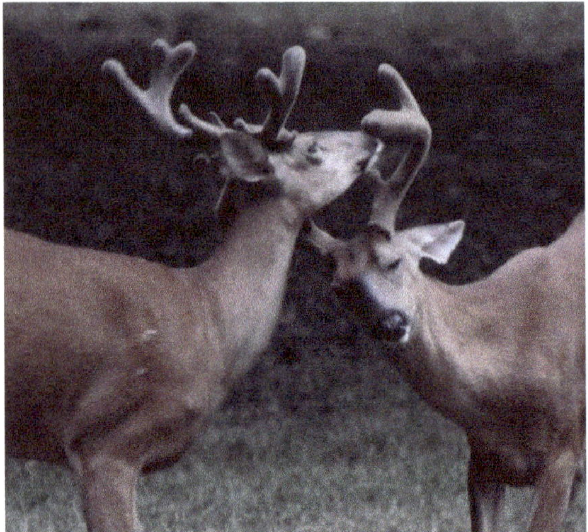
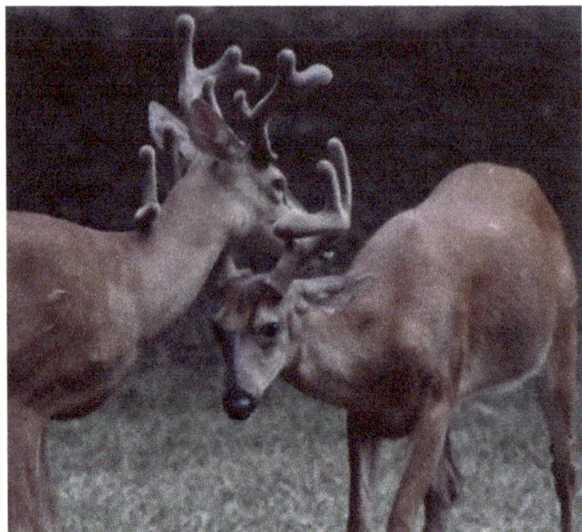

LICKING LIMBS

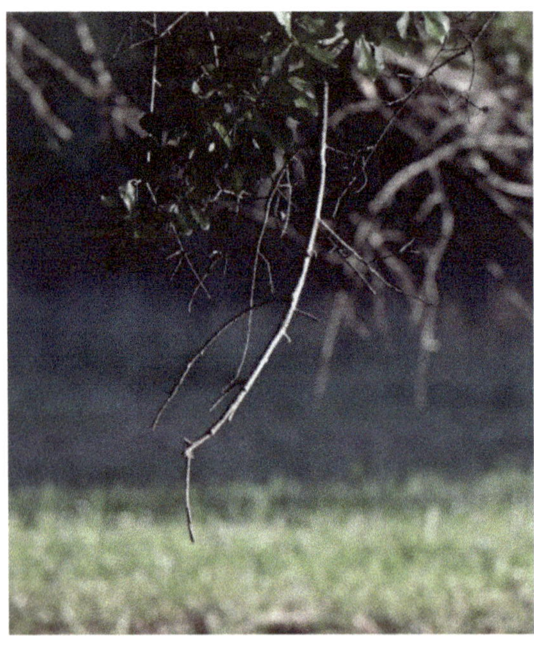
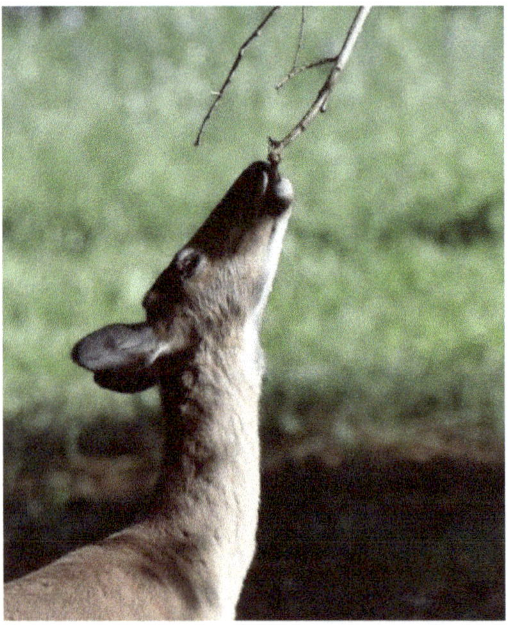

Licking and rubbing facial glands on a limb is another nonreproductive action deer perform, not only as a prelude to breeding season, but year around. They thereby leave messages for others to know they have passed by. In the spring of 2021, my yard deer selected a limb hanging above a 2020-fall scrape. Winter winds tore out most of the limb, but the deer utilized the remainder.

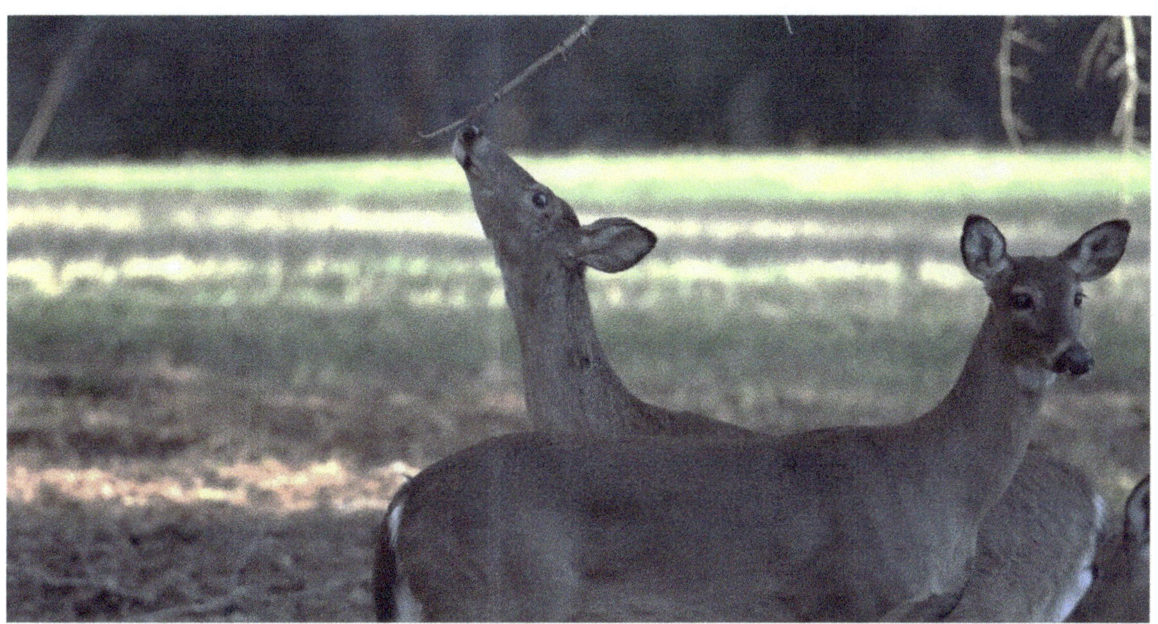

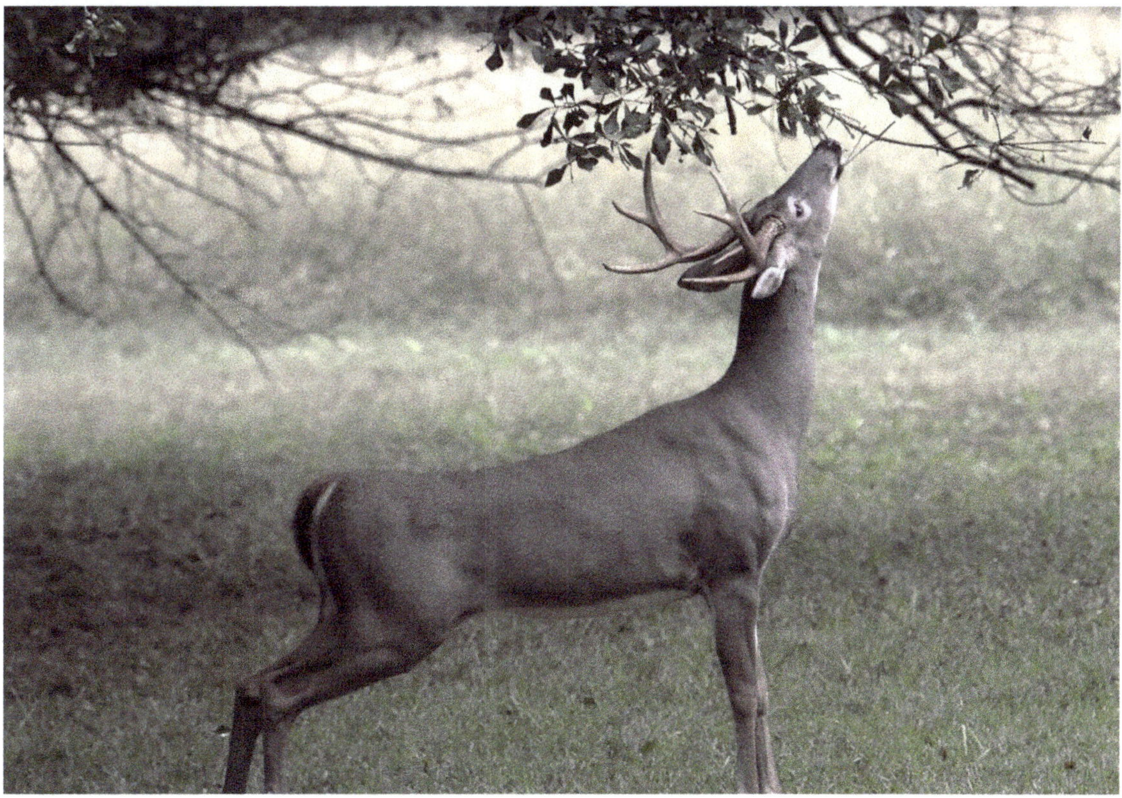

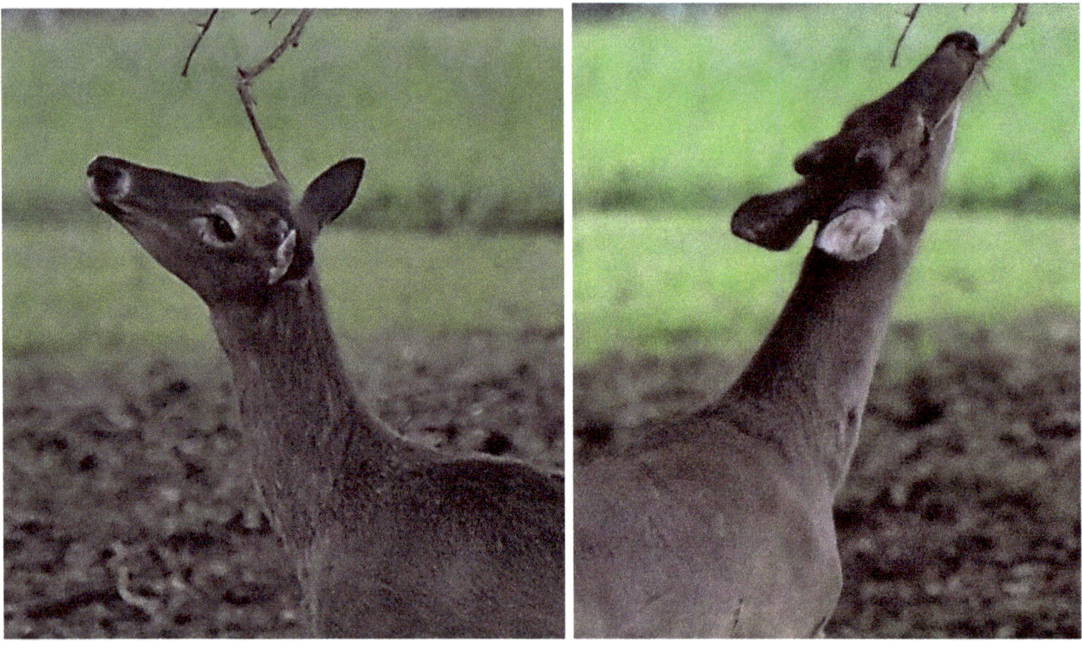

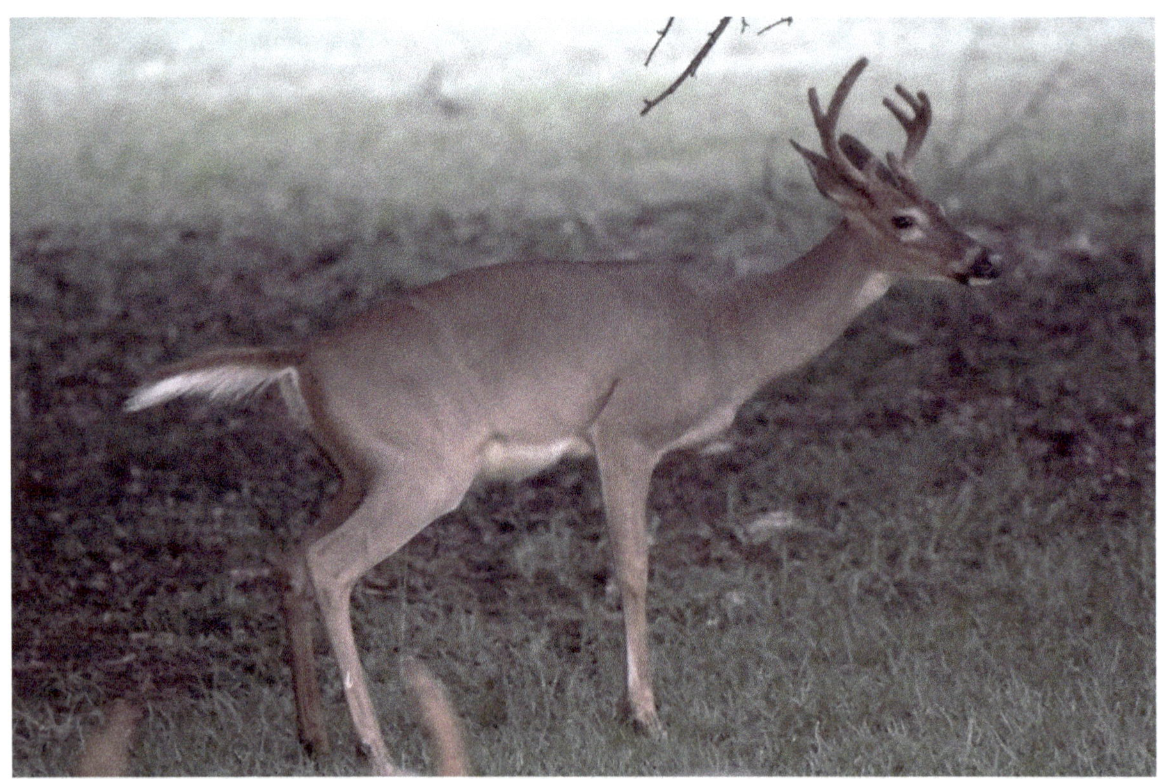

Some urinate beneath the limb to ensure other deer get the message, "I was here." They thus kept the scrape under the limb semi-active before the rut began and long after it ended.

As the rut approached, bucks shoved each other as they sought control of the area under the licking limb. This spot became a frequently used scrape.

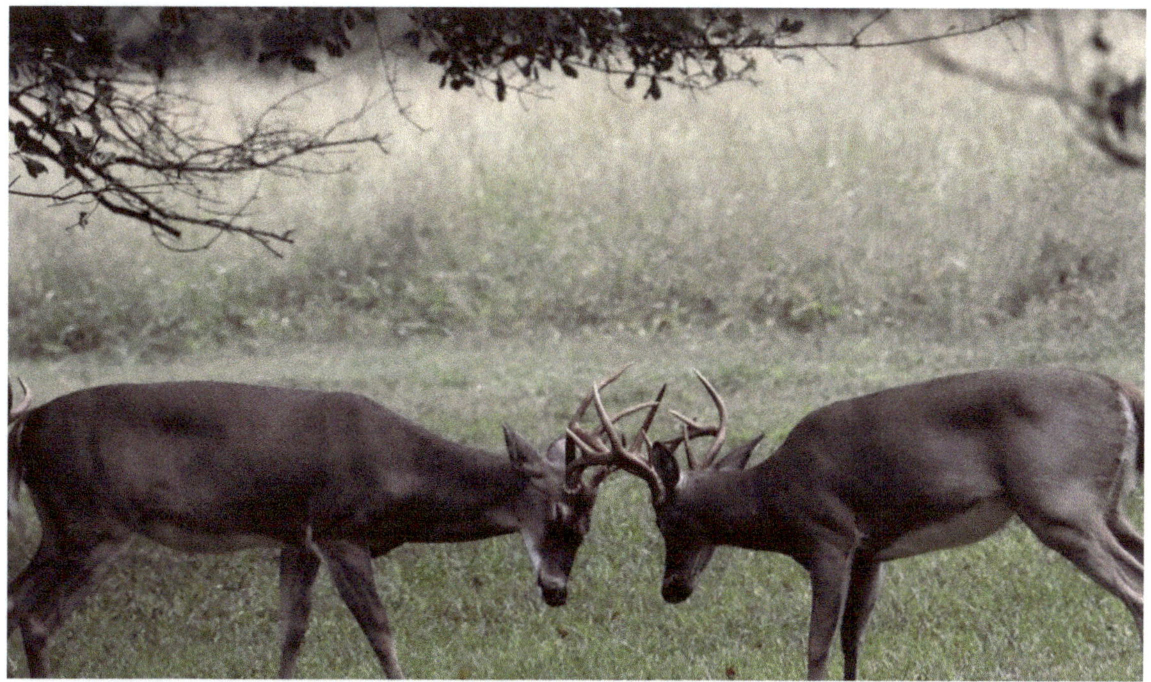

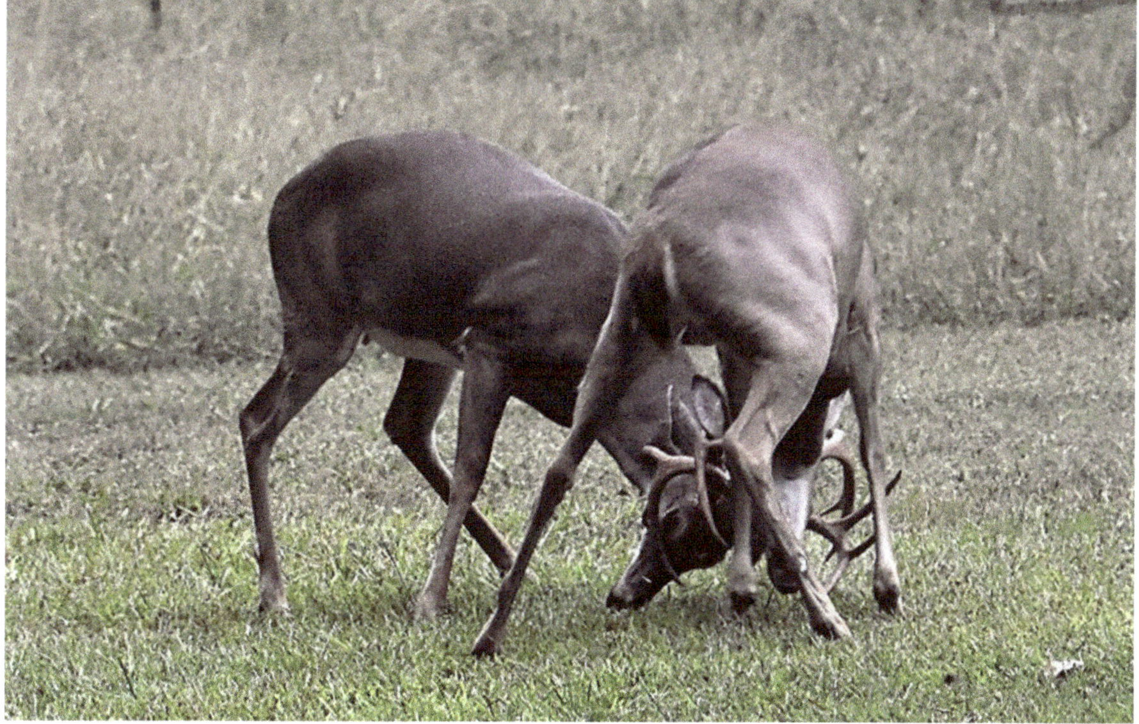

SCROTUM AND TESTICLES OVER THE MONTHS

He may be six or seven years old and the father of a dozen offspring, but come spring, his testosterone levels drop, his testicles shrink and his antlers fall off. In spite of the low sperm level, however, the buck is still able to breed until March or perhaps into April, just as a stallion can sire a foal for about two months after being castrated.

New antlers begin to show as smooth rounded knobs. These grow until late summer, and while the antlers are growing, testosterone levels are still low.

The scrotum looks empty or almost so. These are different bucks but show the changes in the scrotum over the weeks of summer and into the rut.

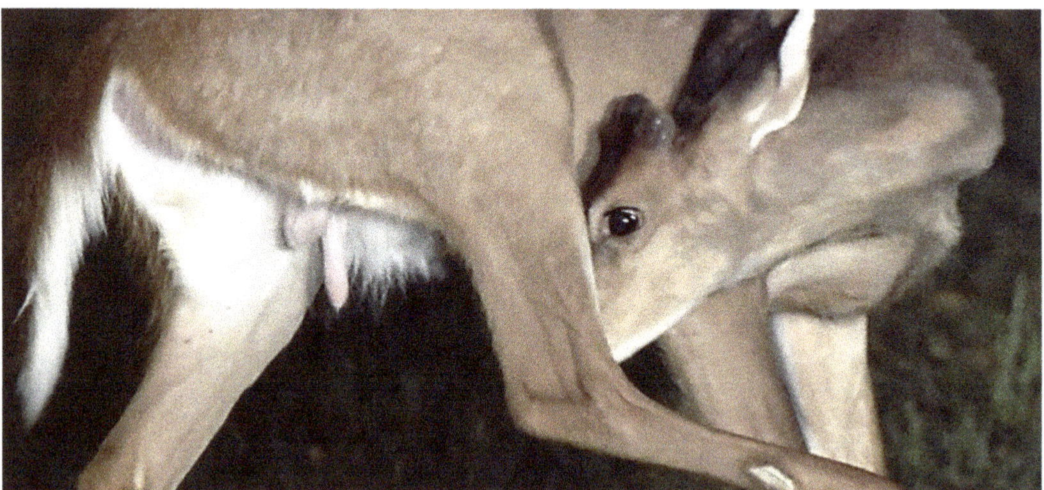

April 9

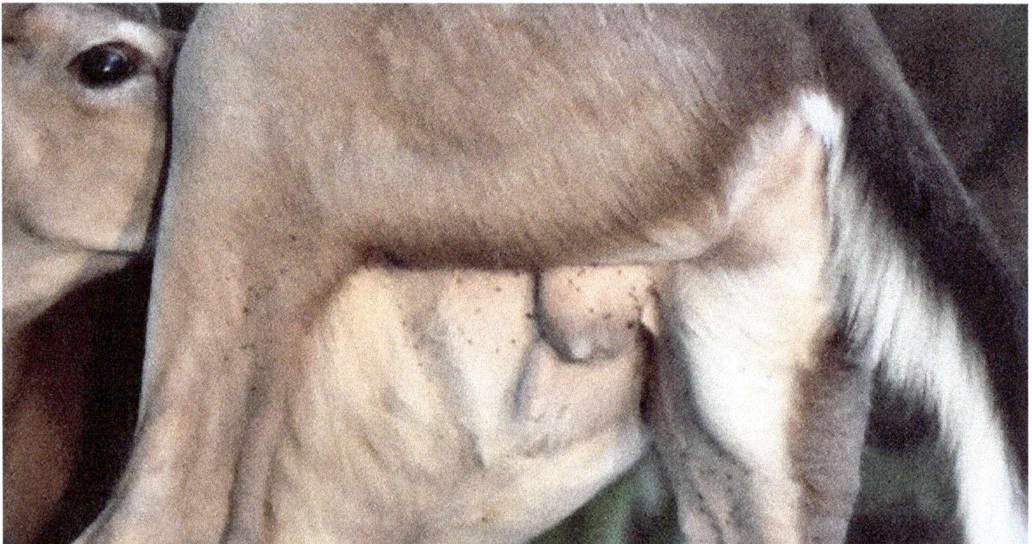

April 30. His scrotum appears to be swollen; the little black bugs are deer *keds* (a type of wingless fly) that live on deer. They are especially numerous when deer populations are high.

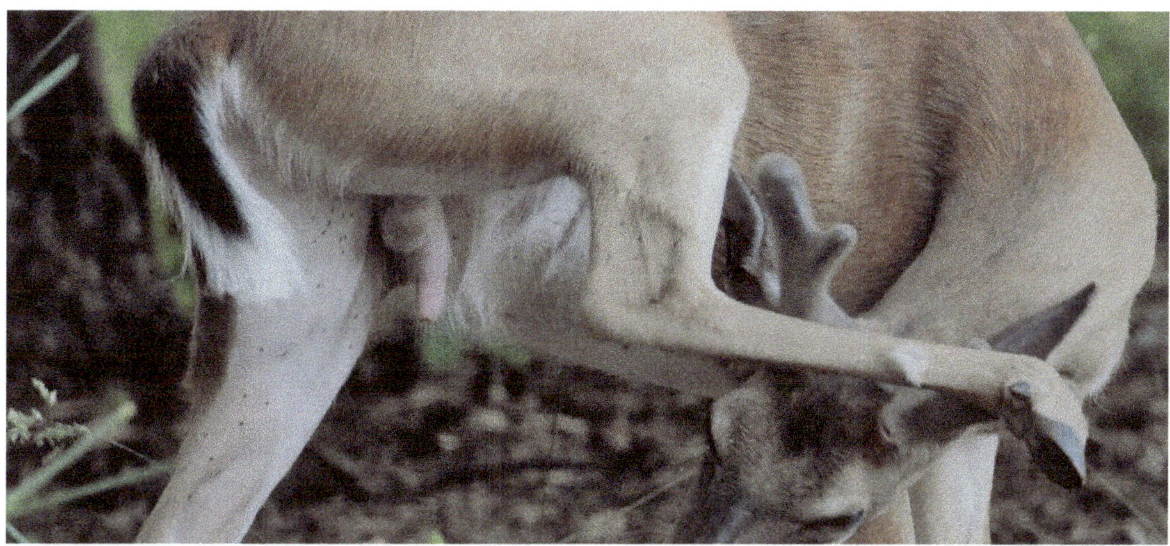

May 6

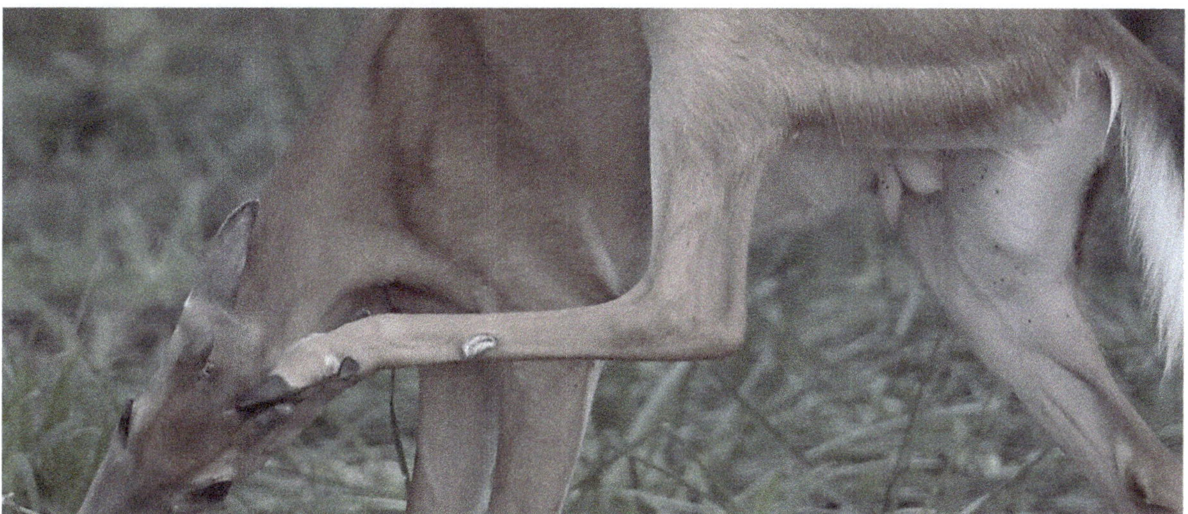

May 8

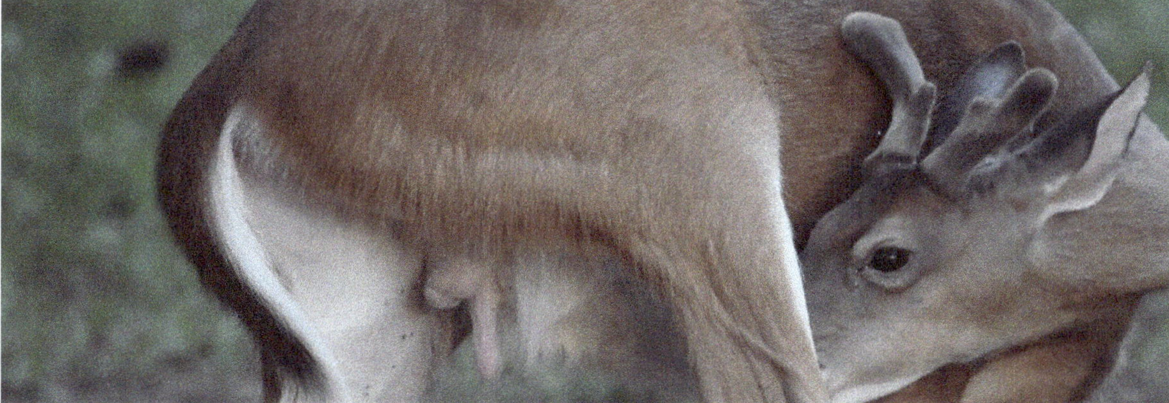

May 16

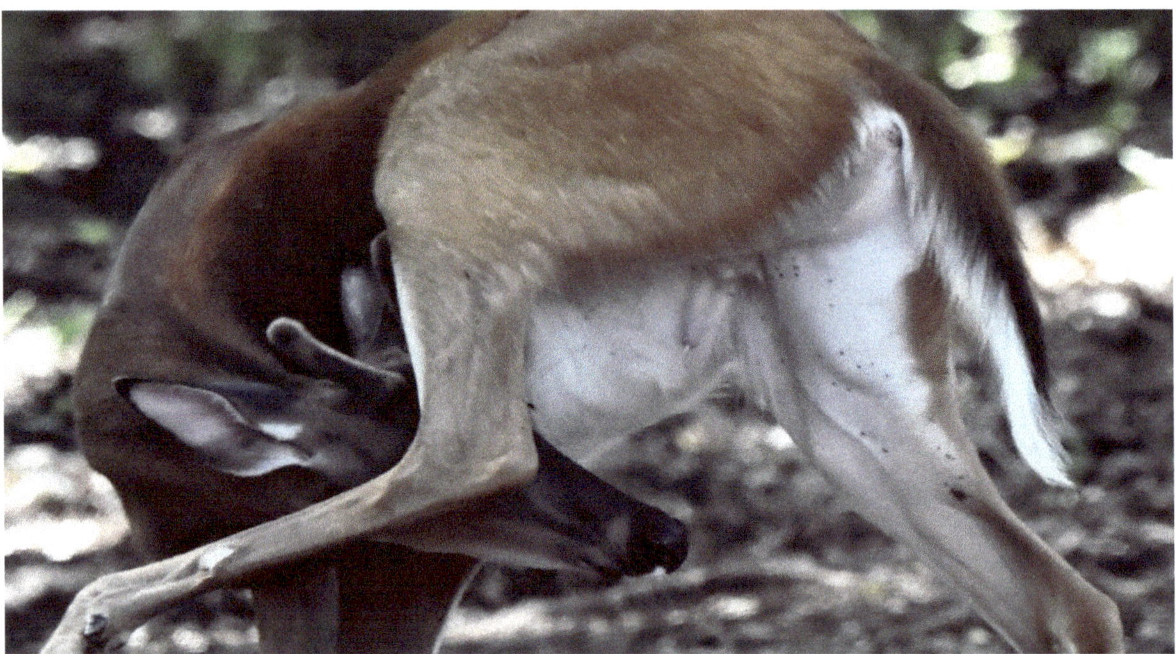

June 20

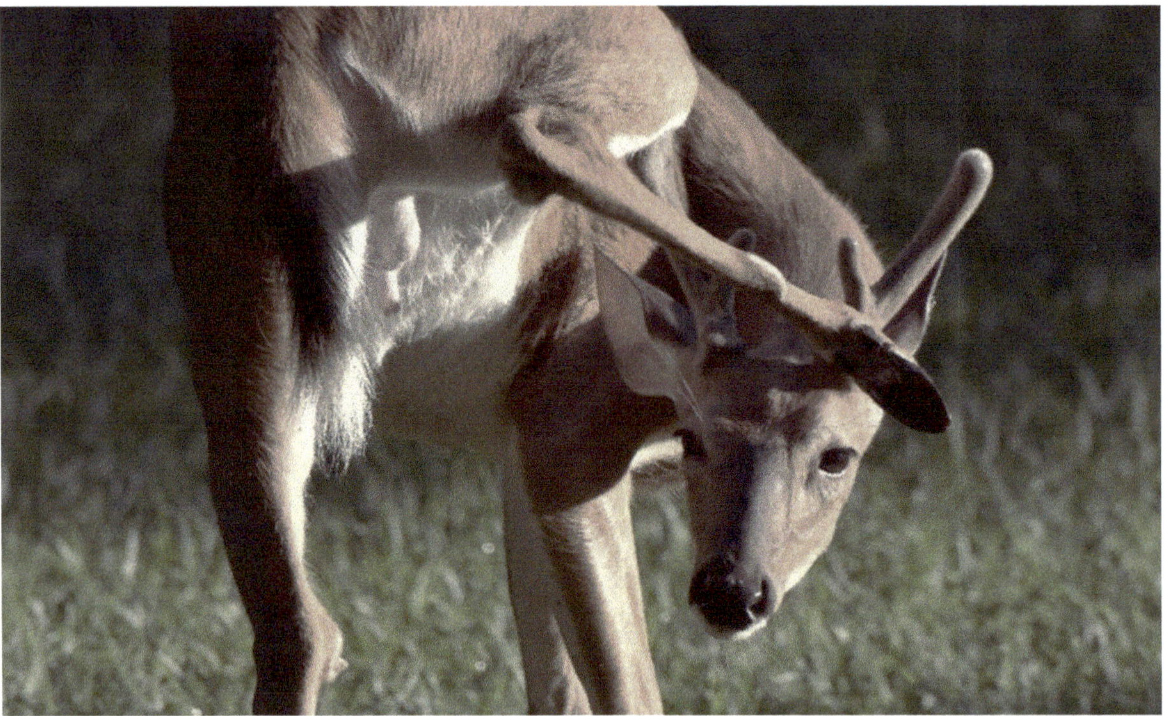

June 25

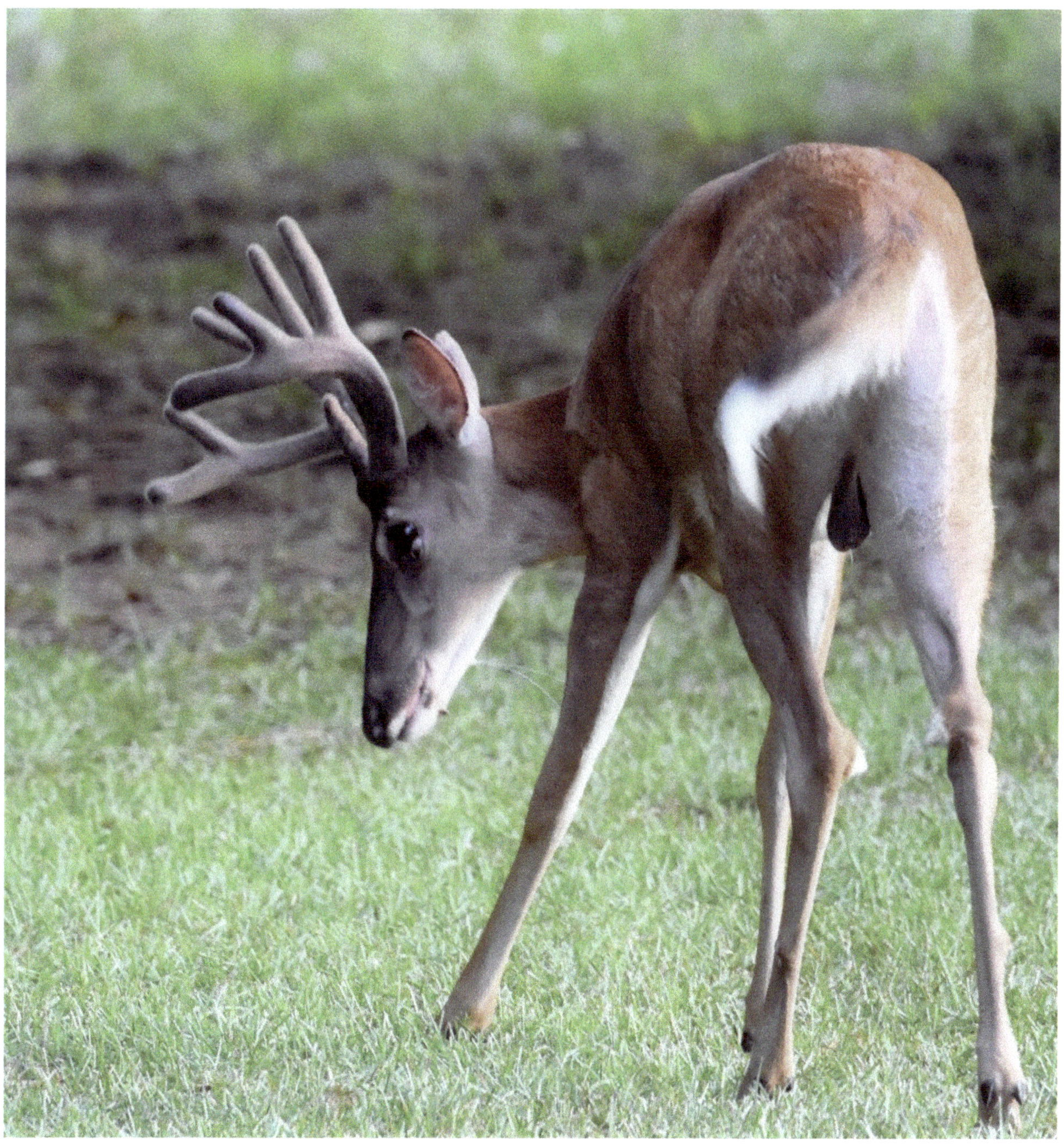

July 16. Pappy

                    Susan Lindsley

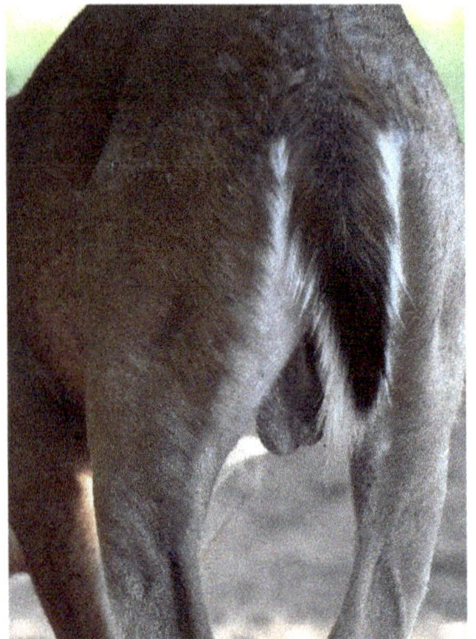
July 24

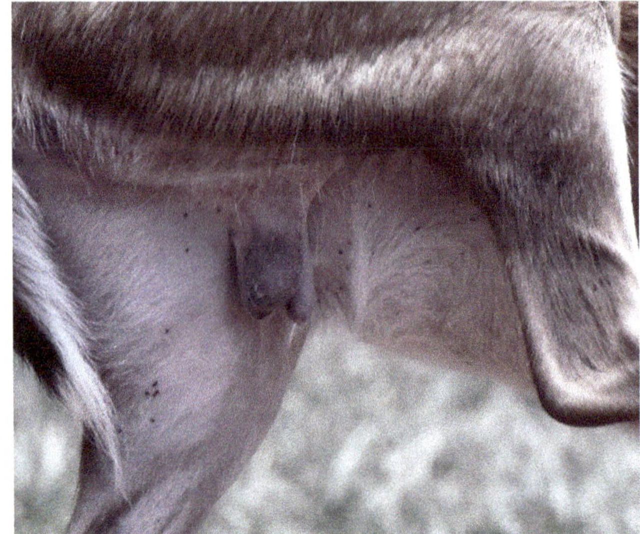
July 30

The testicles begin to expand and increase testosterone levels about the time the antlers begin to harden and the velvet breaks off. Here Pappy's testicles have begun to enlarge but his antlers still carry velvet and he has not begun to urinate onto his musk glands.

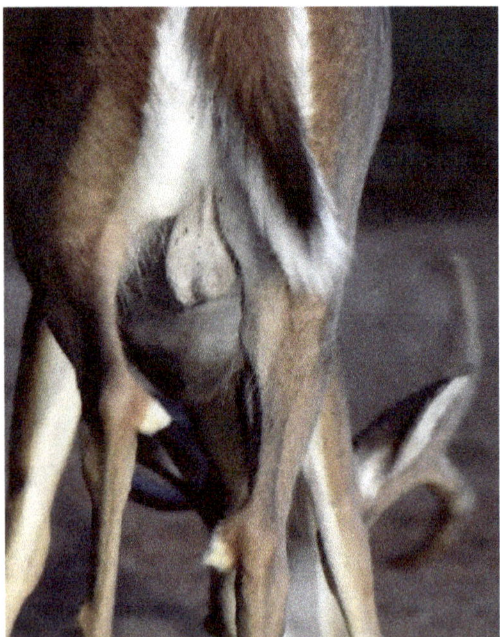
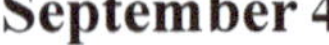
September 4

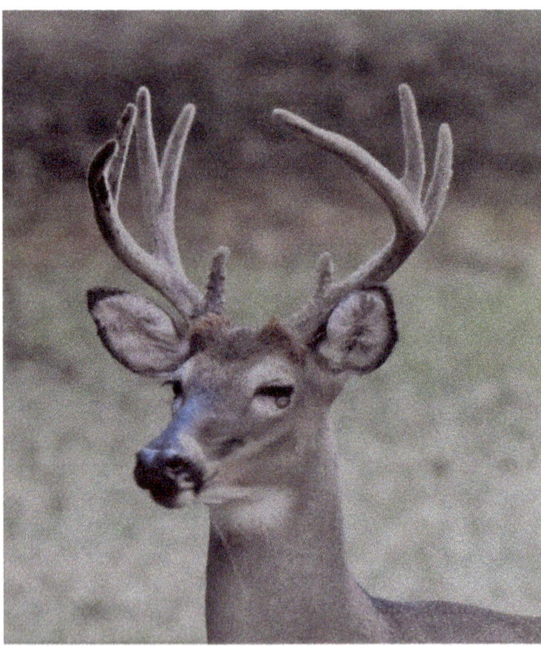
September 10

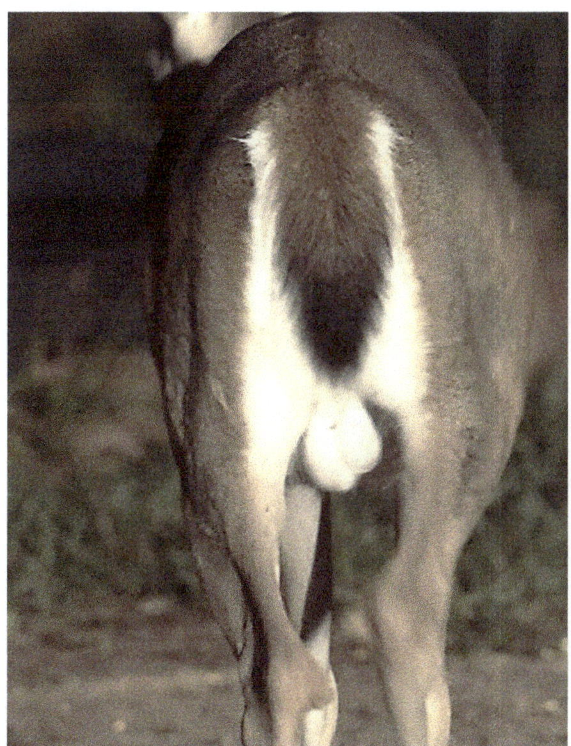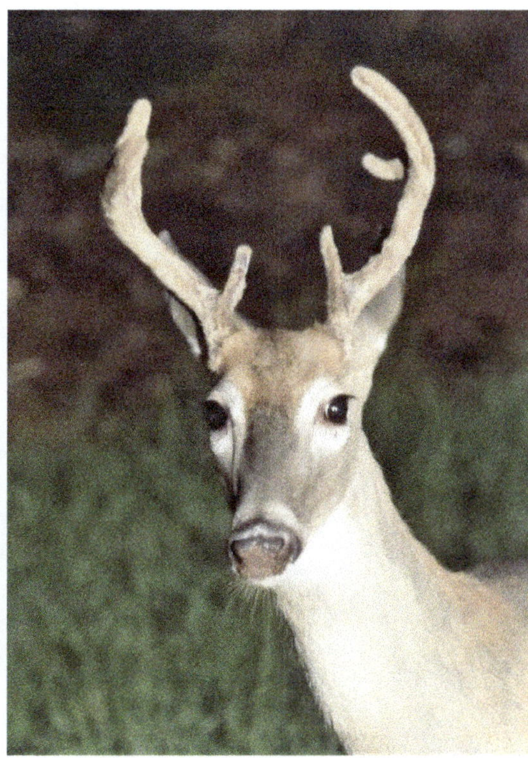

Curly's scrotum enlarged by September 4, while he carried velvet the same evening.

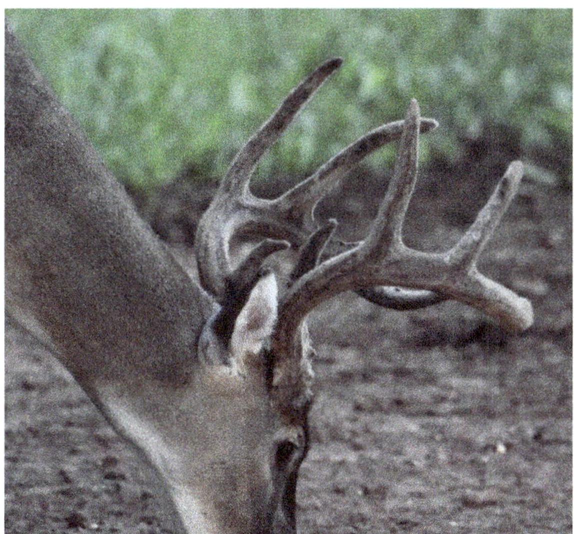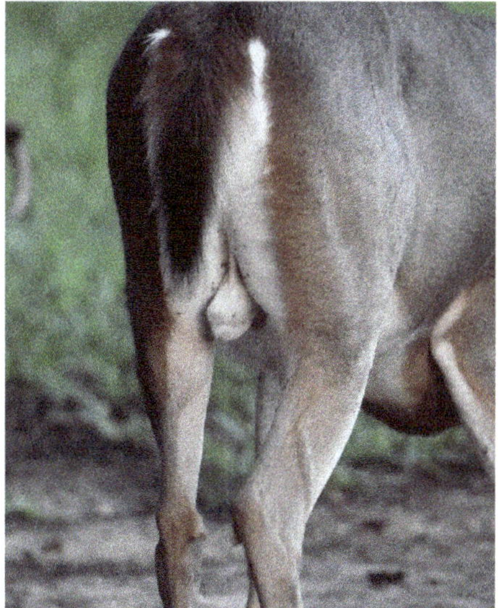

Another dominant type, on September 5, is the eight-pointer.

The size of the antlers has nothing to do with the buck's readiness to breed. This spike on September 14 was ready to mate. He was also the worst bully in the crowd. The Knob was also a breeder (October). Note their tarsal glands.

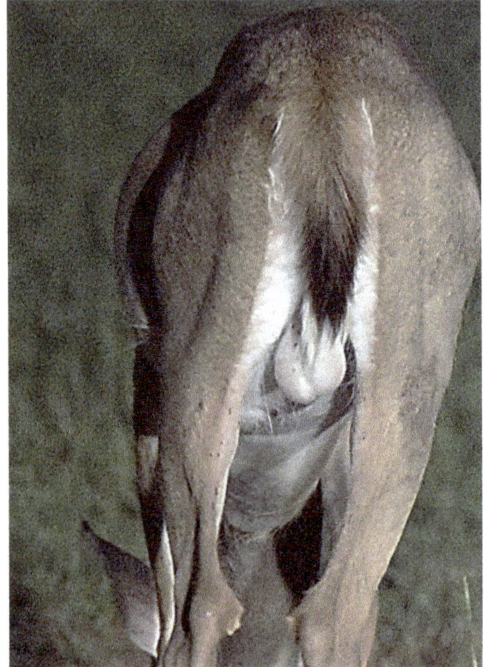

The Bully

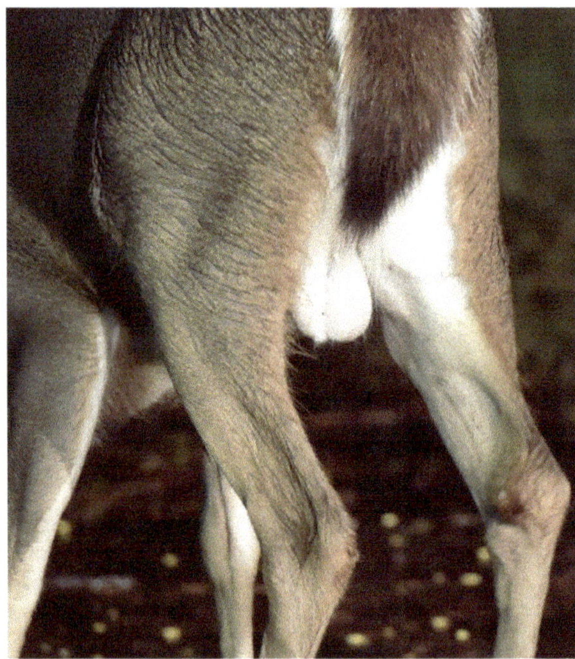

The Knob

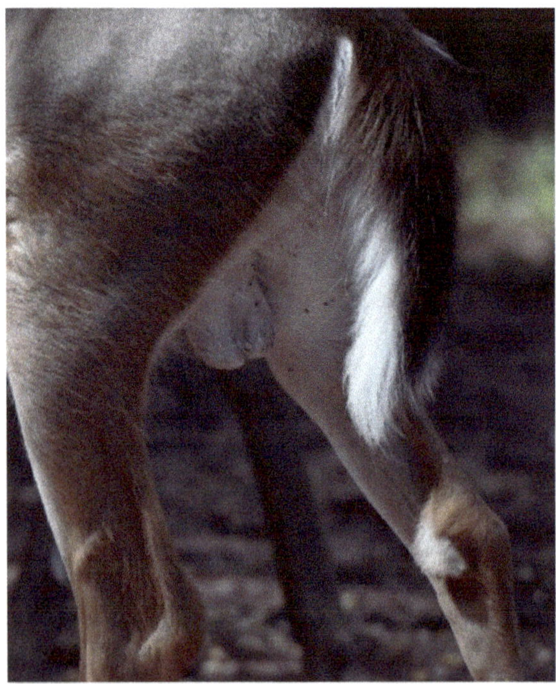

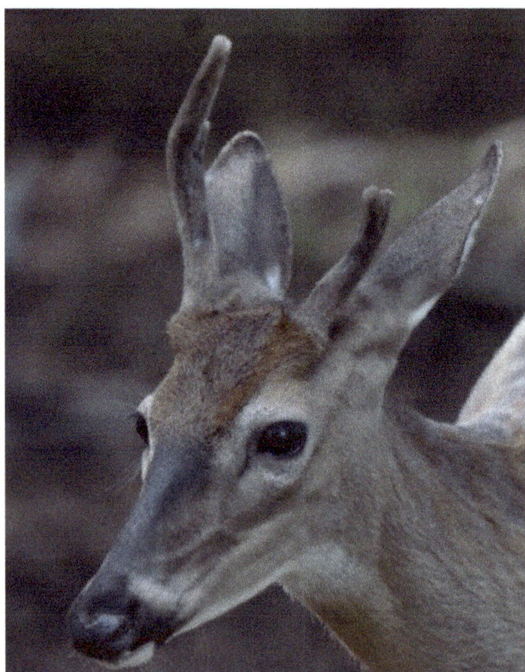

The almost-four spike

TARSAL GLANDS (OFTEN CALLED *MUSK* GLANDS)

All deer urinate down their tarsal glands, bucks as frequently as once a day, does less often, which explains why does also have darkened tarsal glands. During the rut, bucks perform this ritual more often, and almost exclusively. The composition of their urine also changes in response to the increase in testosterone.

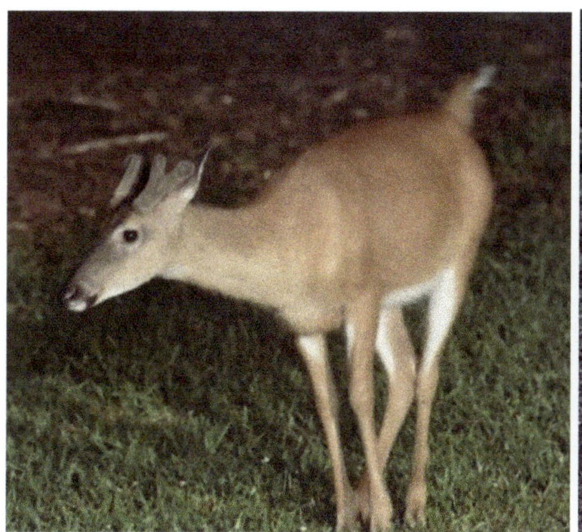

Mid-May

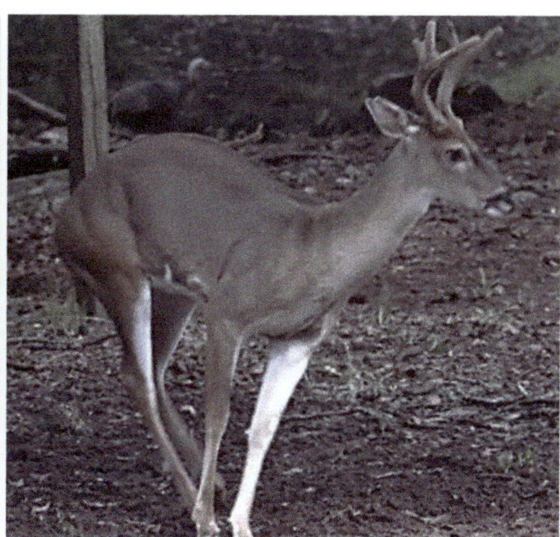

Late August

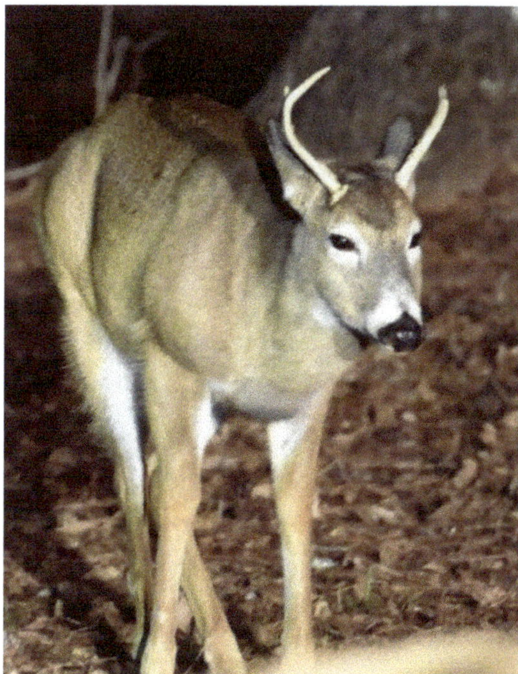

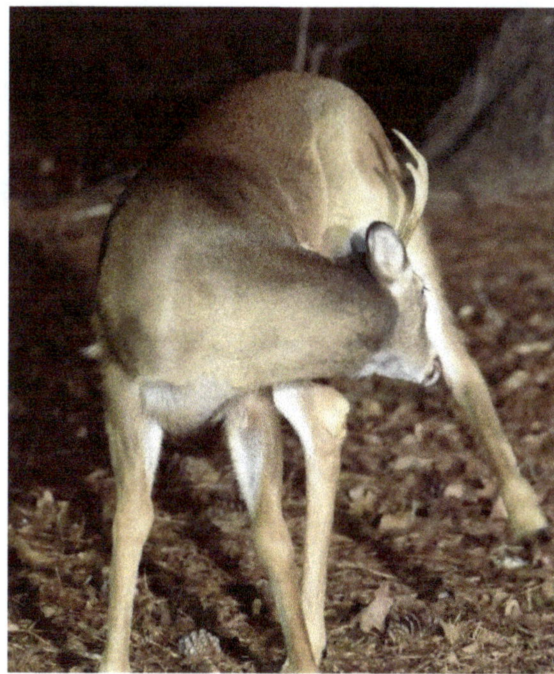

November: They often lick their tarsal glands afterwards.

Every fall a buck undergoes seasonal hormone shifts as his testicles begin to produce more and more testosterone. His neck swells. He spars with his traveling buddies and gets serious with some bucks. He is ready to mate. All he now needs is an available doe. But the buck has to find her first.

He begins his search with a series of scrapes, and constant sniffing, especially when he sees a doe or smells where she has urinated.

SNIFFING THE DOE

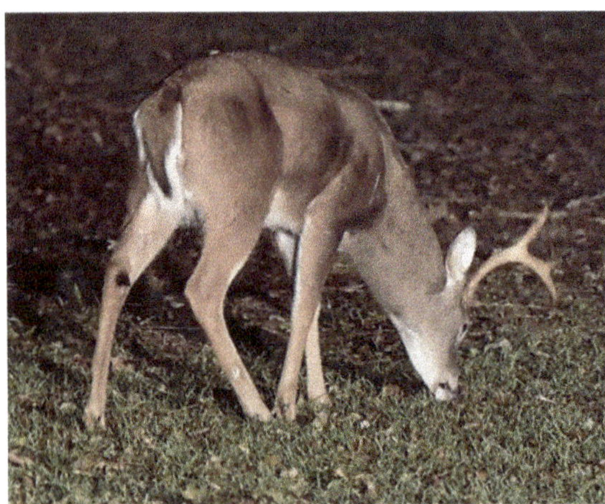
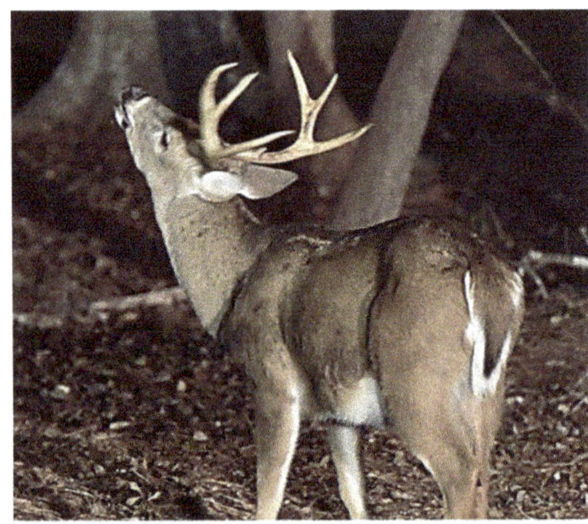

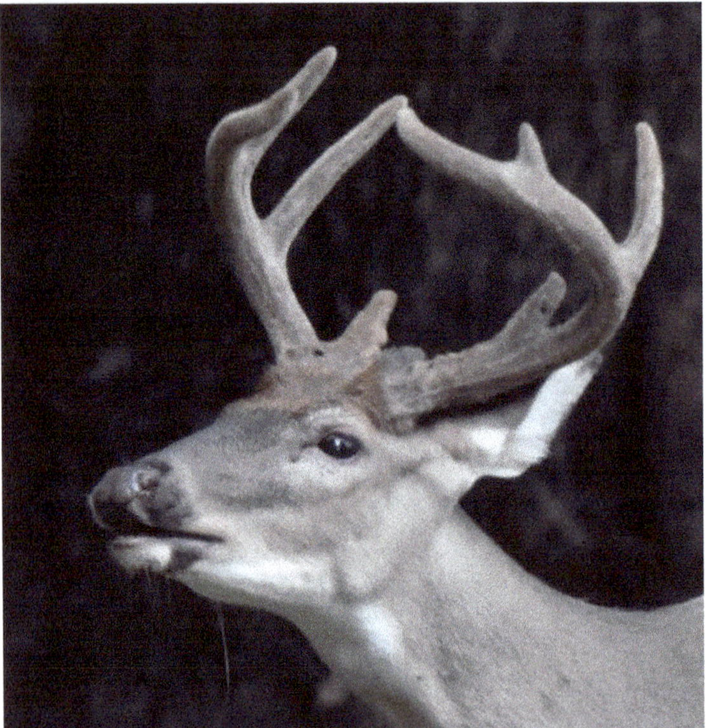

When he smells doe urine in mating season, a buck sniffs up the scent and pulls the scent into his mouth. His upper lip curls away to help the odor enter his mouth and the vomeronasal organ. It tells him what he needs to know about the doe that deposited the urine, on the ground as she passed through or on his scrape in response to his invitation.

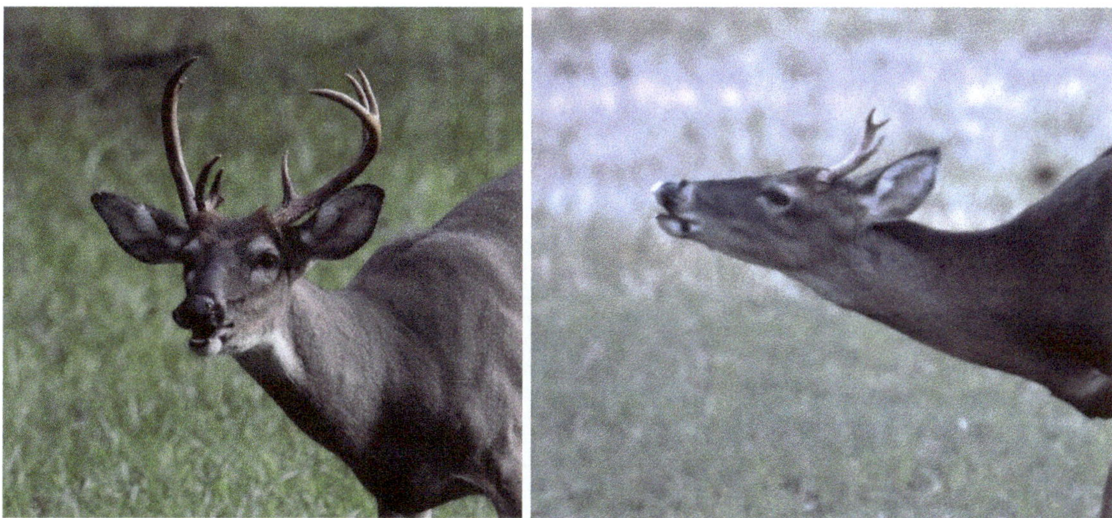

A buck doesn't have to be the dominant guy on campus to go into all stages of the rut and have high hopes for a lady.

He does not need to use this gland when he sniffs the doe herself; his nose can tell him if she is in heat when he sniffs her directly.

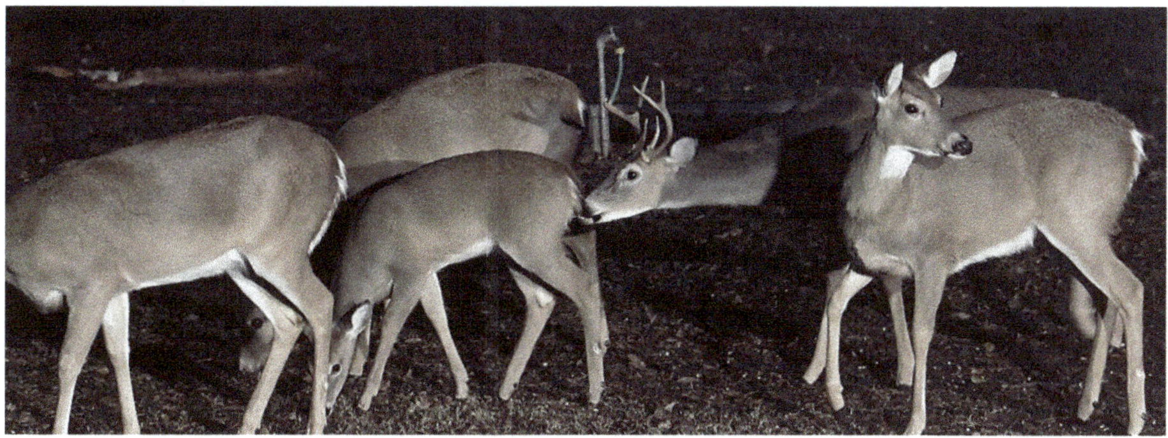

This guy has hopes but no luck here. The doe strode off.

When I began hunting, back in the 1960s, I sought information from anyone who might help me learn about how to hunt. The "facts" included: *Bucks will stay with a doe for three days; he will hit his scrape as soon as the doe leaves him. So hunt a scrape for three days and you will get that buck.*

Dr. Karl Miller, Professor Emeritus of University of Georgia and our deer expert, has corrected these misconceptions: The unbred doe will be in heat about 2 to 2.5 days, but if she is bred, she will go out of heat sooner, 1 to 1.5 days.

The buck doesn't tend to his scrape constantly. In fact, most scraping activity occurs in the two weeks before the peak of the rut and scraping activity almost disappears when most does are in heat.

Yes, multiple bucks will visit and mark scrapes; these visits communicate to others who is in the neighborhood and transmit information about dominance.

 Susan Lindsley

COMPETITION FOR MATING RIGHTS

Many disputes over the food supply result in dominance practically determined during the summer. Usually the one who flees in July will also yield to the one who dominated at the food table when the rut competition begins.

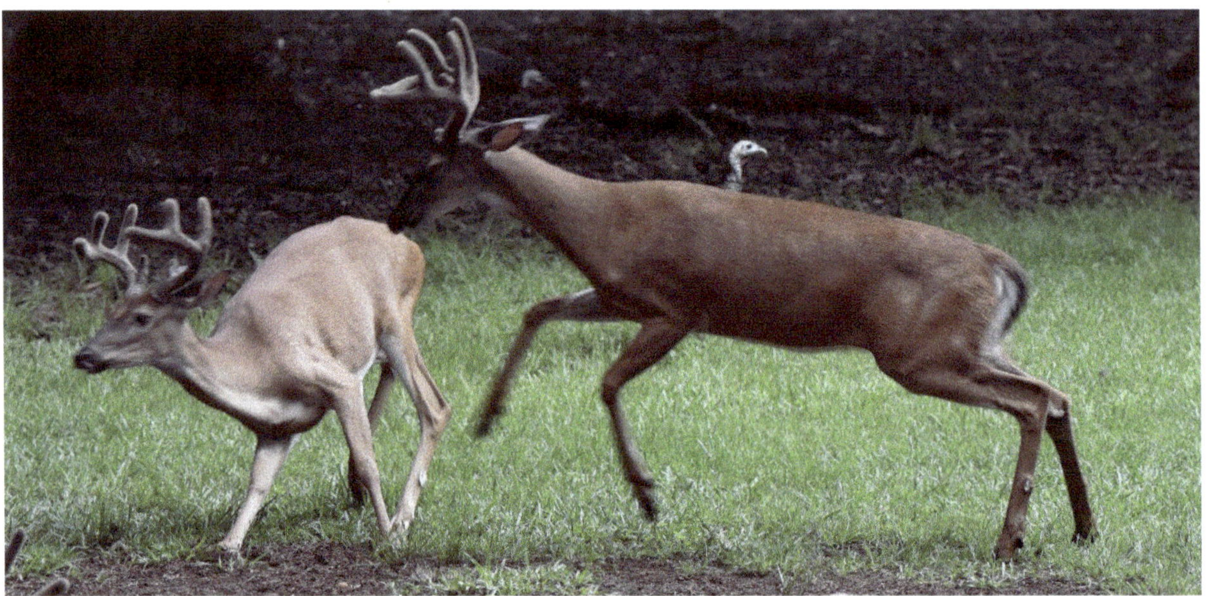

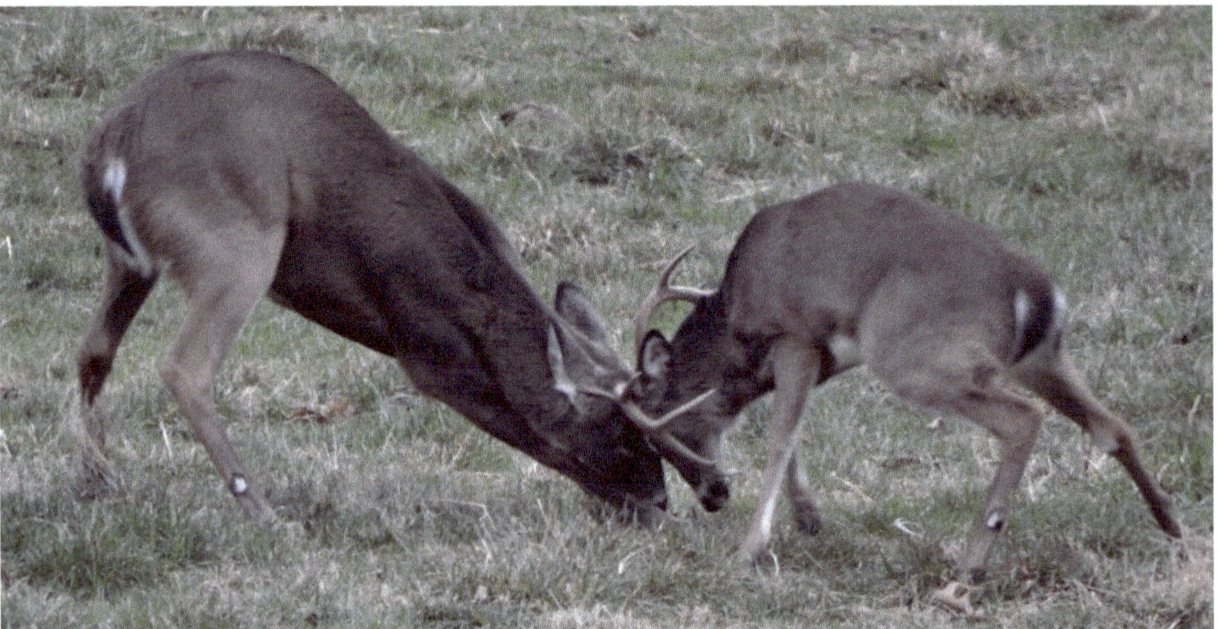

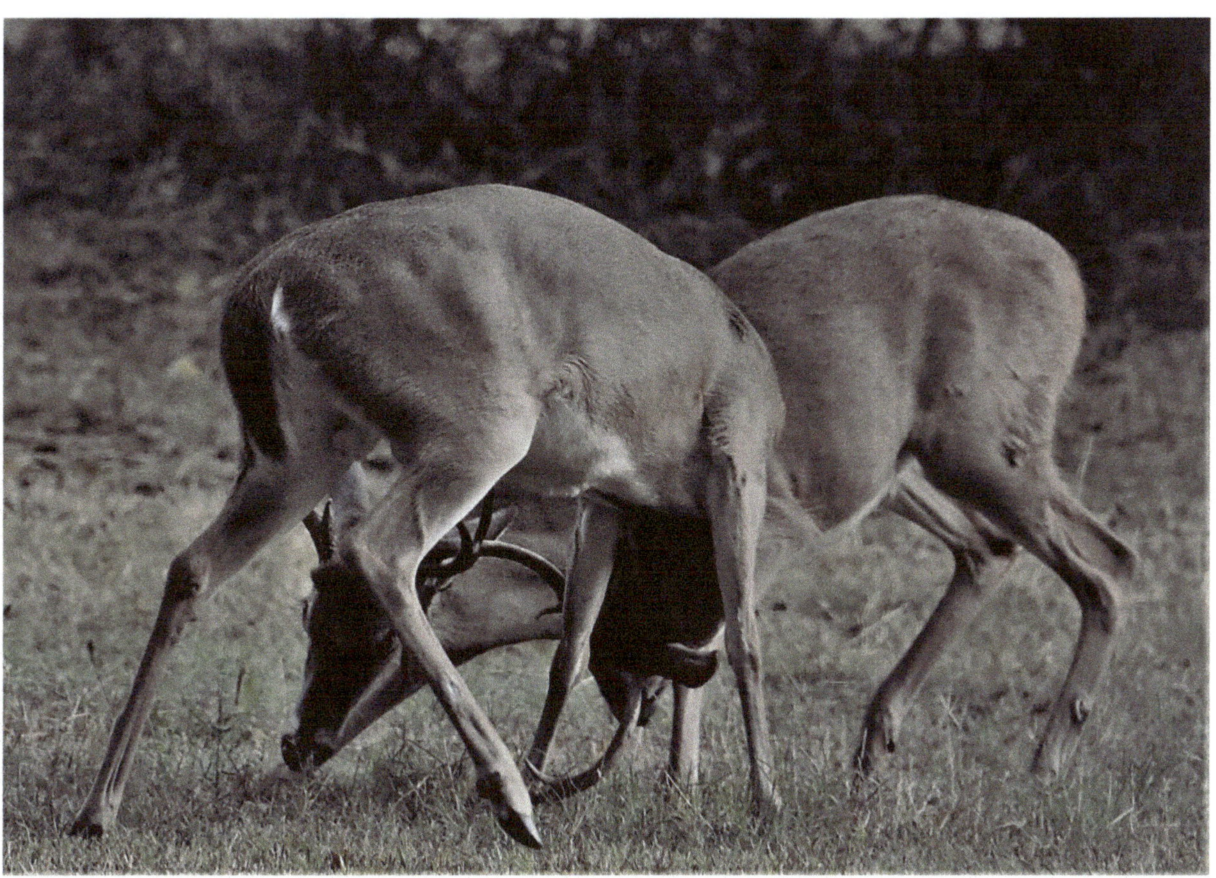

Although bucks may greet each other before they battle, the fights are often push and shove to determine who has the greatest potential to be the boss. In 2022, nine bucks with racks ranging from eight to ten points frequented my yard. By midsummer, they had determined who fell where in the power list. A lifted head sent others moving out. I saw the same behaviors in previous years, with the dominance settled by midsummer. Most fights as the rut approached were greet and push/shove/and "okay, you win."

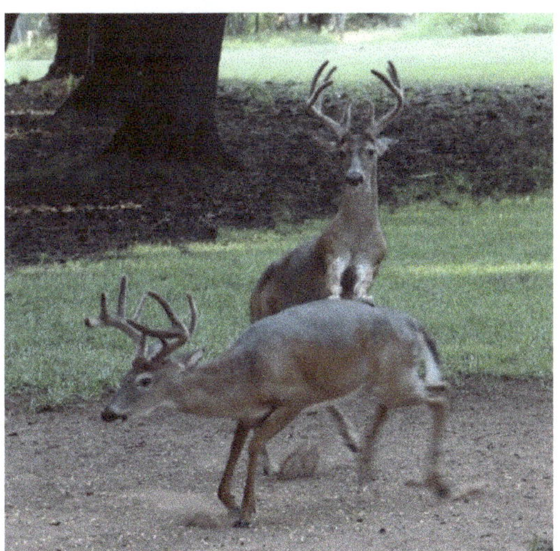

Ironically, the nine-point Bad Jaw Buck fled a smaller one on each encounter. Was he afraid of injured antlers or just afraid of the other buck? The next summer, Pappy 2 fled from a smaller buck.

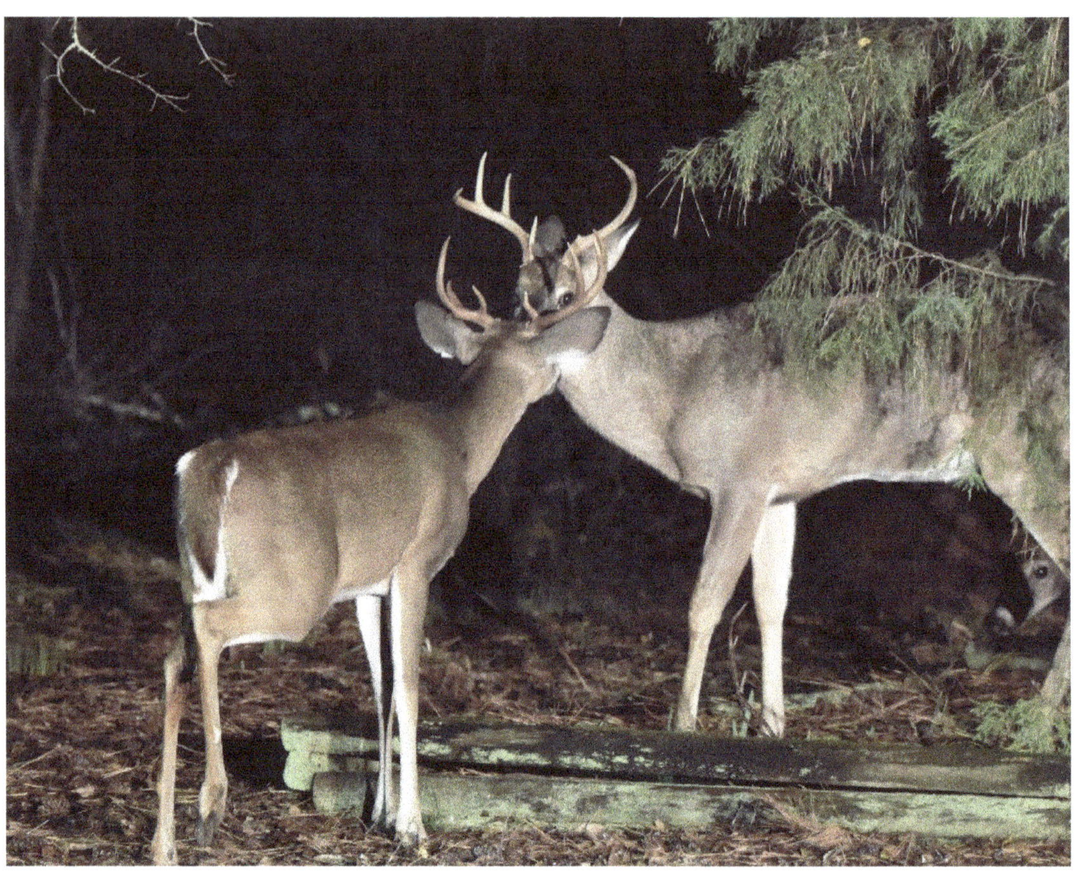

Sometimes they say "Hello, want to rumble?"

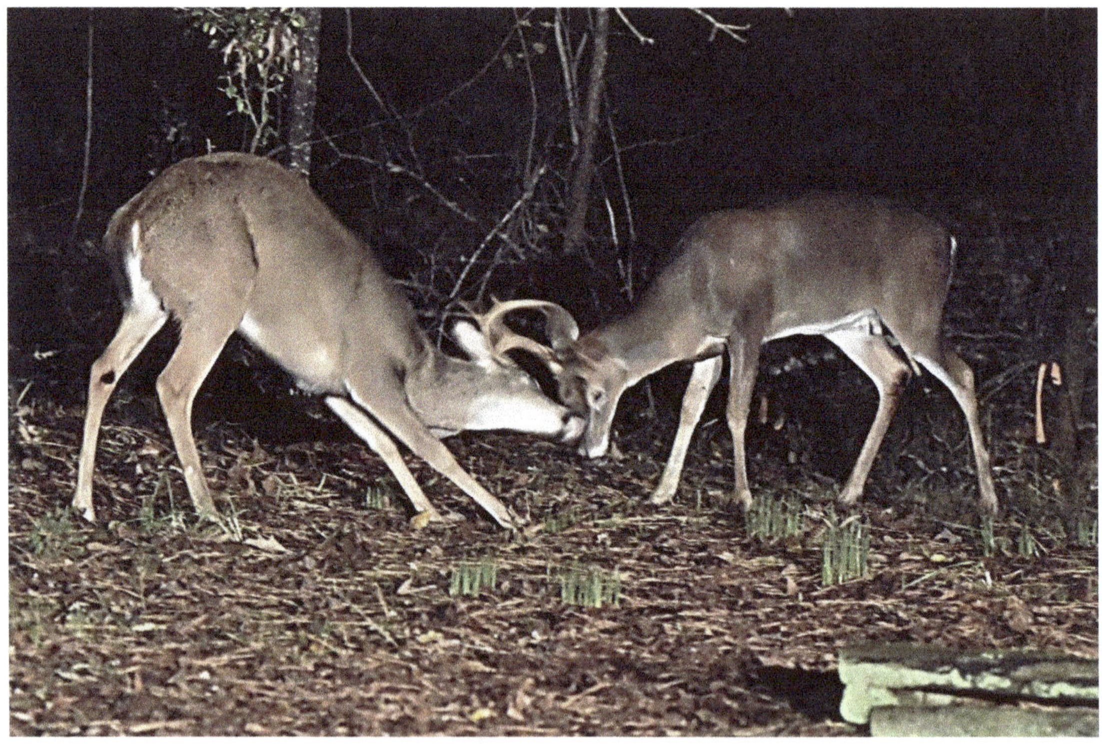

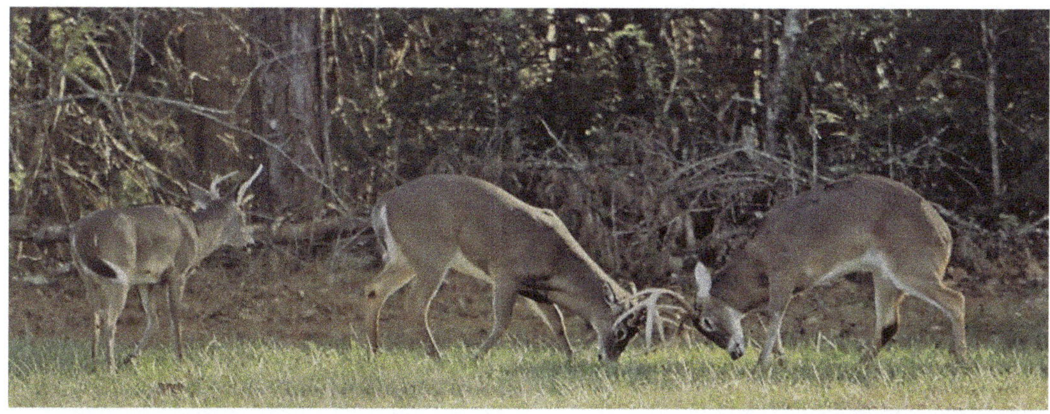

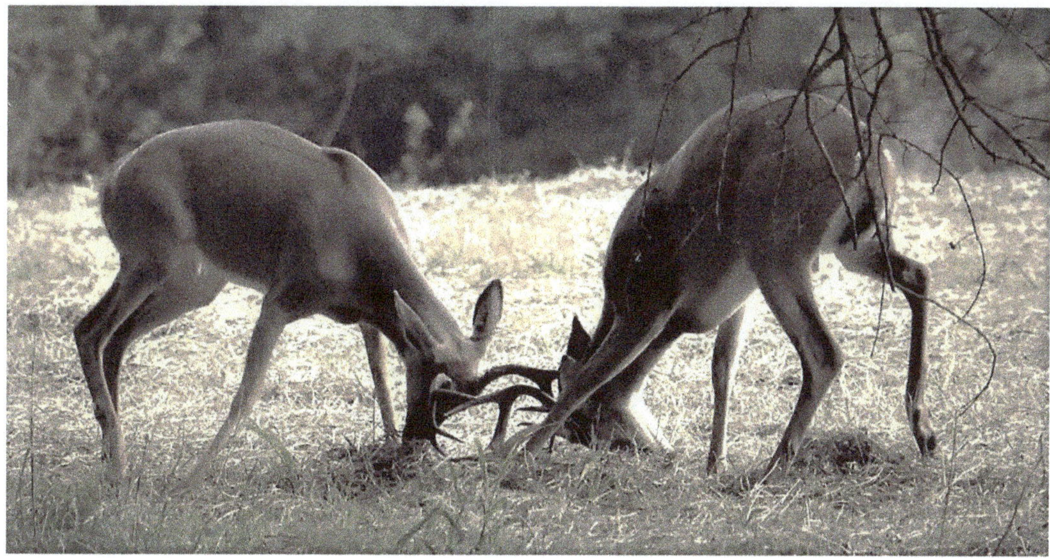

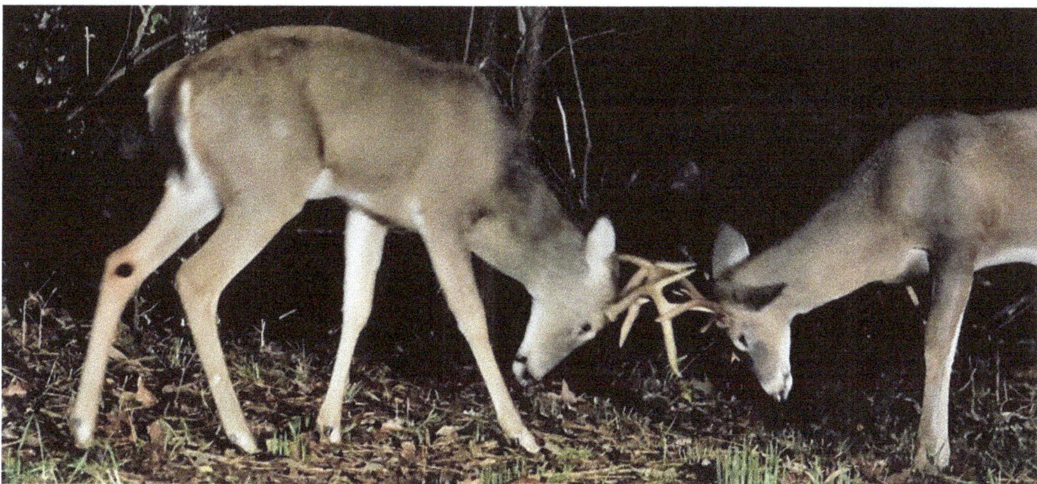

I saw more serious shoving in late December 2022 than any other time during the rut. Numerous times, a big guy shoved another twenty or more feet one way and out of sight, still pushing.

                    Susan Lindsley

Pappy tangled with Two Spot three times. Two Spot, on the left, decided he had enough and loped for other parts. They destroyed the small persimmon.

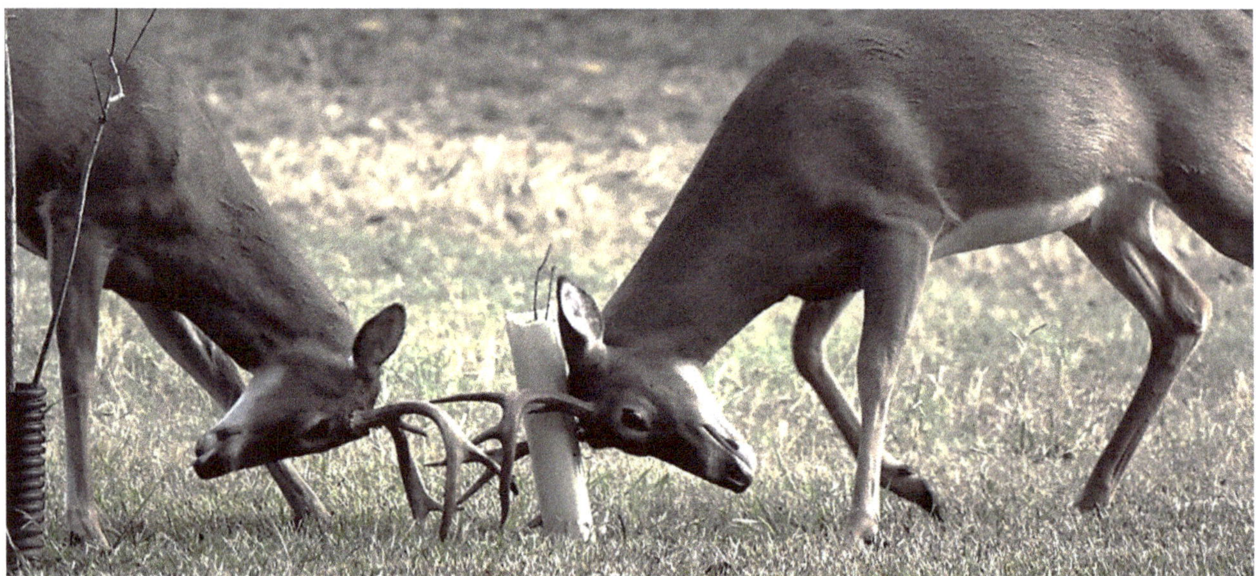

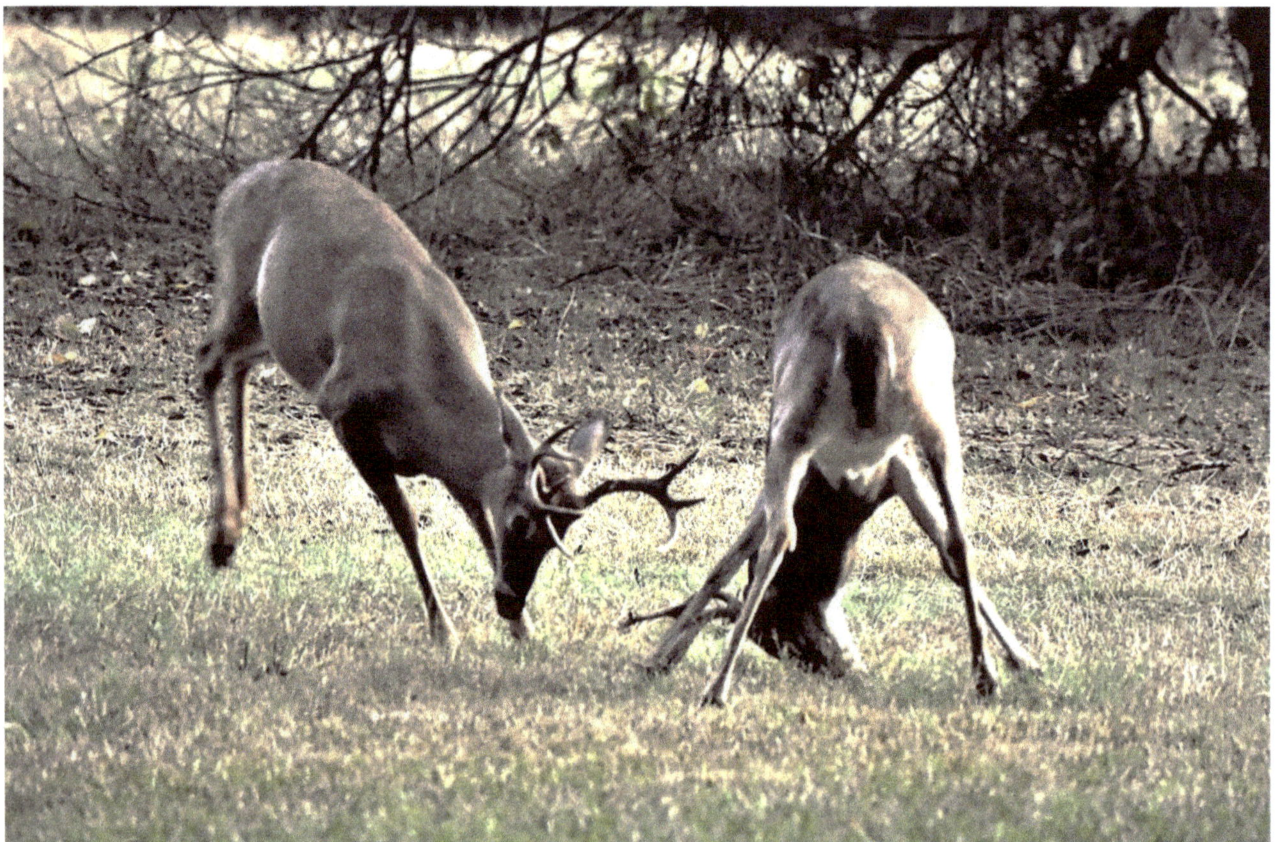

Winner or not, sometimes one just jumps for joy.

MATING

The act itself lasts only seconds. He mounts, thrusts, and it's over. But they might mate several times during the hours they run together. If the doe does not become pregnant, she will recycle in 21-30 days. She would accept another buck at that time.

I was not hunting about ten years ago when I saw my first sexual encounter between buck and doe. I was in my kitchen and watching some yard deer. No camera. A doe came across the field toward the feeder, and a buck followed. She stopped about thirty yards from the feeder, in the wide-open meadow. He stuck his nose to her rear and then mounted her. The mating lasted about three seconds; he dropped off, and they meandered on across the field.

In October 2019 I saw a doe amble behind the oak/tube feeder and I expected her to continue on into the woods and to the adjacent meadow as others did nightly. Instead, she stopped at the edge of the woods, almost out of sight in the small area behind the barn and oak where she was barely visible. I knew a scrape was in that area but I had such a narrow camera window there and the area was in shadow so I paid her little heed. When I saw one of the big bucks head her way, I tried to focus the camera on her and not on the surroundings. Most of my shots wound up focused on either the oak, the close-up feeder or the barn but I did manage to get a few half-decent pictures of the mating. I was able to photograph only their "front ends" since the rest of the bodies was behind the oak tree holding the tube feeder.

She did not move when buck approached her. He mounted, thrust, and was done. She went her way, and he stood panting and slobbering nearby for a few seconds. He then began a frantic search for another doe, as if the mating had stimulated him. He for sure was not satiated. The times below the pictures show the act is over quickly.

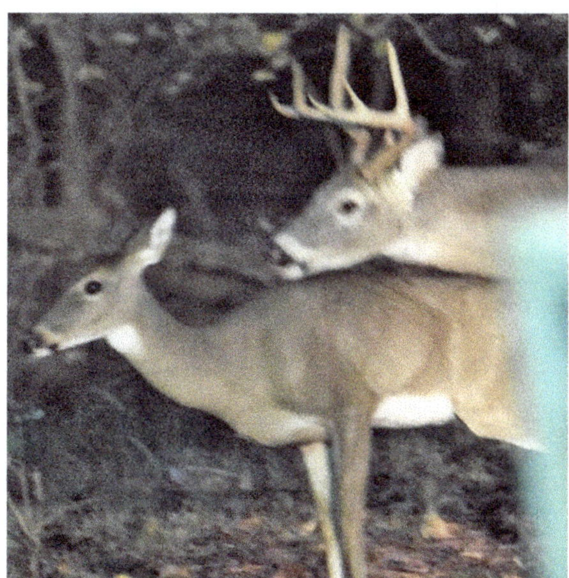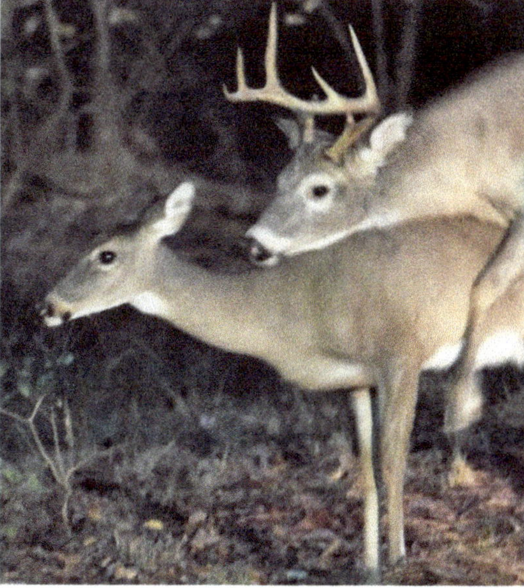

6:02:22

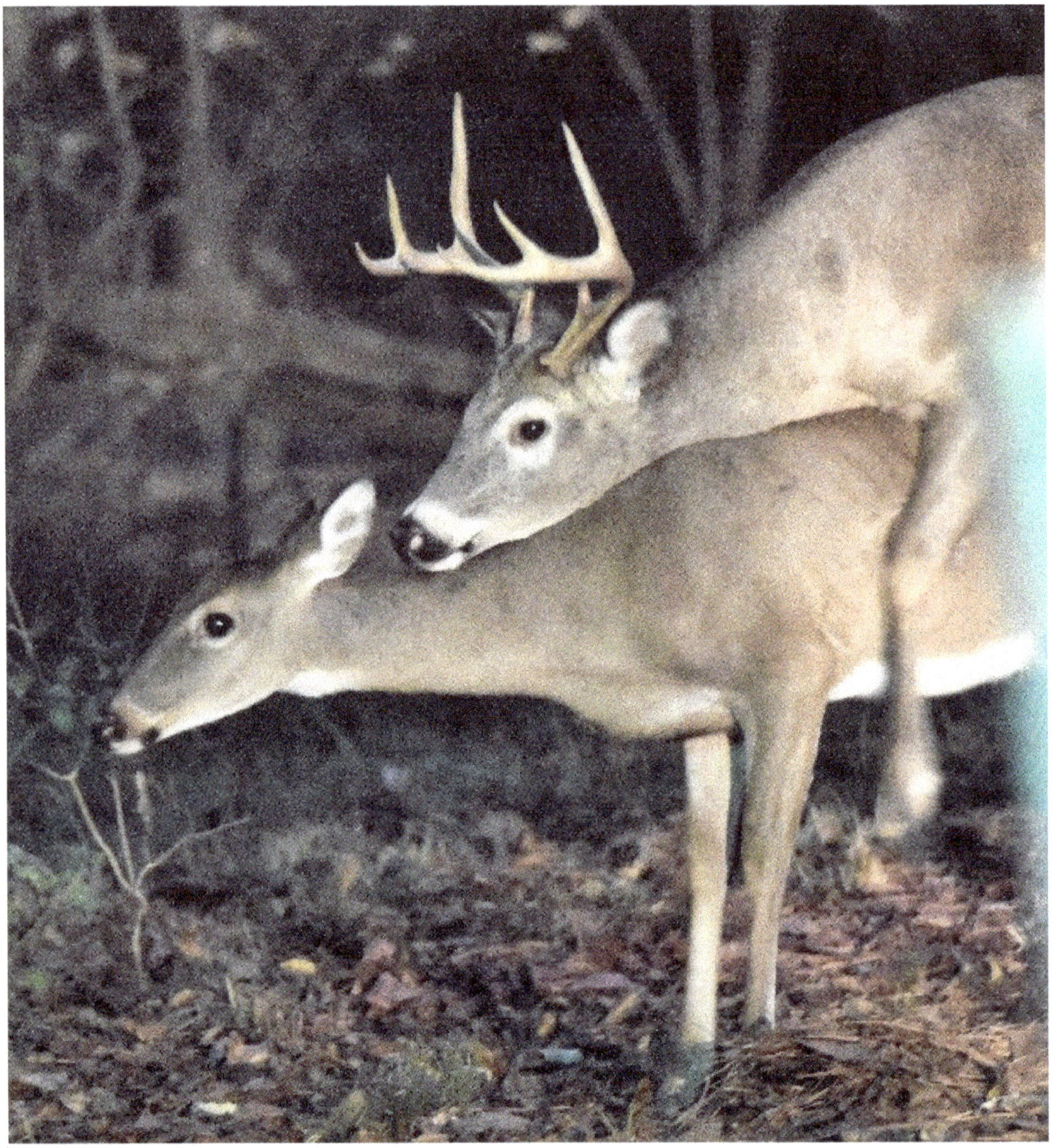

Susan Lindsley

6:02:30

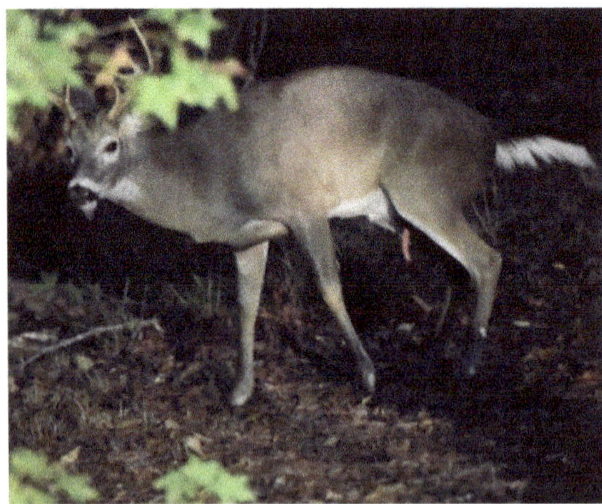

6:02:44

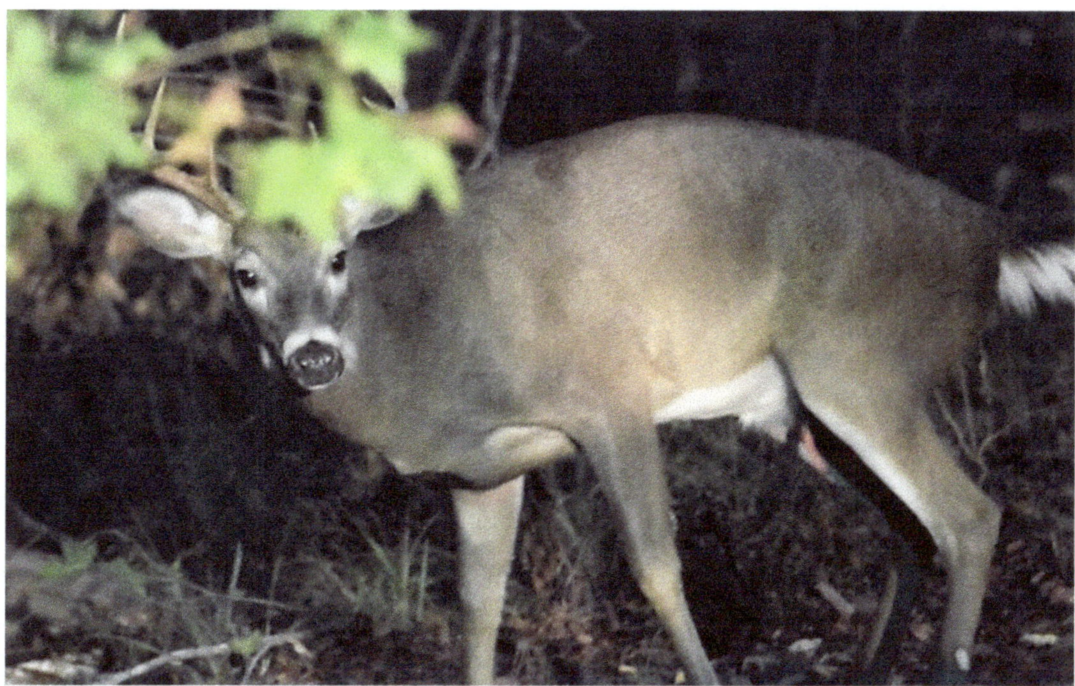

As soon as he caught his breath, he began to look for another opportunity. He seemed frantic as he raced around, across the ditch and back toward the scrape. He paused frequently to look around as if he expected another doe to come to the scrape. He finally returned to the scrape at 7:03 and hung around for another ten minutes before he left for the woods.

AFTER THE RUT

As the rut winds down and winter looks to spring, does relax and don't flee at the sight of an approaching buck. Dominance having been settled in the fall, fewer spats occur over food… the dominant buck lifts his head and others back off. One antler and body odor are often enough to remind others the guy coming is still the one they fled earlier. Some boys never give up hope. This boy checks out possibilities in late January.

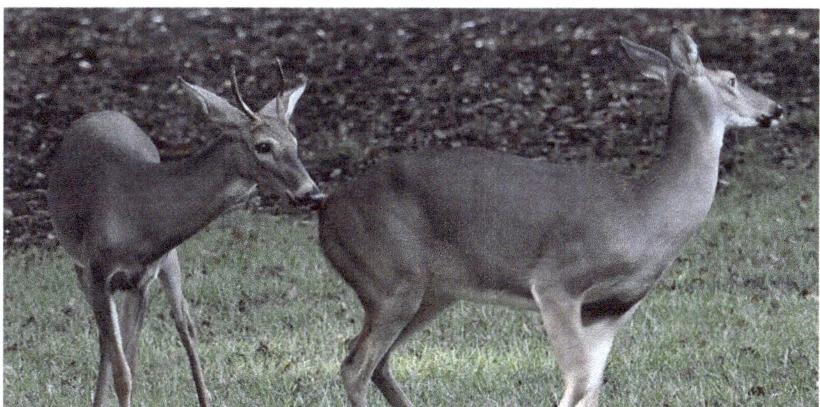

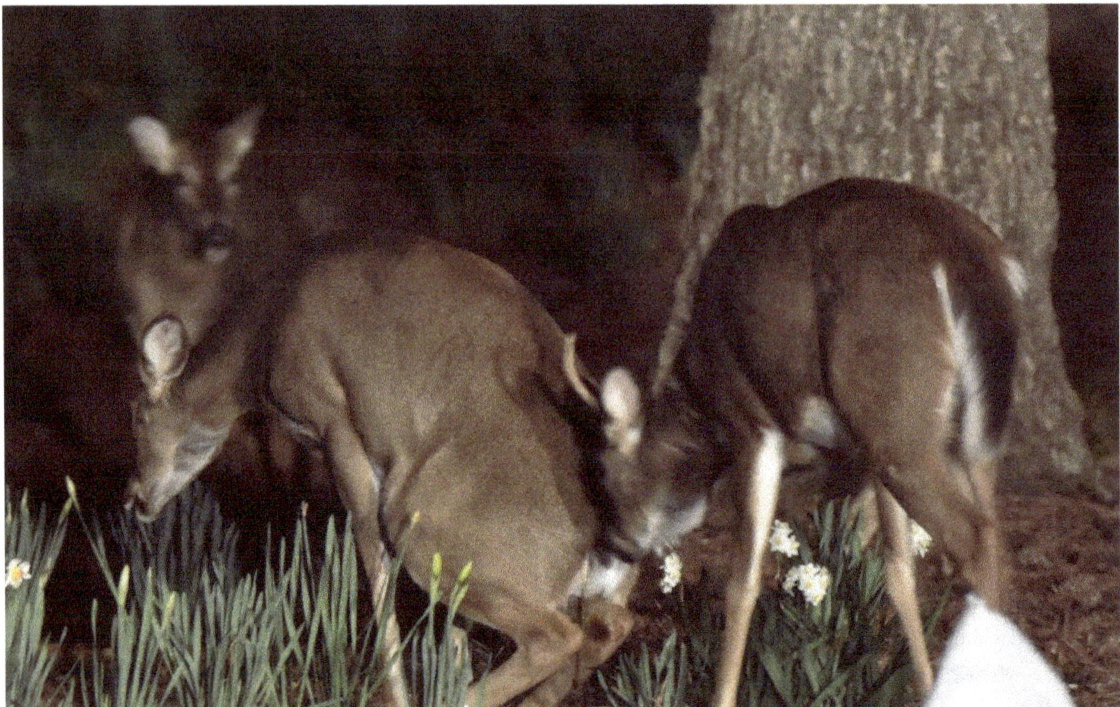

February 25

A few bucks greet and make a sort of mutual agreement to have one more rumble and shove each other again. These boys had their last fling shoving on February 26.

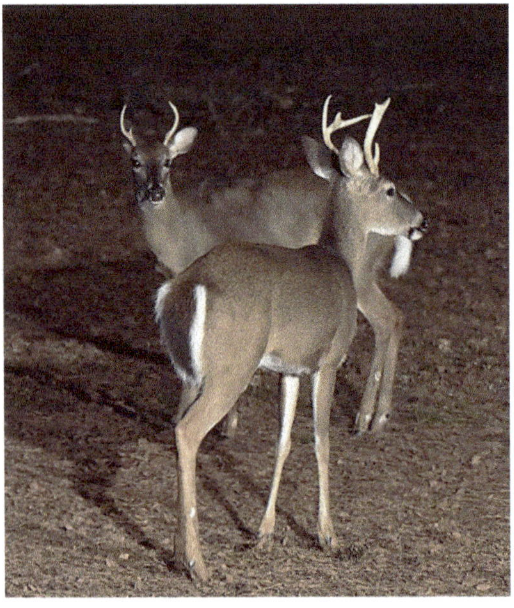

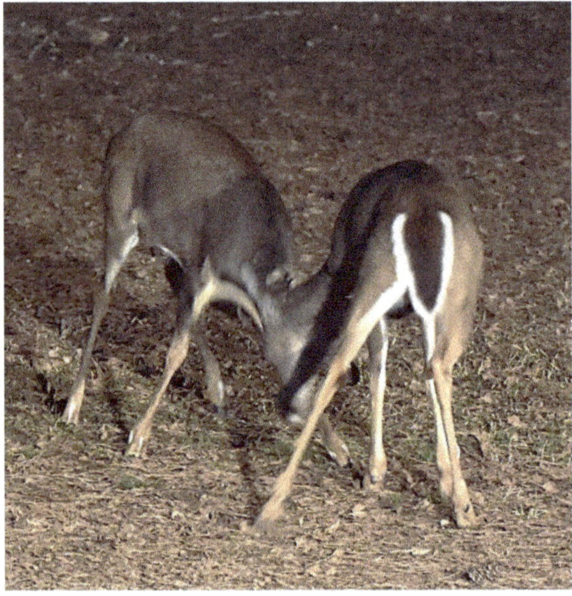

January 26, what is her interest in the young buck? Perhaps she is just wondering if this is her son or a stranger in the territory, or is she still in estrus?

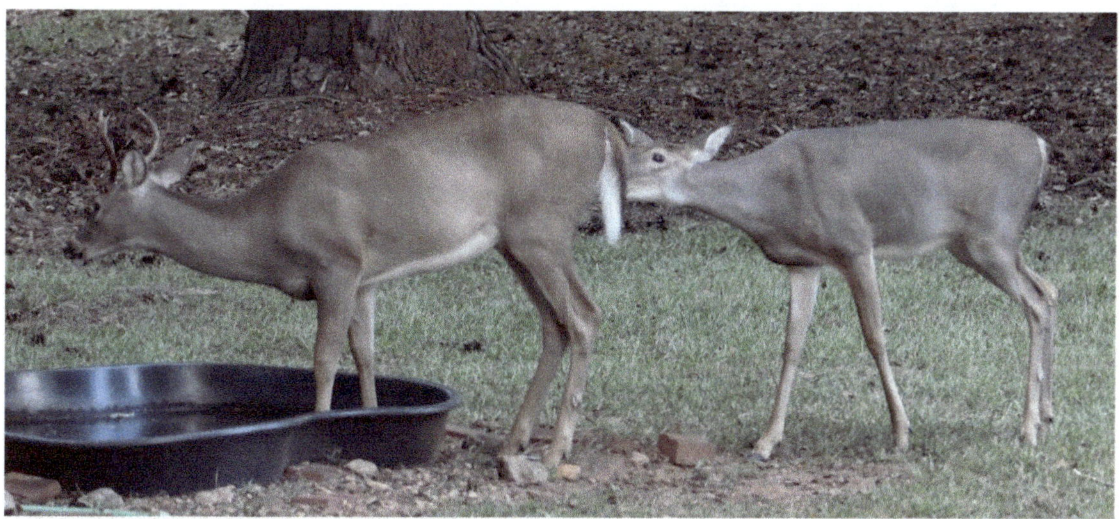

Testosterone production slows, testicles shrink, and thick hair covers external genitals and udders to protect against the cold. Antlers fall, coats begin to turn orange-brown, and the bucks' necks return to their summer svelte size. In days, new antlers begin to bulge.

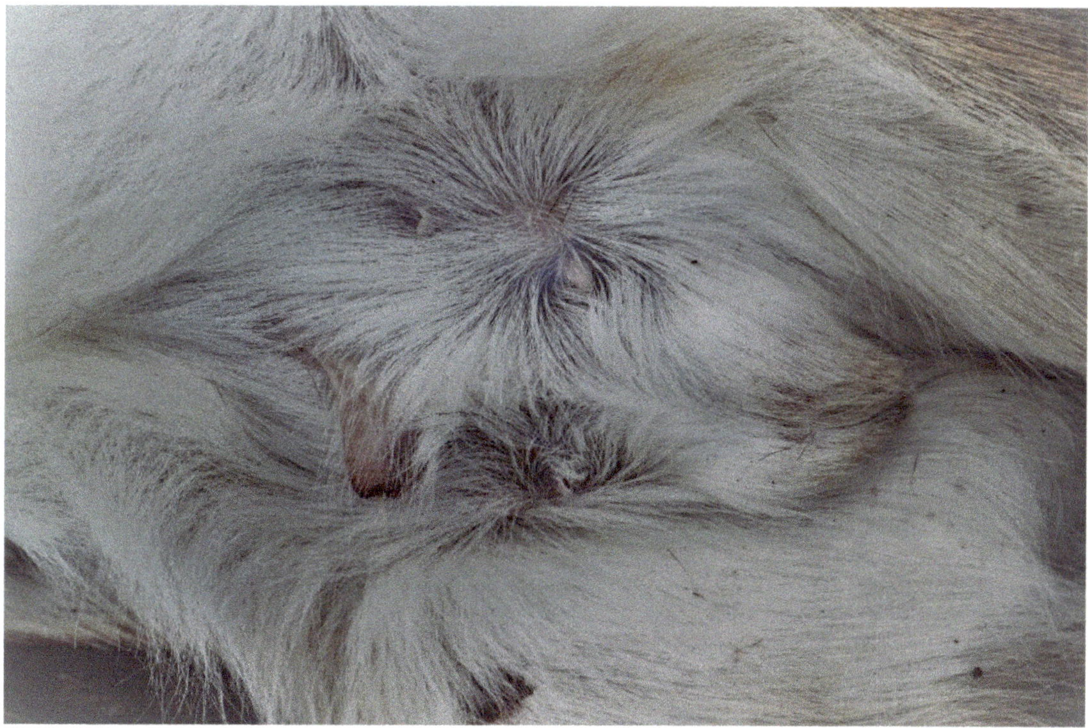

Men and women who hunted for food or trophies in the fall begin to hunt the land for shed antlers.

The cycle of life begins again as summer approaches and fawns are born.

Somewhere in the herd a buck who last fall retreated from others is growing a massive rack and growing in confidence to become the boss buck of the neighborhood in September.

ALL IS WELL IN THE DEER YARD

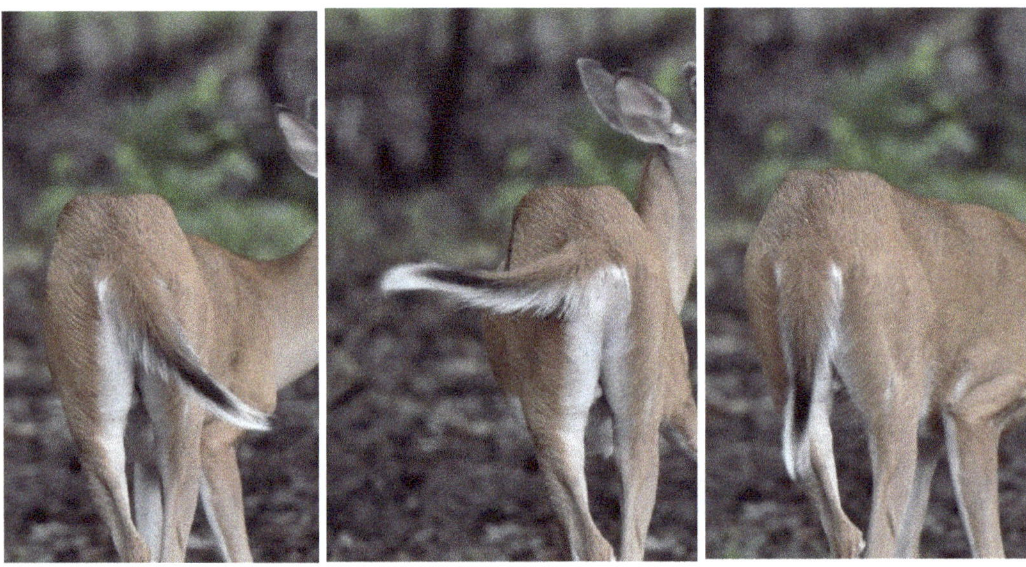

LET'S DO THE HOKEY POKEY

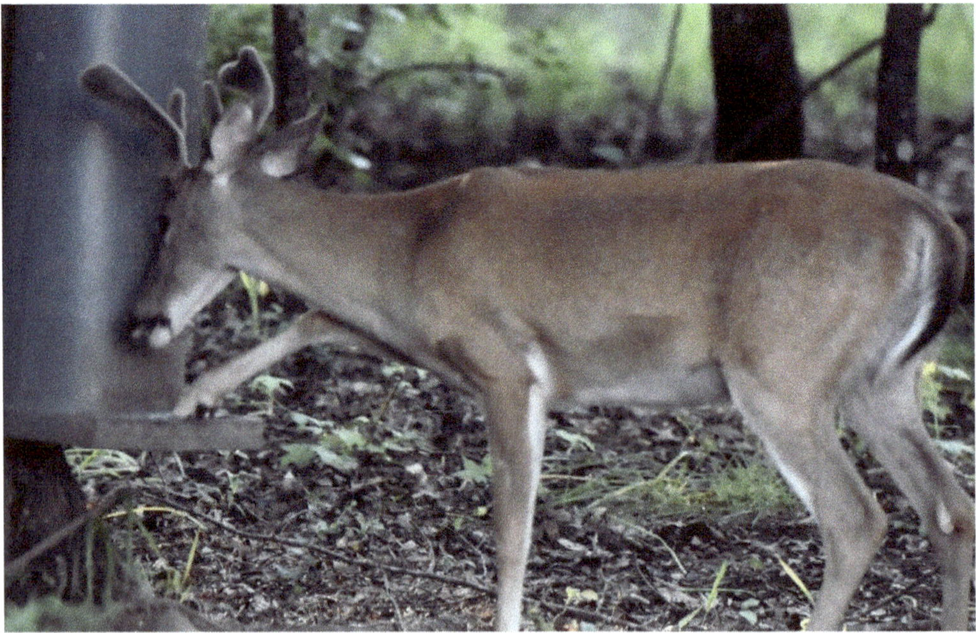

Put your right foot in….

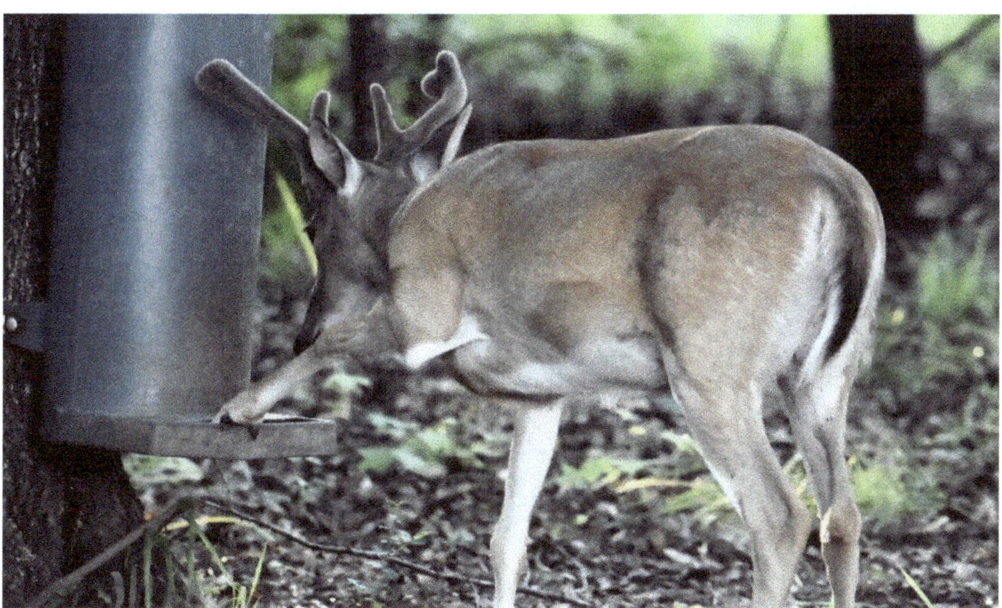

Put your left foot in…

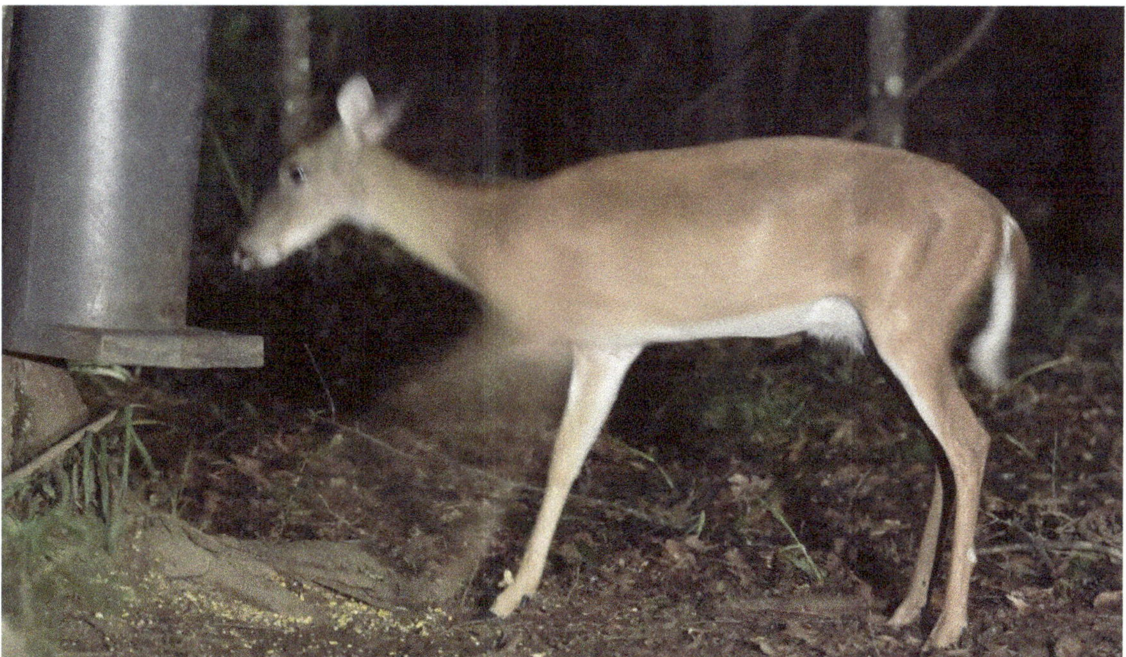

Take your left foot out and shake it all about….

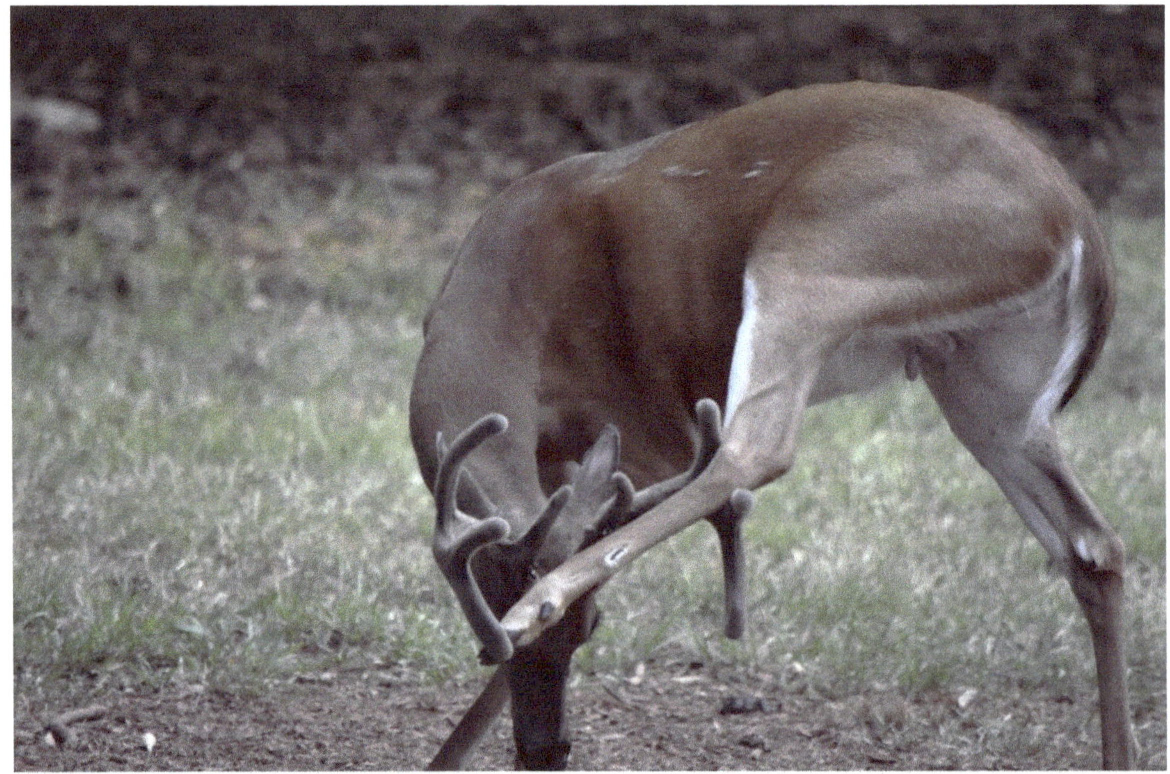

One way to knock yourself down.

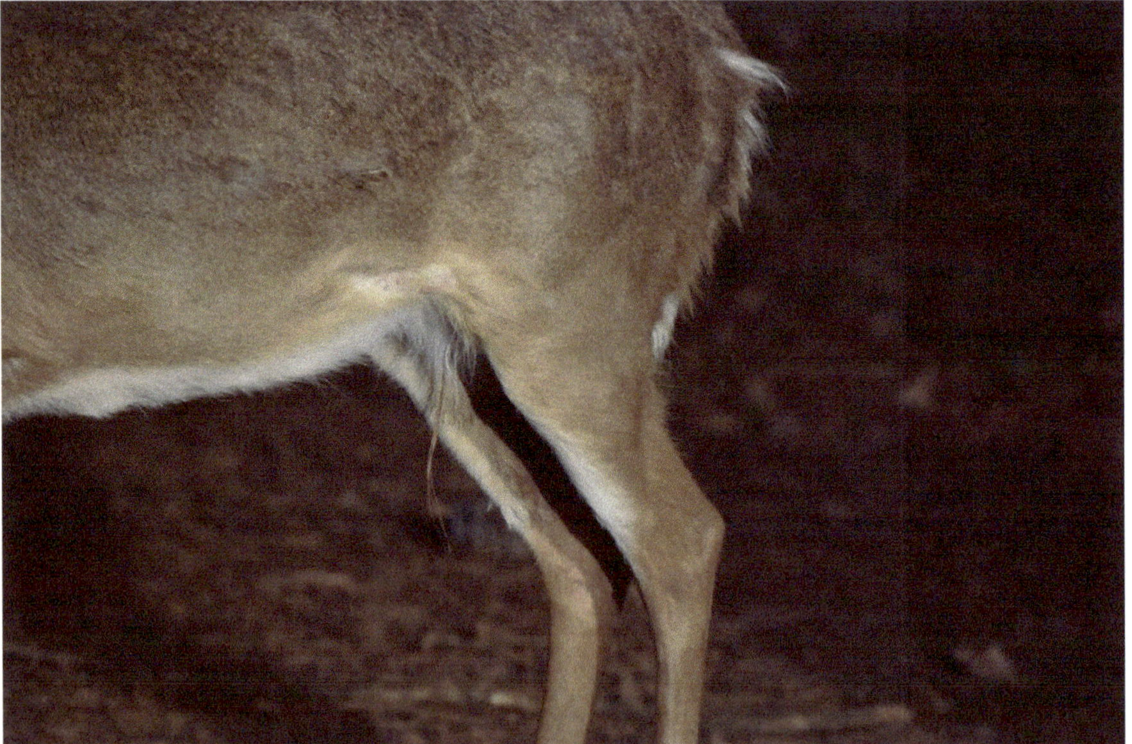

Pine straw won't produce an offspring.

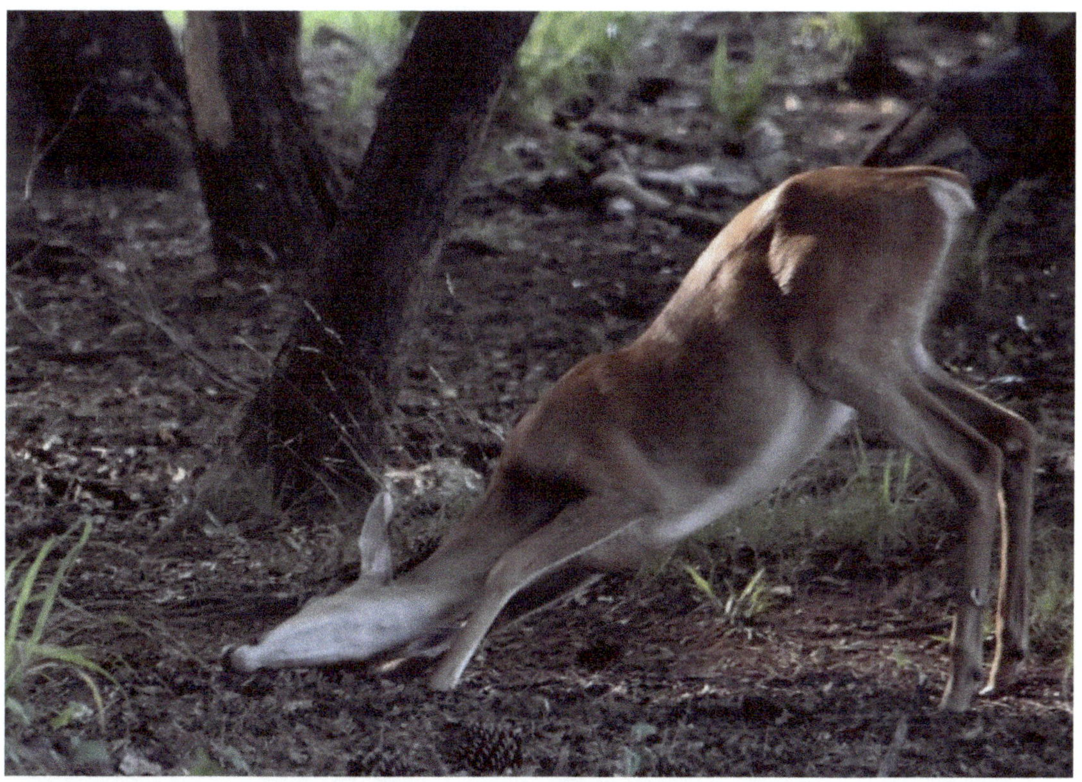

Oh what fun it is to rub my face into the doe urine.

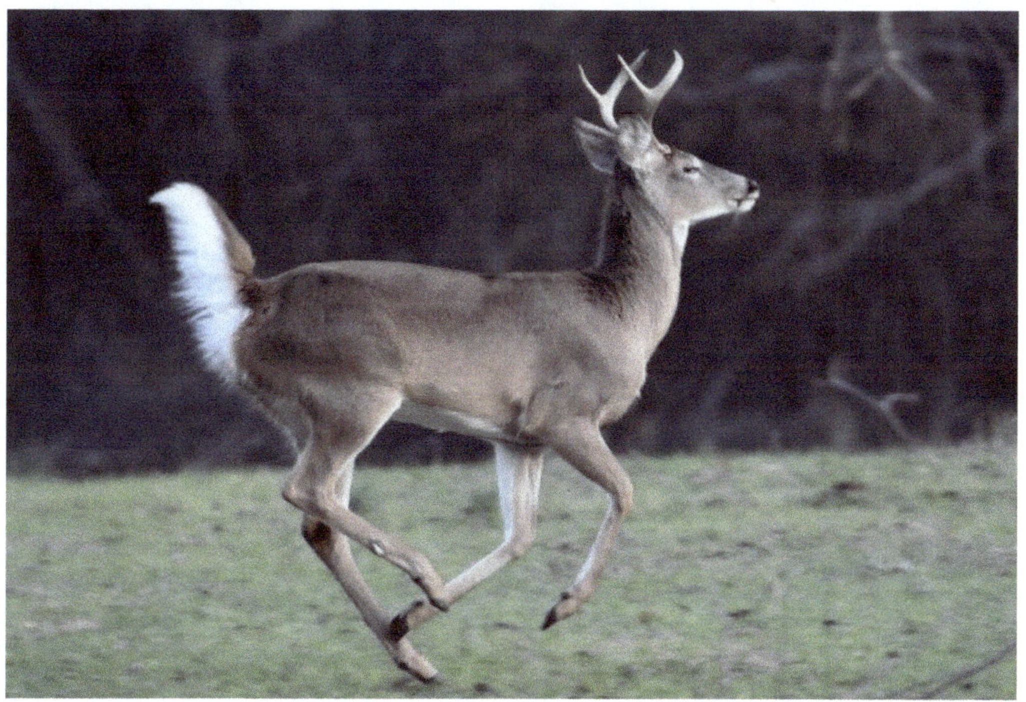

"I'm off for WHITETAIL SECRETS, FAMILY LIFE"

WHITETAIL SECRETS

Family Life

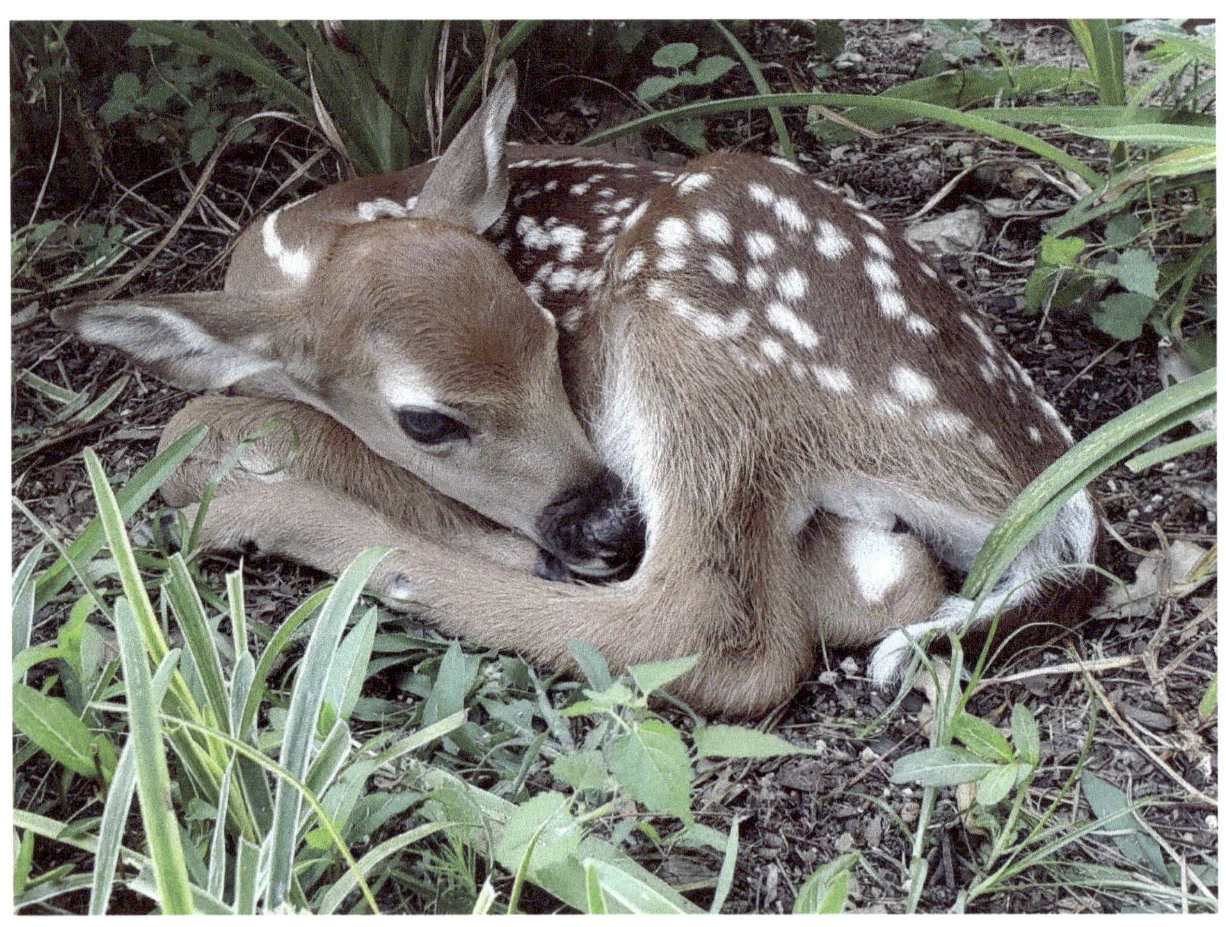

SUSAN LINDSLEY

ABOUT THE AUTHOR

Susan Lindsley's wildlife books and photographs have earned praise from America's premier wildlife photographer Leonard Lee Rue III, from Georgia's deer god Dr. Karl Miller, and from American's Deer Doctor Peter Fiduccia, as well as members of the Georgia Wildlife Federation and Georgia Department of Natural Resources. Her short stories, novels, poetry and nonfiction have received more than eighty awards from state, regional, national and international literary contests. Reared on a 2500-acre farm in middle Georgia, she is surrounded by the wildlife she writes about. When not concentrating on wild critters, she bases her work on characters who populated the rural community of childhood and local events from bootlegging to murder and politics, and combined the trio in the nonfiction book *Milledgeville's Sesquicentennial Murders.*

She has lived many of the events she writes about. As a counterfeit game warden, she pursued hunters who shot deer at night from the road, and her pursuits led to arrests and convictions. She spoke in the Georgia House chambers to hunters to help Game and Fish gain support from Georgia hunters for changes in regulations. When another need arose, Lindsley's recommendations to Game and Fish for an unprecedented action were accepted and the changes made. Lindsley was instrumental in getting wild turkeys reintroduced into her home county; three flocks were released on her family land and another on the farm of the local wildlife ranger. The flocks have thrived. Her photograph of a dead turkey took home the winning ribbon at the Macon Cherry Blossom Festival. She has held numerous photography shows throughout Georgia, including at the Buckarama held by the Georgia Wildlife Federation.

A member of the Georgia Outdoor Writers Association, she contributes to the newly established digital magazine *Georgia Outdoor Adventures.* Lindsley is an honorary life member of the Georgia Wildlife Federation.

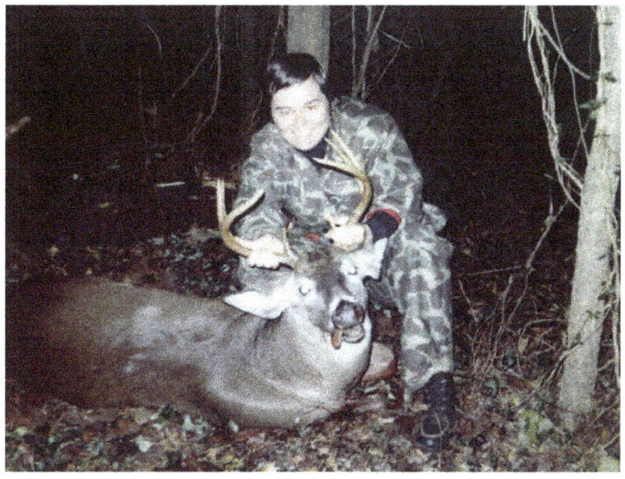

Susan with her first scrape buck, 1968